# THE MERCURY READER

## A CUSTOM PUBLICATION

English Department
Hudson Valley Community College
Composition II
Volume Two

PEARSON
Custom Publishing

*Director of Database Publishing:* Michael Payne
*Sponsoring Editor:* Natalie Danner
*Development Editor:* Katherine R. Gehan
*Editorial Assistant:* Laura Krier
*Marketing Manager:* Kerry Chapman
*Operations Manager:* Eric M. Kenney
*Production Project Manager:* Marianne C. Groth
*Database Project Specialist:* Jason Cohen
*Rights Editor:* Francesca Marcantonio
*Cover Designer:* Renée Sartell

*Cover Art:* "Clouds," by Kathi Mirza and Scott Olsen; "Starry Night Sky," copyright © Orion Press; "Sunset," by Darryl Torksler, and "Gigantia Mountains & Sea of Cortes," by R.G.K. Photography, copyright © Tony Stone Images. "Dime," courtesy of the Shaw Collection.



Printed in the United States of America

Please visit our website at *www.pearsoncustom.com*
Attention bookstores: For permission to return any unsold stock, contact Pearson Custom Publishing at 1-800-777-6872.

ISBN: **0536691754**

PEARSON Custom Publishing

PEARSON CUSTOM PUBLISHING
75 Arlington St., Suite 300
Boston, MA 02116

# General Editors


Janice Neuleib
*Illinois State University*

Kathleen Shine Cain
*Merrimack College*

Stephen Ruffus
*Salt Lake Community College*

In Memoriam:
Maurice Scharton (†)
*Illinois State University*

# CONTENTS

English Department Grading Guidelines For Use In Evaluating Student Writing ........ 1

NONFICTION SELECTIONS

Should the State Know Your HIV Status?
RoseMarie Gionta Alfieri ........ 3

Finishing School
Maya Angelou ........ 12

Pornography
Margaret Atwood ........ 20

Little Red Riding Hood Revisited
Russell Baker ........ 29

School vs. Education
Russell Baker ........ 34

The Case Against College
Caroline Bird ........ 38

The Gender Blur
Deborah Blum ........ 44

The Dehumanization of the Indian
Haig A. Bosmajian ........ 54

The Myth of Sisyphus
Albert Camus ........ 57

Why We Don't Need Animal Experimentation
Peggy Carlson ........ 62

My Father's Life
Raymond Carver ........ 66

Marrying Absurd
Joan Didion .......... 77

So This Was Adolescence
Annie Dillard .......... 82

Adam Goes to School
Michael Dorris .......... 87

Kiss Me, I'm Gay
Barbara Ehrenreich .......... 94

The Tapestry of Friendship
Ellen Goodman .......... 99

Shame
Dick Gregory .......... 103

Don't Let Stereotypes Warp Your Judgments
Robert Heilbroner .......... 110

That Word Black
Langston Hughes .......... 115

The Americanization Ideal
Barbara Jordan .......... 119

A Case of Assisted Suicide
Jack Kevorkian .......... 122

Learning the Language
Perri Klass .......... 130

Are the Homeless Crazy?
Jonathan Kozol .......... 136

The Scheme of Color
Mary Mebane .......... 143

Religion Makes a Comeback. (Belief to Follow)
Jack Miles .......... 148

Gay Teachers, Gay Students
Neil Miller........................................................................................ 157

The Way to Rainy Mountain
N.Scott Momaday........................................................................................ 168

On Boxing
Joyce Carol Oates........................................................................................ 177

Shooting an Elephant
George Orwell........................................................................................ 182

Rape: A Bigger Danger Than Feminists Know
Camille Paglia........................................................................................ 192

The Allegory of the Cave
Plato........................................................................................ 199

Why I Hate "Family Values" (Let Me Count the Ways)
Katha Pollitt........................................................................................ 205

Future Shlock
Neil Postman........................................................................................ 215

The C Word in the Hallways
Anna Quindlen........................................................................................ 227

The Fear of Losing a Culture
Richard Rodriguez........................................................................................ 233

The Rewards of Living a Solitary Life
May Sarton........................................................................................ 239

The Knife
Richard Selzer........................................................................................ 242

Beauty
Susan Sontag........................................................................................ 248

The Jacket
Gary Soto........................................................................................ 253

The Importance of Work
Gloria Steinem........................................................................................ 258

Notes on Punctuation
Lewis Thomas.......................................................................................... 266

The Place Where I Was Born
Alice Walker............................................................................................ 272

Once More to the Lake
E.B. White............................................................................................... 277

Hate Radio
Patricia J. Williams................................................................................. 286

The Library Card
Richard Wright........................................................................................ 296

College Pressures
William Zinsser....................................................................................... 306

| | A | B | C | D | F |
|---|---|---|---|---|---|
| **General** | The **A** paper is generally excellent. It is characterized by maturity, insightfulness, originality, or creativity in developing the central idea. A strong sense of purpose, a keen awareness of audience, clear organization, effective language and full development are the hallmarks of the **A** paper. | The **B** paper organizes well thought-out material into coherent unified paragraphs that have clear topic sentences in support of a central idea. Overall, the **B** paper, while not as insightful as an **A** paper, is above average. | The **C** paper generally demonstrates satisfactory work and is not seriously deficient in any way. It may meet all of the requirements of the assignment, but it does not distinguish itself as having exceeded those requirements. Though adequacy in content, organization, style, and mechanics may be evident, the **C** paper may lack the originality of ideas, fluency, and inventiveness of the **A** or **B** paper. In addition, the **C** paper may have mechanical errors. | The **D** paper is deficient in content, organization, style, and/or mechanics. Its sentences and ideas may be incoherent and/or loosely connected. The **D** paper's problems impair its overall effectiveness. | The **F** paper contains excessive weaknesses in content, organization, sentence structure, diction, and/or mechanics. It may contain numerous errors that impede comprehension and compromise clarity. A paper may also receive an **F for failure to fulfill** assignment requirements or for plagiarism. |
| | **The instructor will apply the criteria below as appropriate within the context of the assignment.** | | | | |
| **Content** | The **A** paper develops an engaging, focused topic with thoroughness, clarity, and creativity. It exhibits interesting and well-developed examples, explanations, and supporting evidence. | The **B** paper contains a focused topic, strong development with evidence that is detailed and well supported, and an above average level of sophistication. | The **C** paper develops and supports ideas in a satisfactory manner. Ideas are convincing but may lack appropriate development and depth. | The **D** paper may have vague, unsophisticated, undeveloped, or inappropriate content. | The **F** paper may have insufficient development of topic and/or little or no specific detail. |
| **Organization** | Beyond a well organized introduction, body, and conclusion in support of the central idea, the **A** paper is characterized by a logical sequence of ideas; graceful transitions; and balanced, thorough development. | The **B** paper is well organized; it contains an introduction, well-developed paragraphs, and a conclusion. A logical sequence and balance of ideas as well as appropriate transitions are evident. | The **C** paper evidences a recognizable pattern with a central idea; unified, coherent paragraphs; and transitions. | The **D** paper is often unclear, indirect, or illogical. | The **F** paper lacks a central idea, a clear organizational plan, and development. |
| **Style** | The **A** paper exhibits a sophisticated use of sentence structure and language, including sentence variety as well as precise, appropriate diction, tone, and figures of speech. | The **B** paper demonstrates effective diction, sentence variety, and tone. | The **C** paper may not be engaging, but the style is appropriate to the subject matter and audience. Inconsistent tone, unsuitable diction, and/or unsophisticated sentence structure may occasionally weaken the paper. | The **D** paper is characterized by simplistic, undeveloped, or inappropriate style. | The **F** paper has inconsistent, incoherent, monotonous or awkward sentence structure or diction that results in a loss of clarity. |
| **Mechanics** | The **A** paper is virtually free of mechanical problems, including sentencing, spelling, punctuation, and grammar errors. It demonstrates careful proofreading and adherence to format conventions. | The **B** paper does not contain serious or numerous mechanical errors. It demonstrates generally correct grammar, punctuation, spelling, and sentence structure. | The **C** paper demonstrates a basic knowledge and application of grammar, spelling, sentence structure, and punctuation. However, it may have errors that detract from the overall effectiveness of the paper. | The **D** paper may include significant problems in spelling, punctuation, sentence structure, and diction that interfere with communication. | The **F** paper contains many errors in sentencing, grammar, punctuation, and spelling that block communication. |

## ENGLISH DEPARTMENT GRADING GUIDELINES FOR USE IN EVALUATING STUDENT WRITING

**The English Department has prepared the following guidelines for use in evaluating student writing. It is assumed that before the following criteria are applied, the work has met the stated requirements of the assignment and is submitted in the appropriate format.**

# SHOULD THE STATE KNOW YOUR HIV STATUS?

## RoseMarie Gionta Alfieri

*In this article originally published in* Ms. *magazine, freelance writer RoseMarie Gionta Alfieri points out the potential for undesirable effects if women are subjected to compulsory HIV tests. A rhetorical question, "Should the state know your HIV status?" serves both as her title and as an implied threat that the government is meddling in the personal lives of citizens to a dangerous degree. As you read the article, note that the arrangement of facts can create an emotional argument as effectively as direct persuasion. By the end of the article, the reader who accepts Alfieri's message will feel the familiar X-Files paranoia of life in the post-modern age.*

1 Last October, the case of Nushawn Williams hit the front pages. 1
He is believed to have infected at least 13 girls and women in Jamestown, New York, with HIV, the virus that causes AIDS. His face and name appeared all over the media, shredding the accepted norm of keeping HIV status confidential. In breaking this tradition, public health officials sought to identify and reach the young women he may have infected.

In the wake of the Williams identification, renewed attention was cast on a hot debate among government officials, public health professionals, and AIDS advocates on the need for new policies to better track HIV infection. Under discussion are HIV status reporting, mandatory testing, and contact tracing.

---

"Should the State Know Your HIV Status?" by RoseMarie Gionta Alfieri, published in *Ms.* September/October 1998.

Until recently, reporting the results of HIV tests was not routinely done, with only full-blown AIDS cases reported. These cases are sent to state health departments, which use the information to help develop treatment and health care priorities, for prevention education, and to study, track, and monitor the course of the disease. Often the reporting is anonymous, but 29 states now have name reporting systems through which the state collects the names of those who test positive. In July, New York became the latest state to enact name-based reporting—a significant development because New York has the largest number of AIDS cases in the country. In addition, unlike most other state policies, New York's law also includes mandatory partner notification.

Federal law already requires states to have in place programs for voluntary partner notification (also called contact tracing) for HIV, but it is not done routinely by most physicians. The process involves informing the sexual or needle-sharing partners of people who test positive for HIV that they, too, may be infected with the virus.

The Centers for Disease Control and Prevention (CDC) has urged states to implement some sort of HIV reporting system. At issue is how that should be done. Both Gay Men's Health Crisis (GMHC), the nation's oldest nonprofit AIDS organization, and the American Civil Liberties Union endorse the use of a unique identifier—a code that preserves anonymity while enabling the collection of data for epidemiologists, who study disease patterns and trends.

GMHC's position marks a shift in its long-held stance against any formal reporting of HIV test results. Ronald S. Johnson, GMHC's managing director for public policy, communications, and community relations, attributes the controversial new stand to the fact that "shifts in HIV infections and new early treatment options demand new approaches."

However, the National Black Women's Health Project (NBWHP) has serious concerns about any type of formal reporting and is particularly against name-based reporting. "It is a well-known public health fact that if name reporting goes through, women will be less likely to seek the care they need," states Robin Massengale, until recently the program associate for NBWHP. "Instead of being treated, these women will go underground, leaving a great public health risk that the untreated virus will mutate and result in more strains of HIV."

The importance of having monitoring data raises the issue of mandatory testing for HIV. After all, goes one pro-testing argument, if we don't do more testing, how can we really know how many people are infected and where the virus will next present itself? While policies on testing for HIV infection vary by state, in general testing is voluntary. Only certain groups, such as blood donors, military personnel, and federal prisoners are required to be tested. In addition, New York mandates that newborns be tested, and a number of states test convicted prostitutes.

Gerald Stine, professor of genetics and microbiology at the University of North Florida and the author of a series of books on AIDS, notes that the prospect of mandatory testing is a subject of debate among the CDC, public health professionals, and researchers. "Under discussion is whether such testing will be for the general population or only for people at high risk," says Stine.

10 In the past, the prominent argument against such testing, ex- 10
pressed by Paul Goldschmidt in his 1993 article in the journal *AIDS*, held that without a cure for AIDS, mandatory testing could be neither scientifically nor ethically defended. It was argued that such a policy would scare away the very people who need testing most.

Lisa Cox, program and policy director for the National Women's Health Network, believes this concern is relevant today. "HIV/AIDS still carries with it very powerful stigmas, particularly for women," Cox says. "There is the fear that their children may be taken away from them, that they'll be fired from their jobs. Mandatory testing would drive these women underground."

However, times have changed. Robert Fullilove, an associate dean at the School of Public Health at Columbia University, who teaches a course on AIDS education, attributes renewed interest in mandatory testing to the advent of effective new treatments that can keep HIV-positive people healthy for years. These "cocktail" therapies are a combination of drugs that effectively reduce the amount of HIV in the blood. People have the greatest chance of success with these therapies if they begin treatment early on, and they can't be treated if they don't know they are infected.

In addition, the discovery of the long-term asymptomatic period of HIV infection lends weight to the argument for mandatory testing. An infected person may live symptom-free for more than a decade, and consequently may unwittingly transmit the virus through unsafe sex and/or needle sharing.

Finally, epidemiologists would gain valuable data from large-scale testing and reporting. These data would include such information as prevalence of HIV by demographic and lifestyle factors, such as sex, age, and sexual habits—information that is useful in planning treatment programs and targeted public education.

That is all well and good. However, the prospect of mandatory testing is particularly relevant—and troubling—for women. Worldwide, 41 percent of all new HIV infections are occurring in women, which translates to more that 6,500 women becoming infected each day. In the United States, black and Hispanic women, particularly those at lower income levels, are at the highest risk for AIDS. According to the CDC, in 1996 they composed 78 percent of all AIDS cases among U.S. women. They are also traditionally disempowered groups. "Mandatory testing creates an environment of distrust, and rates of HIV infection are rising in underserved black and Latino populations, who have less trust in our government and medical systems," says Cox.

Tylene Harrell, special assistant to the president of NBWHP, echoes this sentiment, noting also that the high cost of the compound drug treatment, estimated at $12,000 to $18,000 per year—for life—can be prohibitive. "A large amount of people in this population do not have health insurance, and they have had problems accessing treatment and staying on the regimen," she says.

Implementation of mandatory testing policies would affect not only those who are infected with HIV, but all women. In 1996, New York became the first (and remains the sole) state to mandate both HIV testing of all newborns and the disclosure of test results to their mothers and physicians. The reason: to protect and treat babies infected with HIV as early as possible. The issue is particularly thorny since in three out of four cases, a newborn testing positive for the virus is merely carrying the mother's antibodies, and in fact is not infected. But the mother definitely is.

"Compulsory newborn testing is tantamount to testing the mother for HIV without her consent," according to Leslie R. Wolfe, president of the Center for Women Policy Studies. "Moreover, newborn testing does not ensure that the child who is infected—or her or his mother—will have access to treatment for HIV-related illness."

However, New York State Assembly-woman Nettie Mayersohn, who supported the state law that mandates testing for newborns, defends it as sound medical practice. "If the mother is not told that she herself is infected, and she breast-feeds, she may actually infect her otherwise healthy newborn," contends Mayersohn.

20 Terry McGovern, executive director of the HIV Law Project, a nonprofit organization that serves HIV-positive people in New York City, has seen problems resulting from the law. "Some women are getting results of the HIV test as late as six to seven weeks after delivering, when they are already breast-feeding. We also are seeing inadequate counseling and access to treatment."

Is testing newborns doing too little too late? After all, wouldn't it be preferable to *prevent* HIV infections in babies in the first place? Current policy in most states does require health care workers to encourage pregnant women and those who are planning to get pregnant to take an HIV test, with the ultimate decision left up to the woman.

Requiring HIV testing of all pregnant women is a policy supported by the American Medical Association because several studies have shown that treating a pregnant woman with the drug zidovudine (AZT) can dramatically reduce the chance (from as high as 30 percent down to 8 percent) that the virus will be passed to her child. While the effectiveness of AZT in preventing HIV infection in newborns is well documented, the cost of obtaining the drug—as much as $800 to $1,000 per pregnancy—is too high for many of the women who are infected.

"The largest-growing segment of HIV and AIDS cases is minority women, especially poorer women, who cannot afford to be sick," says Gerald Stine, who also notes that women tend to wait longer than men to seek treatment.

"Testing is not treatment," stresses McGovern. "Administering a mandatory test without proper counseling and treatments serves as a disincentive to women seeking health care." She also points out that voluntary testing programs for pregnant women have been successful in recent years, decreasing birthrates of babies with HIV.

25 Despite media coverage celebrating the efficacy of "cocktail drug" treatments and potential vaccines, there remains no cure for AIDS. As Stine cautions, the new combination treatments do not permanently

eradicate HIV from the body, nor do they work for every person. The possibility exists that a woman could be tested and treated but not benefit from the treatment, leaving her ill, psychologically and emotionally damaged, and facing possible job loss and discrimination.

For all of these reasons, the Joint United Nations Programme on HIV/AIDS recently released a policy statement encouraging voluntary, confidential testing for HIV and discouraging mandatory testing as "a violation of human rights." The organization also pointed out that there is no evidence to date that mandatory testing achieves public health goals.

However, Nancy MacNeil of Women Alive, an educational and support organization for HIV-positive women (hotline: 800-554-4876), contends that, in a sense, mandatory testing is already being performed on women, noting that many of the calls the hotline receives are from pregnant women who say they were tested without their knowledge or consent. "They find out they are HIV positive and they have not had pretesting counseling," MacNeil says.

Proponents of mandatory testing, however, note that aside from the potential health care and monitoring benefits, mandatory testing could help break the chain of transmission of the virus. The rationale is that a person who knows she or he is HIV positive will alter behavior accordingly and not expose anyone else to the virus.

"In reality, many people who are HIV positive and know their status unfortunately continue to have unprotected sex," states Gerald Stine. "We need major behavior change here, and I haven't seen a disease yet that has brought around behavior change."

Perhaps the most controversial aspect of the testing and reporting issue is the prospect of mandatory partner notification. Contact tracing has long been a valuable public health tool for fighting communicable diseases. Certainly a lot of women would want to know if their partners were infected. But are the costs too great?

New York's new name reporting law also mandates that the health department notify the sexual and needle-sharing partners of HIV-positive people. The law, which exempts those tested in anonymous testing programs, garnered the support of the New York *Times*, which published an editorial stating that people at risk "have a right to information that could prolong their lives and prevent them from unknowingly spreading HIV to others."

"The problem with mandatory partner notification programs," says Terry McGovern, "is that they are completely dependent on the willingness of the infected person to divulge the names of those he or she may have infected." Because of this, she feels that contact tracing is just as effective if done on a voluntary basis, but if mandatory, raises privacy and civil liberties issues, and places women at risk for abuse.

"A couple of women served by our agency had to move because they were threatened by notified partners," says MacNeil, who believes women are being targeted by health officials to name their partners because they are perceived as more vulnerable, and more willing to do so than men.

In the Williams case people generally supported the breach in confidentiality because the person involved had flagrantly disregarded the health of others. Notwithstanding such irresponsible behavior, however, the question remains: Would these public health practices pose too great a threat to the person undergoing mandatory testing or reporting?

In the end, Stine believes, "Mandatory testing for HIV should only be implemented if testing for all other sexually transmitted diseases is made mandatory." He feels that "from the beginning, AIDS has been a political football." Mandatory testing, if done selectively and without the proper checks in place to ensure confidentiality and access to treatment, may end up being just one more game of deadly football, with women—especially disadvantaged women—left on the sidelines.

But what if those checks were ensured? What if women were guaranteed access to counseling, treatment, and protection from discrimination? In such an ideal environment, could mandatory testing, reporting, and partner notification policies be justified, or even called for? Leslie Wolfe doesn't think so. "Mandatory HIV testing deprives women of their moral authority to make medical decisions for themselves and their children and violates the long-standing principle of informed consent," she maintains. "Forcing women to be tested for HIV also leads down a slippery slope toward coercive control of women's reproductive decisions if they test positive—including pressure to undergo abortions, sterilization, and medical treatment to prevent maternal-fetal HIV transmission."

In any case, McGovern doubts a perfect world could exist: "Right now there's supposed to be routine offering of testing and counseling to women, and not even this is being done."

## Questions on Meaning

1. The title of the article asks the question, "Should the state know your HIV status?" What do you think is the author's answer to the question? What is yours?
2. What arguments does Alfieri give in favor of mandatory HIV/AIDS testing? What are some of the rebuttals to those arguments?
3. What reasonable conclusions can you draw from the fact that most women who have AIDS are minorities from low socio-economic groups? State a couple of over-generalizations someone might draw from that information.

## Questions on Rhetorical Strategy and Style

1. Alfieri uses an argumentative sequence to develop her essay. She offers an argument concerning HIV testing and then a counter-argument. Find a couple of examples of this strategy and comment on its effectiveness. Does it inform you or confuse you? Why?
2. Does Alfieri's information seem reliable to you? Explain why or why not with references to specific passages of the essay.

## Writing Assignments

1. Locate a copy of *Ms.* magazine and read through it, noting the subjects of the articles and columns as well as the advertisements. Describe the sort of person who reads *Ms.* magazine, and explain why Alfieri's article is well suited to that person.
2. Locate the agencies in your community that test, treat, or refer people for sexually transmitted diseases. Start with the public health department, free clinics, student health services, crisis hotlines, gay/lesbian organizations, and hospitals. Read the literature they provide and interview people who are willing to talk to you. Write a paper about HIV/AIDS testing and treatment in your community.
3. If you have access to the World Wide Web, enter the phrase "mandatory HIV testing" in a few of the search engines. Write a report that describes and evaluates the HIV/AIDS information that is available on the Web.

# FINISHING SCHOOL

## Maya Angelou

*Maya Angelou (1928– ) was born in St. Louis, Missouri, with the name Marguerite Johnson, but grew up with her grandmother in Stamps, Arkansas, from the age of 3. Her traumatic childhood included being raped at age eight by her mother's boyfriend, after which she became mute for five years. She was shuttled back and forth between mother and grandmother, living for a brief time also with her father and running away to join a group of homeless children. At age 16 she gave birth to her son, Guy. She went through many life changes in the decades that followed, including success as a dancer and actor as well as experiences as a cook, a prostitute, and a chauffeur. Increasingly she focused on her writing, which includes four books of poetry and four plays, as well as the five autobiographical novels for which she is best known:* I Know Why the Caged Bird Sings *(1970),* Gather Together in My Name *(1974),* Swinging' and Swingin' and Gettin' Merry Like Christmas *(1976),* The Heart of a Woman *(1981), and* All God's Children Need Traveling Shoes *(1986). Angelou is an influential African-American author who has received many honors and fellowships. The essay "Finishing School" is excerpted from* I Know Why the Caged Bird Sings, *which describes her early childhood. This essay focuses on the period in her life when she was learning what it meant to be black in a world dominated by whites and to be poor in a world owned by the rich.*

1 Recently a white woman from Texas, who would quickly de- 1
scribe herself as a liberal, asked me about my hometown. When I told her that in Stamps my grandmother had owned

the only Negro general merchandise store since the turn of the century, she exclaimed, "Why, you were a debutante." Ridiculous and even ludicrous. But Negro girls in small Southern towns, whether poverty-stricken or just munching along on a few of life's necessities, were given as extensive and irrelevant preparations for adulthood as rich white girls shown in magazines. Admittedly the training was not the same. While white girls learned to waltz and sit gracefully with a tea cup balanced on their knees, we were lagging behind, learning the mid-Victorian values with very little money to indulge them. . . .

We were required to embroider and I had trunkfuls of colorful dishtowels, pillowcases, runners and handkerchiefs to my credit. I mastered the art of crocheting and tatting, and there was a lifetime's supply of dainty doilies that would never be used in sacheted dresser drawers. It went without saying that all girls could iron and wash, but the finer touches around the home, like setting a table with real silver, baking roasts and cooking vegetables without meat, had to be learned elsewhere. Usually at the source of those habits. During my tenth year, a white woman's kitchen became my finishing school.

Mrs. Viola Cullinan was a plump woman who lived in a three bedroom house somewhere behind the post office. She was singularly unattractive until she smiled, and then the lines around her eyes and mouth which made her look perpetually dirty disappeared, and her face looked like the mask of an impish elf. She usually rested her smile until late afternoon when her women friends dropped in and Miss Glory, the cook, served them cold drinks on the closed-in porch.

The exactness of her house was inhuman. This glass went here and only here. That cup had its place and it was an act of impudent rebellion to place it anywhere else. At twelve o'clock the table was set. At 12:15 Mrs. Cullinan sat down to dinner (whether her husband had arrived or not). At 12:16 Miss Glory brought out the food.

It took me a week to learn the difference between a salad plate, a bread plate and a dessert plate.

Mrs. Cullinan kept up the tradition of her wealthy parents. She was from Virginia. Miss Glory, who was a descendant of slaves that had worked for the Cullinans, told me her history. She had married beneath her (according to Miss Glory). Her husband's family hadn't had their money very long and what they had "didn't 'mount to much."

As ugly as she was, I thought privately, she was lucky to get a husband above or beneath her station. But Miss Glory wouldn't let me say a thing against her mistress. She was very patient with me, however, over the housework. She explained the dishware, silverware and servants' bells. The large round bowl in which soup was served wasn't a soup bowl, it was a tureen. There were goblets, sherbet glasses, ice-cream glasses, wine glasses, green glass coffee cups with matching saucers, and water glasses. I had a glass to drink from, and it sat with Miss Glory's on a separate shelf from the others. Soup spoons, gravy boat, butter knives, salad forks and carving platter were additions to my vocabulary and in fact almost represented a new language. I was fascinated with the novelty, with the fluttering Mrs. Cullinan and her Alice-in-Wonderland house.

Her husband remains, in my memory, undefined. I lumped him with all the other white men that I had ever seen and tried not to see.

On our way home one evening, Miss Glory told me that Mrs. Cullinan couldn't have children. She said that she was too delicate-boned. It was hard to imagine bones at all under those layers of fat. Miss Glory went on to say that the doctor had taken out all her lady organs. I reasoned that a pig's organs included the lungs, heart, and liver, so if Mrs. Cullinan was walking around without those essentials, it explained why she drank alcohol out of unmarked bottles. She was
10 keeping herself embalmed. 10

When I spoke to Bailey about it, he agreed that I was right, but he also informed me that Mr. Cullinan had two daughters by a colored lady and that I knew them very well. He added that the girls were the spitting image of their father. I was unable to remember what he looked like, although I had just left him a few hours before, but I thought of the Coleman girls. They were very light-skinned and certainly didn't look very much like their mother (no one ever mentioned Mr. Coleman).

My pity for Mrs.Cullinan preceded me the next morning like the Cheshire cat's smile. Those girls, who could have been her daughters, were beautiful. They didn't have to straighten their hair. Even when they were caught in the rain, their braids still hung down straight like tamed snakes. Their mouths were pouty little cupid's bows. Mrs. Cullinan didn't know what she missed. Or maybe she did. Poor Mrs. Cullinan.

For weeks after, I arrived early, left late and tried very hard to make up for her barrenness. If she had her own children, she wouldn't have had to ask me to run a thousand errands from her back door to the back door of her friends. Poor old Mrs. Cullinan.

Then one evening Miss Glory told me to serve the ladies on the porch. After I set the tray down and turned toward the kitchen, one of the women asked, "What's your name, girl?" It was the speckled-faced one. Mrs. Cullinan said, "She doesn't talk much. Her name's Margaret."

"Is she dumb?"

"No. As I understand it, she can talk when she wants to but she's usually quiet as a little mouse. Aren't you, Margaret?"

I smiled at her. Poor thing. No organs and couldn't even pronounce my name correctly.

"She's a sweet little thing, though."

"Well, that may be, but the name's too long. I'd never bother myself. I'd call her Mary if I was you."

I fumed into the kitchen. That horrible woman would never have the chance to call me Mary because if I was starving I'd never work for her. . . .

That evening I decided to write a poem on being white, fat, old and without children. It was going to be a tragic ballad. I would have to watch her carefully to capture the essence of her loneliness and pain.

The very next day, she called me by the wrong name. Miss Glory and I were washing up the lunch dishes when Mrs. Cullinan came to the doorway. "Mary?"

Miss Glory asked, "Who?"

Mrs. Cullinan, sagging a little, knew and I knew. "I want Mary to go down to Mrs. Randall's and take her some soup. She's not been feeling well for a few days."

Miss Glory's face was a wonder to see. "You mean Margaret, ma'am. Her name's Margaret."

"That's too long. She's Mary from now on. Heat that soup from last night and put it in the china tureen and, Mary, I want you to carry it carefully."

Every person I knew had a hellish horror of being "called out of his name." It was a dangerous practice to call a Negro anything that could be loosely construed as insulting because of the centuries of their having been called niggers, jigs, dinges, blackbirds, crows, boots and spooks.

Miss Glory had a fleeting second of feeling sorry for me. Then as she handed me the hot tureen she said, "Don't mind, don't pay that no mind. Sticks and stones may break your bones, but words . . . You know, I been working for her for twenty years."

She held the back door open for me. "Twenty years. I wasn't much older than you. My name used to be Hallelujah. That's what Ma named me, but my mistress give me 'Glory,' and it stuck. I likes it better too."

I was in the little path that ran behind the houses when Miss Glory shouted, "It's shorter too."

For a few seconds it was a tossup over whether I would laugh (imagine being named Hallelujah) or cry (imagine letting some white woman rename you for her convenience). My anger saved me from either outburst. I had to quit the job, but the problem was going to be how to do it. Momma wouldn't allow me to quit for just any reason.

"She's a peach. That woman is a real peach." Mrs. Randall's maid was talking as she took the soup from me, and I wondered what her name used to be and what she answered to now.

For a week I looked into Mrs. Cullinan's face as she called me Mary. She ignored my coming late and leaving early. Miss Glory was a little annoyed because I had begun to leave egg yolk on the dishes and wasn't putting much heart in polishing the silver. I hoped that she would complain to our boss, but she didn't.

Then Bailey solved my dilemma. He had me describe the contents of the cupboard and the particular plates she liked best. Her favorite piece was a casserole shaped like a fish and the green glass coffee cups. I kept his instructions in mind, so on the next day when Miss Glory was hanging out clothes and I had again been told to serve the old biddies on the porch, I dropped the empty serving tray. When I heard Mrs. Cullinan scream, "Mary!" I picked up the casserole and two of the green glass cups in readiness. As she rounded the kitchen door I let them fall on the tiled floor.

I could never absolutely describe to Bailey what happened next, because each time I got to the part where she fell on the floor and screwed up her ugly face to cry, we burst out laughing. She actually wobbled around on the floor and picked up shards of the cups and cried, "Oh, Momma. Oh, dear Gawd. It's Mamma's china from Virginia. Oh, Momma, I sorry."

Miss Glory came running in from the yard and the women from the porch crowded around. Miss Glory was almost as broken up as her mistress. "You mean to say she broke our Virginia dishes? What we gone do?"

Mrs. Cullinan cried louder. "That clumsy nigger. Clumsy little black nigger."

Old speckled-face leaned down and asked, "Who did it, Viola? Was it Mary? Who did it?"

Everything was happening so fast, I can't remember whether her action preceded her words, but I know that Mrs. Cullinan said, "Her name's Margaret, goddamn it, her name's Margaret." And she threw a wedge of broken plate at me. It could have been the hysteria which put her aim off, but the flying crockery caught Miss Glory right over her ear and she started screaming.

I left the front door wide open so all the neighbors could hear.

Mrs. Cullinan was right about one thing. My name wasn't Mary.

## Questions on Meaning

1. Explain why Marguerite is so upset when Mrs. Cullinan starts calling her Mary. What does her name mean to her?
2. A "finishing school" at the time taught young women, usually of the upper classes, the "social graces" in preparation for adult life. By working in this wealthy household Marguerite is in fact learning *about* some of these things, though obviously not in the same way as well-to-do white debutantes would. In another, ironic sense, however, this experience helps Marguerite graduate to a more "finished" or mature understanding. Explain what she learns from this experience that she will carry on into her adult life.
3. At first Marguerite is sympathetic to Mrs. Cullinan and even wants to write a poem about her. Describe how Marguerite's attitude toward her evolves as the story unfolds. What does she feel for this woman at the end?

## Questions on Rhetorical Strategy and Style

1. Miss Glory, a key character in the narrative, is also an important part of Angelou's writing strategy. Compare and contrast Marguerite and Miss Glory, and comment on Miss Glory's role in the development of the essay's theme about discrimination and exploitation.
2. Symbolism is a literary device that invests something with a meaning usually much greater than the thing itself. What do Mrs. Cullinan's fancy family dishes symbolize to her? Notice how Marguerite seems at first attracted to these dishes, but then chooses to break them; what do they symbolize to *her?*

## Writing Assignments

1. One of the stereotypical racist statements is, "They all look the same to me." Typically this stereotype characterizes how someone in the dominant race views others of the minority race. Notice in this essay, however, that Angelou speaks of Mr. Cullinan in the same way: "I lumped him in with all the other white men." Consider what it means to think this way and view members of other races in this way. Is it different when a minority member says this? Is there an insight here into how people view people of other

races? Is this "racist" to view others this way, even if no prejudice or discrimination is involved?

2. Although Marguerite might seem to desire to have her name kept pure and unchanged, we know that she changed her name to Maya when she was older. Very few of us use the same name in all contexts throughout our lives. Consider your own name and what it means to your identity. How have you modified it from your childhood? How do you feel if someone changes it or calls you now by a childish version of your name? Write an essay in which you define the importance of personal names, using your own and its variations over time as an example.

# PORNOGRAPHY

## Margaret Atwood

*Margaret Atwood (1939– ), born in Ottawa, Canada, attended the University of Toronto, Radcliffe, and Harvard. At a young age she decided to become a writer, and she has published a remarkable list of novels, poetry, and essays, along with forays into other genres such as children's stories and television scripts. She is best known, however, for her novels:* The Edible Woman *(1969),* Surfacing *(1972),* Lady Oracle *(1976),* Life Before Man *(1979),* Bodily Harm *(1982),* The Handmaid's Tale *(1985),* Cat's Eye *(1989),* The Robber Bride *(1994), and* Alias Grace *(1996). In the following selection, first published in 1988, she explores a topic she first became involved in when doing research for a novel. As a gifted stylist, Atwood is well aware of the power of language—which she uses in this essay to describe vividly the violence of pornography.*

1 When I was in Finland a few years ago for an international 1 writers' conference, I had occasion to say a few paragraphs in public on the subject of pornography. The context was a discussion of political repression, and I was suggesting the possibility of a link between the two. The immediate result was that a male journalist took several large bites out of me. Prudery and pornography are two halves of the same coin, said he, and I was clearly a prude. What could you expect from an Anglo-Canadian? Afterward, a couple of pleasant Scandinavian men asked me what I had been so worked up about. All "pornography" means, they said, is graphic depictions of whores, and what was the harm in that?

Not until then did it strike me that the male journalist and I had two entirely different things in mind. By "pornography," he meant naked bodies and sex. I, on the other hand, had recently been doing the research for my novel *Bodily Harm,* and was still in a state of shock from some of the material I had seen, including the Ontario Board of Film Censors' "outtakes." By "pornography," I meant women getting their nipples snipped off with garden shears, having meat hooks stuck into their vaginas, being disemboweled; little girls being raped; men (yes, there are some men) being smashed to a pulp and forcibly sodomized. The cutting edge of pornography, as far as I could see, was no longer simple old copulation, hanging from the chandelier or otherwise: it was death, messy, explicit and highly sadistic. I explained this to the nice Scandinavian men. "Oh, but that's just the United States," they said. "Everyone knows they're sick." In their country, they said, violent "pornography" of that kind was not permitted on television or in movies; indeed, excessive violence of any kind was not permitted. They had drawn a clear line between erotica, which earlier studies had shown did not incite men to more aggressive and brutal behavior toward women, and violence, which later studies indicated did.

Some time after that I was in Saskatchewan, where, because of the scenes in *Bodily Harm,* I found myself on an open-line radio show answering questions about "pornography." Almost no one who phoned in was in favor of it, but again they weren't talking about the same stuff I was, because they hadn't seen it. Some of them were all set to stamp out bathing suits and negligees, and, if possible, any depictions of the female body whatsoever. God, it was implied, did not approve of female bodies, and sex of any kind, including that practised by bumblebees, should be shoved back into the dark, where it belonged. I had more than a suspicion that *Lady Chatterley's Lover,* Margaret Laurence's *The Diviners,* and indeed most books by most serious modern authors would have ended up as confetti if left in the hands of these callers.

For me, these two experiences illustrate the two poles of the emotionally heated debate that is now thundering around this issue. They also underline the desirability and even the necessity of defining the terms. "Pornography" is now one of those catchalls, like "Marxism" and "feminism," that have become so broad they can mean almost anything, ranging from certain verses in the Bible, ads for skin lotion and sex texts for children to the contents of Penthouse, Naughty '90s postcards and films with titles containing the word *Nazi* that show vicious scenes of torture and killing. It's easy to say that sensible people can tell the difference. Unfortunately, opinions on what constitutes a sensible person vary.

5 But even sensible people tend to lose their cool when they start 5 talking about this subject. They soon stop talking and start yelling, and the name-calling begins. Those in favor of censorship (which may include groups not noticeably in agreement on other issues, such as some feminists and religious fundamentalists) accuse the others of exploiting women through the use of degrading images, contributing to the corruption of children, and adding to the general climate of violence and threat in which both women and children live in this society; or, though they may not give much of a hoot about actual women and children, they invoke moral standards and God's supposed aversion to "filth," "smut" and deviated *perversion,* which may mean ankles.

The camp in favor of total "freedom of expression" often comes out howling as loud as the Romans would have if told they could no longer have innocent fun watching the lions eat up Christians. It too may include segments of the population who are not natural bedfellows: those who proclaim their God-given right to freedom, including the freedom to tote guns, drive when drunk, drool over chicken porn and get off on videotapes of women being raped and beaten, may be waving the same anticensorship banner as responsible liberals who fear the return of Mrs. Grundy, or gay groups for whom sexual emancipation involves the concept of "sexual theatre." *Whatever turns you on* is a handy motto, as is *A man's home is his castle* (and if it includes a dungeon with beautiful maidens strung up in chains and bleeding from every pore, that's his business).

Meanwhile, theoreticians theorize and speculators speculate. Is today's pornography yet another indication of the hatred of the body, the deep mind-body split, which is supposed to pervade Western Christian society? Is it a backlash against the women's movement by men who are threatened by uppity female behavior in real life, so like to fantasize about women done up like outsize parcels, being turned into hamburger, kneeling at their feet in slavelike adoration or sucking off guns? Is it a sign of collective impotence, of a generation of men who can't relate to real women at all but have to make do with bits of celluloid and paper? Is the current flood just a result of smart marketing and aggressive promotion by the money men in what has now become a multibillion-dollar industry? If they were selling movies about men getting their testicles stuck full of knitting needles by women with swastikas on their sleeves, would they do as well, or is this penchant somehow peculiarly male? If so, why? Is pornography a power trip rather than a sex one? Some say that those ropes, chains, muzzles and other restraining devices are an argument for the immense power female sexuality still wields in the male imagination: you don't put these things on dogs unless you're afraid of them. Others, more literary, wonder about the shift from the 19th-century Magic Women or Femme Fatale image to the lollipop-licker, airhead or turkey-carcass treatment of women in porn today. The proporners don't care much about theory: they merely demand product. The antiporners don't care about it in the final analysis either: there's dirt on the street, and they want it cleaned up, now.

It seems to me that this conversation, with its *You're-a-prude/You're-a-pervert* dialectic, will never get anywhere as long as we continue to think of this material as just "entertainment." Possibly we're deluded by the packaging, the format: magazine, book, movie, theatrical presentation. We're used to thinking of these things as part of the "entertainment industry," and we're used to thinking of ourselves as free adult people who ought to be able to see any kind of "entertainment" we want to. That was what the First Choice pay-TV debate was all about. After all, it's only entertainment, right? Entertainment means fun, and only a killjoy would be antifun. What's the harm?

This is obviously the central question: *What's the harm?* If there isn't any real harm to any real people, then the antiporners can tsk-tsk and/or throw up as much as they like, but they can't rightfully expect more legal controls or sanctions. However, the no-harm position is far from being proven.

10 (For instance, there's a clear-cut case for banning—as the federal 10
government has proposed—movies, photos and videos that depict children engaging in sex with adults: real children are used to make the movies, and hardly anybody thinks this is ethical. The possibilities for coercion are too great.)

To shift the viewpoint, I'd like to suggest three other models for looking at "pornography"—and here I mean the violent kind.

Those who find the idea of regulating pornographic materials repugnant because they think it's Fascist or Communist or otherwise not in accordance with the principles of an open democratic society should consider that Canada has made it illegal to disseminate material that may lead to hatred toward any group because of race or religion. I suggest that if pornography of the violent kind depicted these acts being done predominantly to Chinese, to blacks, to Catholics, it would be off the market immediately, under the present laws. Why is hate literature illegal? Because whoever made the law thought that such material might incite real people to do real awful things to other real people. The human brain is to a certain extent a computer: garbage in, garbage out. We only hear about the extreme cases (like that of American multimurderer Ted Bundy) in which pornography has contributed to the death and/or mutilation of women and/or men. Although pornography is not the only factor involved in the creation of such deviance, it certainly has upped the ante by suggesting both a variety of techniques and the social acceptability of such actions. Nobody knows yet what effect this stuff is having on the less psychotic.

Studies have shown that a large part of the market for all kinds of porn, soft and hard, is drawn from the 16-to-21-year-old population of young men. Boys used to learn about sex on the street, or (in Italy, according to Fellini movies) from friendly whores, or, in more genteel surroundings, from girls, their parents, or, once upon a time, in school, more or less. Now porn has been added, and sex education in the schools is rapidly being phased out. The buck has been passed, and boys are being taught that all women secretly like to be raped and that real men get high on scooping out women's digestive tracts.

Boys learn their concept of masculinity from other men: is this what most men want them to be learning? If word gets around that rapists are "normal" and even admirable men, will boys feel that in order to be normal, admirable and masculine they will have to be rapists? Human beings are enormously flexible, and how they turn out depends a lot on how they're educated, by the society in which they're immersed as well as by their teachers. In a society that advertises and glorifies rape or even implicitly condones it, more women get raped. It becomes socially acceptable. And at a time when men and the traditional male role have taken a lot of flak and men are confused and casting around for an acceptable way of being male (and, in some cases, not getting much comfort from women on that score), this must be at times a pleasing thought.

15 It would be naïve to think of violent pornography as just harmless entertainment. It's also an educational tool and a powerful propaganda device. What happens when boy educated on porn meets girl brought up on Harlequin romances? The clash of expectations can be

heard around the block. She wants him to get down on his knees with a ring, he wants her to get down on all fours with a ring in her nose. Can this marriage be saved?

Pornography has certain things in common with such addictive substances as alcohol and drugs: for some, though by no means for all, it induces chemical changes in the body, which the user finds exciting and pleasurable. It also appears to attract a "hard core" of habitual users and a penumbra of those who use it occasionally but aren't dependent on it in any way. There are also significant numbers of men who aren't much interested in it, not because they're undersexed but because real life is satisfying their needs, which may not require as many appliances as those of users.

For the "hard core," pornography may function as alcohol does for the alcoholic: tolerance develops, and a little is no longer enough. This may account for the short viewing time and fast turnover in porn theatres. Mary Brown, chairwoman of the Ontario Board of Film Censors, estimates that for every one mainstream movie requesting entrance to Ontario, there is one porno flick. Not only the quantity consumed but the quality of explicitness must escalate, which may account for the growing violence: once the big deal was breasts, then it was genitals, then copulation, then that was no longer enough and the hard users had to have more. The ultimate kick is death, and after that, as the Marquis de Sade so boringly demonstrated, multiple death.

The existence of alcoholism has not led us to ban social drinking. On the other hand, we do have laws about drinking and driving, excessive drunkenness and other abuses of alcohol that may result in injury or death to others.

This leads us back to the key question: what's the harm? Nobody knows, but this society should find out fast, before the saturation point is reached. The Scandinavian studies that showed a connection between depictions of sexual violence and increased impulse toward it on the part of male viewers would be a starting point, but many more questions remain to be raised as well as answered. What, for instance, is the crucial difference between men who are users and men who are not? Does using affect a man's relationship with actual women, and, if so, adversely? Is there a clear line between erotica and violent pornography, or are they on an escalating continuum? Is this a "men versus women" issue, with all men secretly siding with the propomers and all women secretly siding against? (I think not; there *are* lots of men who don't think that running their true love through the Cuisinart is the best way they can think of to spend a Saturday night, and they're just as nauseated by films of someone else doing it as women are.) Is pornography merely an expression of the sexual confusion of this age or an active contributor to it?

20 Nobody wants to go back to the age of official repression, when even piano legs were referred to as "limbs" and had to wear pantaloons to be decent. Neither do we want to end up in George Orwell's *1984,* in which pornography is turned out by the State to keep the proles in a state of torpor, sex itself is considered dirty and the approved practise is only for reproduction. But Rome under the emperors isn't such a good model either.

If all men and women respected each other, if sex were considered joyful and life-enhancing instead of a wallow in germ-filled glop, if everyone were in love all the time, if, in other words, many people's lives were more satisfactory for them than they appear to be now, pornography might just go away on its own. But since this is obviously not happening, we as a society are going to have to make some informed and responsible decisions about how to deal with it.

## Questions on Meaning

1. What does Atwood mean when she says violent pornography is "an educational tool and a powerful propaganda device"?
2. Atwood speculates about the possible causes for what she sees as an explosion of pornography in modern times. List some of these causes. Does she argue for one cause rather than another? Explain why or why not.
3. The essay asks far more questions about pornography than it attempts to answer, but Atwood still has a clear point to make. State her primary theme in your own words.

## Questions on Rhetorical Strategy and Style

1. Atwood's style is quite graphic in some places in this essay, such as in the second paragraph where she describes violent details of the pornographic film out-takes she saw from the Ontario Board of Film Censors. What effect did such descriptions have on you as you read the essay? Explain how this style is appropriate for what she has to say about her subject.
2. One goal of this essay is simply to define pornography. After establishing that different people mean very different things by the word, Atwood does attempt to define it. What writing techniques does she use to define what she means by pornography?
3. To explain the argument that pornography should be regulated by laws, Atwood compares it to hate literature. Examine how she uses this strategy of comparison and contrast explicitly in that part of the essay but also implicitly throughout by associating the concepts of hatred and pornography.

## Writing Assignments

1. The term "date rape" has arisen in the last decade to describe a specific kind of sexual coercion. Date rape has become so common on most college campuses that colleges and universities have developed programs for purposes of education and prevention. Research what is being done on your own campus to help overcome this problem.
2. Atwood comments that when discussing pornography, people "soon stop talking and start yelling." Think of other social issues about which people become highly emotional. Without getting

into a debate on the issue itself, write an essay exploring why you think it is so difficult for people on both sides of such issues to calmly and rationally debate the question.

3. Atwood mentions how much better it would be "if sex were considered joyful and life-enhancing." Consider all the different ways you have seen sex portrayed in reality and in the media. Write an essay in which you compare and contrast different representations of sex.

# LITTLE RED RIDING HOOD REVISITED

Russell Baker

*Russell Baker (1925– ) was born in a rural town in Virginia and grew up in New Jersey and Maryland. He received his B.A. in English from Johns Hopkins University in 1947 and worked as a reporter for* The Baltimore Sun *and then* The New York Times. *In 1962 he began writing his "Observer" column for the* Times, *which was syndicated in over 400 newspapers for more than two decades. His topics range from mundane everyday annoyances to serious social problems, and his style is generally casual but thoughtful. In 1979 he received the Pulitzer Prize for distinguished commentary; he received the Prize again for his autobiography* Growing Up *(1982). His collections of columns and essays include* All Things Considered *(1965),* Poor Russell's Almanac *(1972),* So This is Depravity *(1980)* The Rescue of Miss Yaskell and Other Pipe Dreams *(1983), and* There's a Country in My Cellar *(1990). The following piece, first published in his* New York Times *column in 1980, is an entertaining satire of the prose style of much scholarly writing.*

1 In an effort to make the classics accessible to contemporary readers, I am translating them into the modern American language. Here is the translation of "Little Red Riding Hood": 1

Once upon a point in time, a small person named Little Red Riding Hood initiated plans for the preparation, delivery and transportation of foodstuffs to her grandmother, a senior citizen residing at a place of residence in a forest of indeterminate dimension.

In the process of implementing this program, her incursion into the forest was in mid-transportation process when it attained interface with an alleged perpetrator. This individual, a wolf, made inquiry as to the whereabouts of Little Red Riding Hood's goal as well as inferring that he was desirous of ascertaining the contents of Little Red Riding Hood's foodstuffs basket, and all that.

"It would be inappropriate to lie to me," the wolf said, displaying his huge jaw capability. Sensing that he was a mass of repressed hostility intertwined with acute alienation, she indicated.

"I see you indicating," the wolf said, "but what I don't see is whatever it is you're indicating at, you dig?"

Little Red Riding Hood indicated more fully, making one thing perfectly clear—to wit, that it was to her grandmother's residence and with a consignment of foodstuffs that her mission consisted of taking her to and with.

At this point in time the wolf moderated his rhetoric and proceeded to grandmother's residence. The elderly person was then subjected to the disadvantages of total consumption and transferred to residence in the perpetrator's stomach.

"That will raise the old woman's consciousness," the wolf said to himself. He was not a bad wolf, but only a victim of an oppressive society, a society that not only denied wolves' rights, but actually boasted of its capacity for keeping the wolf from the door. An interior malaise made itself manifest inside the wolf.

"Is that the national malaise I sense within my digestive tract?" wondered the wolf. "Or is it the old person seeking to retaliate for her consumption by telling wolf jokes to my duodenum?" It was time to make a judgment. The time was now, the hour had struck, the body lupine cried out for decision. The wolf was up to the challenge. He took two stomach powders right away and got into bed.

The wolf had adopted the abdominal-distress recovery posture when Little Red Riding Hood achieved his presence.

"Grandmother," she said, "your ocular implements are of an extraordinary order of magnitude."

"The purpose of this enlarged viewing capability," said the wolf, "is to enable your image to register a more precise impression upon my sight systems."

"In reference to your ears," said Little Red Riding Hood, "it is noted with the deepest respect that far from being underprivileged, their elongation and enlargement appear to qualify you for unparalleled distinction."

"I hear you loud and clear, kid," said the wolf, "but what about these new choppers?"

"If it is not inappropriate," said Little Red Riding Hood, "it might be observed that with your new miracle masticating products you may even be able to chew taffy again."

This observation was followed by the adoption of an aggressive posture on the part of the wolf and the assertion that it was also possible for him, due to the high efficiency ratio of his jaw, to consume little persons, plus, as he stated, his firm determination to do so at once without delay and with all due process and propriety, notwithstanding the fact that the ingestion of one entire grandmother had already provided twice his daily recommended cholesterol intake.

There ensued flight by Little Red Riding Hood accompanied by pursuit in respect to the wolf and a subsequent intervention on the part of a third party, heretofore unnoted in the record.

Due to the firmness of the intervention, the wolf's stomach underwent ax-assisted aperture with the result that Red Riding Hood's grandmother was enabled to be removed with only minor discomfort.

The wolf's indigestion was immediately alleviated with such effectiveness that he signed a contract with the intervening third party to perform with the grandmother in a television commercial demonstrating the swiftness of this dramatic relief for stomach discontent.

"I'm going to be on television," cried grandmother.

And they all joined her happily in crying, "What a phenomena!"

## Questions on Meaning

1. Why do we find Baker's retelling of this classic fairy tale funny? What is Baker really making fun of?
2. In addition to the general satirizing of a certain style of writing, Baker's story also makes humorous jabs along the way at specific social attitudes, such as in the comment about the "victim of an oppressive society." Reread the story carefully and note passages that make fun of particular attitudes or aspects of society.

## Questions on Rhetorical Strategy and Style

1. What kinds of writing are you most familiar with that use the style Baker is here satirizing?
2. Pick out two passages in this story you find particularly humorous. Analyze the phrasing and word choices to determine what exactly is so appropriate and effective about Baker's adopted style.
3. Following are five principles for a clear, effective writing style. For each, find one or two sentences in Baker's story that violate the principle.

   Use active rather than passive voice whenever possible.

   Depend on strong nouns and verbs to carry your meaning, rather than using many modifiers.

   Avoid long strings of prepositional phrases.

   Avoid double negatives (e.g., "this is not unlike . . . ").

   Use simple verbs rather than verb-noun phrases ("he stopped it" rather than "he put a stop to it").

## Writing Assignments

1. Visit the periodical room of your library and browse among the scholarly journals in any field. Do you find articles written in language such as what is satirized in Baker's story? Is such a pretentious style common or rare? What conclusions do you reach about such writing?
2. Try your hand at writing a satire of language such as Baker has done. Choose two classified advertisements from a newspaper—one a help wanted ad describing the kind of person sought for an

employment position, and the other an ad describing an automobile for sale—and rewrite both in pretentious, complicated language that seeks to sound very impressive.

# SCHOOL VS. EDUCATION

## Russell Baker

*Russell Baker (1925– ) was born in a rural town in Virginia and grew up in New Jersey and Maryland. He received his B. A. in English from Johns Hopkins University in 1947 and worked as a reporter for the* Baltimore Sun *and then the* New York Times. *In 1962 he began writing his "Observer" column for the* Times, *which was syndicated in over 400 newspapers for more than two decades. His topics range from the mundane everyday annoyances to serious social problems, and his style is generally casual but thoughtful. In 1979 he received the Pulitzer Prize for distinguished commentary; he received the Prize again for his autobiography* Growing Up *(1982). His collections of columns and essays include* All Things Considered *(1965),* Poor Russell's Almanac *(1972),* So This is Depravity *(1980)* The Rescue of Miss Yaskell and Other Pipe Dreams *(1983), and* There's a Country in My Cellar *(1990). The following piece, first published in his* New York Times *column in 1975, intertwines serious commentary on American education and values with a spoof on what our schools teach. As you read it, think about the serious message Baker wants to communicate to us.*

1 By the age of six the average child will have completed the basic 1
American education and be ready to enter school. If the child has been attentive in these preschool years, he or she will already have mastered many skills.

From television, the child will have learned how to pick a lock, commit a fairly elaborate bank holdup, prevent wetness all day long, get the laundry twice as white, and kill people with a variety of sophisticated armaments.

From watching his parents, the child, in many cases, will already know how to smoke, how much soda to mix with whiskey, what kind of language to use when angry, and how to violate the speed laws without being caught.

At this point, the child is ready for the second stage of education, which occurs in school. There, a variety of lessons may be learned in the very first days.

The teacher may illustrate the economic importance of belonging to a strong union by closing down the school before the child arrives. Fathers and mothers may demonstrate to the child the social cohesion that can be built on shared hatred by demonstrating their dislike for children whose pigmentation displeases them. In the latter event, the child may receive visual instruction in techniques of stoning buses, cracking skulls with a nightstick, and subduing mobs with tear gas. Formal education has begun.

During formal education, the child learns that life is for testing. This stage lasts twelve years, a period during which the child learns that success comes from telling testers what they want to hear.

Early in this stage, the child learns that he is either dumb or smart. If the teacher puts intelligent demands upon the child, the child learns he is smart. If the teacher expects little of the child, the child learns he is dumb and soon quits bothering to tell the testers what they want to hear.

At this point, education becomes more subtle. The child taught by school that he is dumb observes that neither he, she, nor any of the many children who are even dumber, ever fails to be promoted to the next grade. From this, the child learns that while everybody talks a lot about the virtue of being smart, there is very little incentive to stop being dumb.

What is the point of school, besides attendance? the child wonders. As the end of the first formal stage of education approaches, school answers this question. The point is to equip the child to enter college.

Children who have been taught they are smart have no difficulty. They have been happily telling testers what they want to hear for twelve years. Being artists at telling testers what they want to hear, they are admitted to college joyously, where they promptly learn that they are the hope of America.

Children whose education has been limited to adjusting themselves to their schools' low estimates of them are admitted to less joyous colleges which, in some cases, may teach them to read.

At this stage of education, a fresh question arises for everyone. If the point of lower education was to get into college, what is the point of college? The answer is soon learned. The point of college is to prepare the student—no longer a child now—to get into graduate school. In college the student learns that it is no longer enough simply to tell the testers what they want to hear. Many are tested for graduate school; few are admitted.

Those excluded may be denied valuable certificates to prosper in medicine, at the bar, in the corporate boardroom. The student learns that the race is to the cunning and often, alas, to the unprincipled.

Thus, the student learns the importance of destroying competitors and emerges richly prepared to play his role in the great simmering melodrama of American life.

Afterward, the former student's destiny fulfilled, his life rich with Oriental carpets, rare porcelain, and full bank accounts, he may one day find himself with the leisure and the inclination to open a book with a curious mind, and start to become educated.

## Questions on Meaning

1. What kinds of things does Baker say children learn before going to school?
2. Does Baker use any positive examples of what children learn either in or out of school? Why do you think Baker is so critical of both American society and our system of education?
3. Reread the essay's closing paragraph. Why does he say "*start* to become educated" (emphasis added)? What is different about the learning described at that moment from the schooling and lessons learned previously?

## Questions on Rhetorical Strategy and Style

1. Analyze Baker's newspaper column style in this essay. What are the effects of short paragraphs, simple sentences, sweeping generalizations, and so on? How would you describe his tone?
2. Baker does not explicitly define schooling or education in a definitive way, but his meanings emerge clearly by the end of the essay. Summarize in your own words Baker's definitions of school learning and education.
3. Although Baker does not use all the rhetorical devices of persuasion in this essay, he does argue different points along the way. How does he develop his arguments that schools primarily teach one how to take tests, and that college teaches one how to succeed in a rapacious world?

## Writing Assignments

1. How would you evaluate the American educational system as you have experienced it? To what extent is Baker correct in his judgment? What other statements about school and education do you think are necessary to add in order to complete a fair description of American education?
2. What does it mean to be truly educated—apart from having a college degree? Write an essay in which you define your own ideas about what education—at its best—really means.

# THE CASE AGAINST COLLEGE


## Caroline Bird


*Caroline Bird (1915- ) was born in New York City. In addition to writing about business issues affecting women, she has taught at Vassar College and worked in public relations. Her books include* Born Female *(1968),* What Women Want *(1979),* The Two-Paycheck Marriage *(1982),* The Good Years: Your Life in the 21st Century *(1983), and* Lives of Our Own: Secrets of Salty Old Women *(1995). In this essay, which was excerpted from* The Case Against College *(1975), Bird questions the value of college and a college education.*

1 The case *for* college has been accepted without question for more than a generation. All high school graduates ought to go, says Conventional Wisdom and statistical evidence, because college will help them earn more money, become "better" people, and learn to be more responsible citizens than those who don't go.

But college has never been able to work its magic for everyone. And now that close to half our high school graduates are attending, those who don't fit the pattern are becoming more numerous, and more obvious. College graduates are selling shoes and driving taxis; college students sabotage each other's experiments and forge letters of recommendation in the intense competition for admission to graduate school. Others find no stimulation in their studies, and drop out—often encouraged by college administrators.

Some observers say the fault is with the young people themselves—they are spoiled, stoned, overindulged, and expecting too much. But that's mass character assassination, and doesn't explain all campus unhappiness. Others blame the state of the world, and they are partly right. We've been told that young people have to go to college because our economy can't absorb an army of untrained eighteen-year-olds. But disillusioned graduates are learning that it can no longer absorb an army of trained twenty-two-year-olds, either. . . .

The ultimate defense of college has always been that while it may not teach you anything vocationally useful, it will somehow make you a better person, able to do anything better, and those who make it through the process are initiated into the "fellowship of educated men and women." In a study intended to probe what graduates seven years out of college thought their colleges should have done for them, the Carnegie Commission found that most alumni expected the "development of my abilities to think and express myself." But if such respected educational psychologists as Bruner and Piaget are right, specific learning skills have to be acquired very early in life, perhaps even before formal schooling begins.

5 So, when pressed, liberal-arts defenders speak instead about something more encompassing, and more elusive. "College changed me inside," one graduate told us fervently. The authors of a Carnegie Commission report, who obviously struggled for a definition, concluded that one of the common threads in the perceptions of a liberal education is that it provides "an integrated view of the world which can serve as an inner guide." More simply, alumni say that college should have "helped me to formulate the values and goals of my life,"

In theory, a student is taught to develop these values and goals himself, but in practice, it doesn't work quite that way. All but the wayward and the saintly take their sense of the good, the true, and the beautiful from the people around them. When we speak of students acquiring "values" in college, we often mean that they will acquire the values—and sometimes that means only the tastes—of their professors. The values of professors may be "higher" than many students will encounter elsewhere, but they may not be relevant to situations in which students find themselves in college and later.

Of all the forms in which ideas are disseminated, the college professor lecturing a class is the slowest and most expensive. You don't have to go to college to read the great books or learn about the great ideas of Western Man. Today you can find them everywhere—in paperbacks, in the public libraries, in museums, in public lectures, in adult-education courses, in abridged, summarized, or adapted form in magazines, films, and television. The problem is no longer one of access to broadening ideas; the problem is the other way around: how to choose among the many courses of action proposed to us, how to edit the stimulations that pour into our eyes and ears every waking hour. A college experience that piles option on option and stimulation on stimulation merely adds to the contemporary nightmare.

What students and graduates say that they did learn on campus comes under the heading of personal, rather than intellectual, development. Again and again I was told that the real value of college is learning to get along with others, to practice social skills, to "sort out my head," and these have nothing to do with curriculum.

For whatever impact the academic experience used to have on college students, the sheer size of many undergraduate classes . . . dilutes faculty-student dialogue, and, more often than not, they are taught by teachers who were hired when colleges were faced with a shortage of qualified instructors, during their years of expansion and when the big rise in academic pay attracted the mediocre and the less than dedicated.

10 On the social side, colleges are withdrawing from responsibility for feeding, housing, policing, and protecting students at a time when the environment of college may be the most important service it could render. College officials are reluctant to "intervene" in the personal lives of the students. They no longer expect to take over from parents, but often insist that students—who have, most often, never lived away from home before—take full adult responsibility for their plans, achievements, and behavior.

Most college students do not live in the plush, comfortable country-clublike surroundings their parents envisage, or, in some cases, remember. Open dorms, particularly when they are coeducational, are noisy, usually overcrowded, and often messy. Some students desert the institutional "zoos" (their own word for dorms) and move into run-down, overpriced apartments. Bulletin boards in student centers are littered with notices of apartments to share and the drift of conversation suggests that a lot of money is dissipated in scrounging for food and shelter.

Taxpayers now provide more than half of the astronomical sums that are spent on higher education. But less than half of today's high school graduates go on, raising a new question of equity: Is it fair to make all the taxpayers pay for the minority who actually go to college? We decided long ago that it is fair for childless adults to pay school taxes because everyone, parents and nonparents alike, profits by a literate population. Does the same reasoning hold true for state-supported higher education? There is no conclusive evidence on either side.

Young people cannot be expected to go to college for the general good of mankind. They may be more altruistic than their elders, but no great numbers are going to spend four years at hard intellectual labor, let alone tens of thousands of family dollars, for "the advancement of human capability in society at large," one of the many purposes invoked by the Carnegie Commission report. Nor do any considerable number of them want to go to college to beat the Russians to Jupiter, improve the national defense, increase the Gross National Product, lower the crime rate, improve automobile safety, or create a market for the arts—all of which have been suggested at one time or other as benefits taxpayers get for supporting higher education.

One sociologist said that you don't have to have a reason for going to college because it's an institution. His definition of an institution is something everyone subscribes to without question. The burden of proof is not on why you should go to college, but why anyone thinks there might be a reason for not going. The implication—and some educators express it quite frankly—is that an eighteen-year-old high school graduate is still too young and confused to know what he wants to do, let alone what is good for him.

Mother knows best, in other words.

It had always been comfortable for students to believe that authorities, like Mother, or outside specialists, like educators, could determine what was best for them. However, specialists and authorities no longer enjoy the credibility former generations accorded them. Patients talk back to doctors and are not struck suddenly dead. Clients question the lawyer's bills and sometimes get them reduced. It is no longer self-evident that all adolescents must study a fixed curriculum that was constructed at a time when all educated men could agree on precisely what it was that made them educated.

The same with college. If high school graduates don't want to continue their education, or don't want to continue it right away, they may perceive more clearly than their elders that college is not for them.

College is an ideal place for those young adults who love learning for its own sake, who would rather read than eat, and who like nothing better than writing research papers. But they are a minority, even at the prestigious colleges, which recruit and attract the intellectually oriented.

The rest of our high school graduates need to look at college more closely and critically, to examine it as a consumer product, and decide if the cost in dollars, in time, in continued dependency, and in future returns, is worth the very large investment each student—and his family—must make.

## Questions on Meaning

1. What is Bird's thesis in this essay? Where does she summarize her key point?
2. Bird states that many people believe college is beneficial simply because of "conventional wisdom." What does she cite as standard reasons for going to college? How has this "conventional wisdom" changed since the mid-1970s, when Bird wrote this essay?
3. Bird states that *access* to "ideas" is not a problem, but that college is the "slowest and most expensive" way to disseminate "ideas." What *is* the problem with "ideas" according to Bird?

## Questions on Rhetorical Strategy and Style

1. Bird uses a number of rhetorical strategies to support her argument. Find where she presents examples (facts, statistics, opinions, etc.) and when she uses cause and effect in building her case.
2. In the second paragraph, Bird states that "close to half" of high school graduates attend college. Later in the essay (in the paragraph beginning, "Taxpayers now provide . . . "), she states that "less than half" of high school graduates go on. What is her reason for stating the same statistic in two different ways? What is your reaction to that writing strategy?

## Writing Assignments

1. Describe your decision to attend college or take college courses. What college experiences have other members of your family had? What alternatives did you explore? What would you do if you discover, part way through college, that it is not for you—would you leave or try to graduate?
2. Bird states that there is no evidence to justify state-supported higher education. What is your opinion of taxpayer subsidies for college? What benefits do you feel society gains by encouraging young people to attend college that offsets the cost?
3. Conventional wisdom drives a lot of our decisions—in addition to whether or not we attend college. We try to stay warm in the winter to keep from catching a cold—although cold temperatures per se don't cause the common cold. We assume that churchgoing folks have high morals and ethics, although a lot of crooks and scoundrels have sat in pews. Write an essay about some

"conventional wisdom" that you take issue with. Use facts and statistics, where possible, to argue against this dictum.

# THE GENDER BLUR

## Deborah Blum

*Deborah Blum (1954-) was born in Urbana, Illinois to an entomologist and a legal scholar. Educated in journalism at the University of Georgia (B.A.) and the University of Wisconsin (M.A.), she has worked as a reporter for several newspapers in Georgia and Florida, and as a science writer for the Sacramento, California* Bee. *Currently Blum is professor of journalism at the University of Wisconsin. Her first book,* The Monkey Wars, *explored the issue of medical and psychological experimentation on primates. Lauded for its balanced approach, the book grew out of a Pulitzer Prize-winning series she had written on the subject in 1992. Her work has also earned her other awards, among them a Westinghouse Award from the American Academy of Arts and Sciences and a Clarion Award for Investigative Reporting, both in 1992; and a National Award for Non-Deadline Reporting from the Society of Professional Journalists in 1996. In 1997 she co-edited* A Field Guide for Science Writers. *Her most recent book,* Sex on the Brain: The Biological Differences Between Men and Women *(1997), explores the roles of biology and environment in determining gender. In this selection, based on that book, Blum describes how imprecise biological determiners of sex can be. Using extensive examples of indeterminate sexual identity, Blum raises questions about the rigid classification of male and female in the human race.*

---

"The Gender Blur" by Deborah Blum from *Utne Reader*, No. 45, September–October, 1998

1 I was raised in one of those university-based, liberal elite families 1
that politicians like to ridicule. In my childhood, every human being—regardless of gender—was exactly alike under the skin, and I mean exactly, barring his or her different opportunities. My parents wasted no opportunity to bring this point home. One Christmas, I received a Barbie doll and a softball glove. Another brought a green enamel stove, which baked tiny cakes by the heat of a lightbulb, and also a set of steel-tipped darts and competition-quality dartboard. Did I mention the year of the chemistry set and the ballerina doll?

It wasn't until I became a parent—I should say, a parent of two boys—that I realized I had been fed a line and swallowed it like a sucker (barring the part about opportunities, which I still believe). This dawned on me during my older son's dinosaur phase, which began when he was about 2 1/2. Oh, he loved dinosaurs, all right, but only the blood-swilling carnivores. Plant-eaters were wimps and losers, and he refused to wear a T-shirt marred by a picture of a stegosaur. I looked down at him one day, as he was snarling around my feet and doing his toddler best to gnaw off my right leg, and I thought: This goes a lot deeper than culture.

Raising children tends to bring on this kind of politically incorrect reaction. Another friend came to the same conclusion watching a son determinedly bite his breakfast toast into the shape of a pistol he hoped would blow away—or at least terrify—his younger brother. Once you get past the guilt part—Did I do this? Should I have bought him that plastic allosaur with the oversized teeth?—such revelations can lead you to consider the far more interesting field of gender biology, where the questions take a different shape: Does love of carnage begin in culture or genetics, and which drives which? Do the gender roles of our culture reflect an underlying biology, and, in turn, does the way we behave influence that biology?

The point I'm leading up to—through the example of my son's innocent love of predatory dinosaurs—is actually one of the most straightforward in this debate. One of the reasons we're so fascinated by childhood behaviors is that, as the old saying goes, the child becomes the man (or woman, of course.) Most girls don't spend their preschool years snarling around the house and pretending to chew off their companion's legs. And they—mostly—don't grow up to be as aggressive as men. Do the ways that we amplify those early differences in childhood shape the adults we become? Absolutely. But it's worth exploring the starting place—the faint signal that somehow gets amplified.

"There's plenty of room in society to influence sex differences," says Marc Breedlove, a behavioral endocrinologist at the University of California at Berkeley and a pioneer in defining how hormones can help build sexually different nervous systems. "Yes, we're born with predispositions, but it's society that amplifies them, exaggerates them. I believe that—except for the sex differences in aggression. Those [differences] are too massive to be explained simply by society."

Aggression does allow a straightforward look at the issue. Consider the following statistics: Crime reports in both the United States and Europe record between 10 and 15 robberies committed by men for every one by a woman. At one point, people argued that this was explained by size difference. Women weren't big enough to intimidate, but that would change, they predicted, with the availability of compact weapons. But just as little girls don't routinely make weapons out of toast, women—even criminal ones—don't seem drawn to weaponry in the same way that men are. Almost twice as many male thieves and robbers use guns as their female counterparts do.

Or you can look at more personal crimes: domestic partner murders. Three-fourths of men use guns in those killings; 50 percent of women do. Here's more from the domestic front: In conflicts in which a woman killed a man, he tended to be the one who had started the fight—in 51.8 percent of the cases, to be exact. When the man was the killer, he again was the likely first aggressor, and by an even more dramatic margin. In fights in which women dies, they had started the argument only 12.5 percent of the time.

Enough. You can parade endless similar statistics but the point is this: Males are more aggressive, not just among humans but among almost all species on earth. Male chimpanzees, for instance, declare war on neighboring troops, and one of their strategies is a warning strike: They kill females and infants to terrorize and intimidate. In terms of simple, reproductive genetics, it's an advantage of males to be aggressive: You can muscle you way into dominance, winning more sexual encounters, more offspring, more genetic future. For the female—especially in a species like ours, with time for just one successful pregnancy a year—what's the genetic advantage in brawling?

Thus the issue becomes not whether there is a biologically influenced sex difference in aggression—the answer being a solid, technical "You betcha"—but rather how rigid that difference is. The best science, in my opinion, tends to align with basic common sense. We all know that there are extraordinarily gentle men and murderous women. Sex differences are always generalizations: They refer to a behavior, with some evolutionary rationale behind it. They never define, entirely, an individual. And that fact alone should tell us that there's always—even in the most biologically dominated traits—some flexibility, an instinctive ability to respond, for better and worse, to the world around us.

10 This is true even with physical characteristics that we've often assumed are nailed down by genetics. Scientists now believe height, for instance, is only about 90 percent heritable. A person's genes might code for a six-foot-tall body, but malnutrition could literally cut that short. And there's also some evidence, in girls anyway, that children with stressful childhoods tend to become shorter adults. So while some factors are predetermined, there's evidence that the prototypical male/female body design can be readily altered.

It's a given that humans, like most other species—bananas, spiders, sharks, ducks, any rabbit you pull out of a hat—rely on two sexes for reproduction. So basic is that requirement that we have chromosomes whose primary purpose is to deliver the genes that order up a male or a female. All other chromosomes are numbered, but we label the sex chromosomes with the letters X and Y. We get one each from our mother and our father, and the basic combinations are these: XX makes female, XY makes male.

There are two important—and little known—points about these chromosomal matches. One is that even with this apparently precise system, there's nothing precise—or guaranteed—about the physical construction of male and female. The other point makes that possible. It appears that sex doesn't matter in the early stages of embryonic development. We are unisex at the point of conception.

If you examine an embryo at about six weeks, you see that it has the ability to develop in either direction. The fledgling embryo has two sets of ducts—Wolffian for male, Muellerian for female—an either/or structure, held in readiness for further development. If testosterone and other androgens are released by hormone-producing cells, then the Wolffian ducts develop into the channel that connects penis to testes, and the female ducts wither away.

Without testosterone, the embryo takes on a female form; the male ducts vanish and the Muellerian ducts expand into oviducts, uterus, and vagina. In other words, in humans, anyway (the opposite is true in birds), the female is the default sex. Back in the 1950s, the famed biologist Alfred Jost showed that if you castrate a male rabbit fetus, choking off testosterone, you produce a completely feminized rabbit.

We don't do these experiments in humans—for obvious reasons—but there are naturally occurring instances that prove the same point. For instance: In the fetal testes are a group of cells called Leydig cells, that make testosterone. In rare cases, the fetus doesn't make enough of these cells (a defect known as Leydig cell hypoplasia). In this circumstance we see the limited power of the XY chromosome. These boys have the right chromosomes and the right genes to be boys; they just don't grow a penis. Obstetricians and parents often think they see a baby girl, and these children are routinely raised as daughters. Usually, the "mistake" is caught about the time of puberty, when menstruation doesn't start. A doctor's examination shows the child to be internally male; there are usually small testes, often tucked with the abdomen. As the researchers put it, if the condition had been know from the beginning, "the sisters would have been born as brothers."

Just to emphasize how tricky all this body-building can get, there's a peculiar genetic defect that seems to be clustered by heredity in a small group of villages in the Dominican Republic. The result of the defect is a failure to produce an enzyme that concentrates testosterone, specifically for building genitals. One obscure little enzyme only, but here's what happens without it: You get a boy with undescended testes and a penis so short and stubby that it resembles an oversized clitoris.

In the mountain villages of this Caribbean nation, people are used to it. The children are usually raised as "conditional" girls. At puberty, the secondary tide of androgens rises and is apparently enough to finish the construction project. The scrotum suddenly descends, the phallus grows, and the child develops a distinctly male body—narrow hips, muscular build, and even slight beard growth. At that point, the family shifts the child over from daughter to son. The dresses are thrown out. He begins to wear male clothes and starts dating girls. People in the Dominican Republic are so familiar with this condition that there's a colloquial name for it: *guevedoces*, meaning "eggs (or testes) at 12."

It's the comfort level with this slip-slide of sexual identity that's so remarkable and, I imagine, so comforting to the children involved. I'm positive that the sexual transition of these children is less traumatic than the abrupt awareness of the "sisters who would have been brothers." There's a message of tolerance there, well worth repeating, and there are some other key lessons too.

These defects are rare and don't alter the basic male-female division of our species. They do emphasize how fragile those divisions can be. Biology allows flexibility, room to change, to vary and grow. With that comes room for error as well. That it's possible to live with these genetic defects, that they don't merely kill us off, is a reminder that we, male and female alike, exist on a continuum of biological possibilities that can overlap and sustain either sex.

Marc Breedlove points out that the most difficult task may be separating how the brain responds to hormones from how the brain responds to the *results* of hormones. Which brings us back, briefly, below the belt: In this context, the penis is just a result, the product of androgens at work before birth. "And after birth," says Breedlove, "virtually everyone who interacts with that individual will note that he has a penis, and will, in many instances, behave differently than if the individual was a female."

Do the ways that we amplify physical and behavioral differences in childhood shape who we become as adults? Absolutely. But to understand that, you have to understand the differences themselves—their beginning and the very real biochemistry that may lie behind them.

Here is a good place to focus on testosterone—a hormone that is both well-studied and generally underrated. First, however, I want to acknowledge that there are many other hormones and neurotransmitters that appear to influence behavior. Preliminary work shows that fetal boys are a little more active than fetal girls. It's pretty difficult to argue socialization at that point. There's a strong suspicion that testosterone may create the difference.

And there are a couple of relevant animal models to emphasize the point. Back in the 1960s, Robert Goy, a psychologist at the University of Wisconsin at Madison, first documented that young male monkeys play much more roughly than young females. Goy went on to show that if you manipulate testosterone level—raising it in females, damping it down in males—you can reverse those effects, creating sweet little male monkeys and rowdy young females.

Is testosterone the only factor at work here? I don't think so. But clearly we can argue a strong influence, and, interestingly, studies have found that girls with congenital adrenal hypoplasia—who run high in testosterone—tend to be far more fascinated by trucks and toy weaponry than most little girls are. They lean toward rough-and-tumble play, too. As it turns out, the strongest influence on this "abnormal" behavior is not parental disapproval, but the company of other little girls, who tone them down and direct them toward more routine girl games.

25 And that reinforces an early point: If there is indeed a biology to sex differences, we amplify it. At some point—when it is still up for debate—we gain a sense of our gender, and with it a sense of "gender-appropriate" behavior.

Some scientists argue for some evidence of gender awareness in infancy, perhaps by the age of 12 months. The consensus seems to be that full-blown "I'm a girl" or "I'm a boy" instincts arrive between the ages of 2 and 3. Research shows that if a family operates in a very traditional, Beaver Cleaver kind of environment, filled with awareness of and association with "proper" gender behaviors, the "boys do trucks, girls do dolls" attitude seems to come very early. If a child grows up in a less traditional family, with an emphasis on partnership and sharing—"We all do the dishes, Joshua"—children maintain a more flexible sense of gender roles until about age 6.

In this period, too, relationships between boys and girls tend to fall into remarkably strict lines. Interviews with children find that 3-year-olds say that about half their friendships are with the opposite sex. By the age of 5, that drops to 20 percent. By 7, almost no boys or girls have, or will admit to having, best friends of the opposite sex. They still hang out on the same playground, play on the same soccer teams. They may be friendly, but the real friendships tend to be boy-to-boy or girl-to-girl.

There's some interesting science that suggests that the space between boys and girls is a normal part of development; there are periods during which children may thrive and learn from hanging out with peers of the same sex. Do we, as parents, as a culture at large, reinforce such separations? Is the pope Catholic? One of my favorite studies looked at little boys who asked for toys. If they asked for a heavily armed action figure, they got the soldier about 70 percent of the time. If they asked for a "girl" toy, like a baby doll or a Barbie, their parents purchased it maybe 40 percent of the time. Name a child who won't figure out to work *that* system.

How does all this fit together—toys and testosterone, biology and behavior, the development of the child into the adult, the way that men and women relate to one another?

30 Let me make a cautious statement about testosterone: It not only has some body-building functions, it influences some behaviors as well. Let's make that a little less cautious: These behaviors include rowdy play, sex drive, competitiveness, and an in-your-face attitude. Males tend to have a higher baseline of testosterone than females—in our species, about seven to ten times as much—and therefore you would predict (correctly, I think) that all of those behaviors would be more generally found in men than in women.

But testosterone is also one of my favorite examples of how responsive biology is, how attuned it is to the way we live our lives. Testosterone, it turns out, rises in response to competition and threat. In the days of our ancestors, this might have been hand-to-hand combat or high-risk hunting endeavors. Today, scientists have measured testosterone rise in athletes preparing for a game, in chess players awaiting a match, in spectators following a soccer competition.

If a person—or even just a person's favored team—wins, testosterone continues to rise. It falls with a loss. (This also makes sense in an evolutionary perspective. If one was being clobbered with a club, it would be extremely unhelpful to have a hormone urging one to battle on.) Testosterone also rises in the competitive world of dating, settles down with a stable and supportive relationship, climbs again if the relationship starts to falter.

It's been know for years that men in high-stress professions—say, police work or corporate law—have higher testosterone levels than men in the ministry. It turns out that women in the same kind of strong-attitude professions have higher testosterone than women who choose to stay home. What I like about this is the chicken-or-egg aspect. If you argue that testosterone influenced the behavior of those women, which came first? Did they have high testosterone and choose the law? Or did they choose the law, and the competitive environment ratcheted them up on the androgen scale? Or could both be at work?

And, returning to children for a moment, there's an ongoing study by Pennsylvania researchers, tracking that question in adolescent girls, who are being encouraged by their parents to engage in competitive activities that were once for boys only. As they do so, the researchers are monitoring, regularly, two hormones: testosterone and cortisol, a stress hormone. Will these hormones rise in response to this new, more traditionally male environment? What if more girls choose the competitive path; more boys choose the other? Will female testosterone levels rise, male levels fall? Will that wonderful, unpredictable, flexible biology that we've been given allow a shift, so that one day, we will literally be far more alike?

35 We may not have answers to all those questions, but we can ask 35 them, and we can expect that the answers will come someday, because science clearly shows us that such possibilities exist. In this most important sense, sex differences offer us a paradox. It is only through exploring and understanding what makes us different that we can begin to understand what binds us together.

## Questions on Meaning

1. According to Blum, why are males naturally more aggressive than females? What evidence does she offer to support this conclusion?
2. What does Blum mean when she says that "the female is the default sex" in humans? How do the examples she provides explain the importance of understanding this biological fact?
3. Blum and the experts she cites emphasize the significance of culture and environment "amplifying" biological differences. What biologically determined behaviors are often amplified in male and female children? How are those behaviors amplified?

## Questions on Rhetorical Strategy and Style

1. Effective classification demands that each part of an identified group share the same features. How does Blum's analysis call into question the classifications "male" and "female"? What generally accepted features of each group does she question?
2. Blum employs several examples to illustrate her point. Choose two of those examples and explain how they work with the scientific data to underscore the imprecision of sex determiners in humans.
3. What is the impact of Blum's opening her essay with the story of her own childhood and her son's? How do you react as a reader to those stories? What would be the effect on the essay by beginning with a more scientific discussion?

## Writing Assignments

1. Think about your own childhood: In what ways did your family reinforce traditionally accepted sex roles? To what extent were you free to exhibit behaviors of the opposite sex? Write an essay in which you use these examples to support or challenge Blum's conclusions.
2. Although Blum does not discuss the political implications of her work, it is clear that sex roles are important to many political discussions. Find articles in magazines and newspapers on sex-discrimination, "family values," the feminist movement, the promise-keepers movement, and other sex-related issues. What groups are more likely to embrace a biological explanation of sex roles? What groups emphasize cultural influences? To what extent do any of these groups use scientific evidence to support their positions?

# THE DEHUMANIZATION OF THE INDIAN

## Haig A. Bosmajian

*Haig A. Bosmajian (1927– ), a speech educator, was born in Fresno, California. Educated at the University of California at Berkeley (B.A., 1949), the University of the Pacific (M.A., 1951), and Stanford University (Ph.D., 1960), Bosmajian has taught at the University of Idaho, the University of Connecticut, and the University of Washington. In 1991, he received the Bicentennial of the Bill of Rights award from the Western States Communication Association. His publications include* The Language of Oppression *(1973) (recipient of the Orwell Award),* Justice Douglas *(1980),* Freedom of Speech *(1982), and* The Freedom Not to Speak *(1994), as well as the* First Amendment in the Classroom Series. *This essay, from* The Language of Oppression, *describes how words can be dehumanizing and brutalizing.*

1 While the state and church as institutions have defined the 1
Indian into subjugation, there has been in operation the use of a suppressive language by society at large which has perpetuated the dehumanization of the Indian. Commonly used words and phrases relegate the Indian to an inferior, infantile status: "The only good Indian is a dead Indian"; "Give it back to the Indians"; "drunken Indians"; "dumb Indians"; "Redskins"; "Indian giver." Writings and speeches include references to the "Indian problem" in the same manner that references have been made by whites to "the Negro problem" and by the Nazis to "the Jewish problem." There was no "Jewish problem" in Germany until the Nazis linguistically created the myth; there was no "Negro problem" until white Americans

created the myth; similarly, the "Indian problem" has been created in such a way that the oppressed, not the oppressor, evolve as "the problem."

As the list of negative "racial characteristics" of the "Indian race" grew over the years, the redefinition of the individual Indian became easier and easier. He or she was trapped by the racial definitions, stereotypes, and myths. No matter how intelligent, how "civilized" the Indian became, he or she was still an Indian.

## Questions on Meaning

1. What does Bosmajian mean when he says that the state and church have "defined the Indian into subjugation"?
2. What is the "Indian problem"? Why is it similar to the "Negro problem" and the "Jewish problem"?
3. How have negative stereotypes hurt Indians' efforts to improve themselves?

## Questions on Rhetorical Strategy and Style

1. What denigrating words and phrases does Bosmajian cite that have been used to create negative definitions of Indians?
2. Describe your reaction to Bosmajian relating the term "Indian problem" to "Negro problem" and "Jewish problem." How persuasive were these other examples of creating myths to oppress?
3. Describe the image most people you know have of Native Americans. How has this image changed in the last decade? How does this image differ from the image described in this 1974 essay?

## Writing Assignments

1. Research the incomes, educational levels, home ownership, and other measures of "success" in America for whites, African-Americans, Asian-Americans, and Hispanics, and compare them to Indians. What do you think could be done to help improve the lot of Native Americans?
2. Write an essay defining oppression. Explain the different ways in which oppression can occur—such as verbal and economic. Characterize oppressors and the oppressed.

# THE MYTH OF SISYPHUS

## Albert Camus

*Albert Camus (1913–1960) was born in Mondovi, Algeria (at that time a colony of France). Camus attended the University of Algeria, where he majored in philosophy. He wrote for the* Alger-Republicain, *a socialist paper, between 1937 and 1939, and edited* Soir-Republicain, *another socialist paper, from 1939–1940. He moved to France during World War II, joined the Resistance, and wrote for and edited the underground publication* Combat. *A leading proponent of existentialism, Camus is perhaps best remembered for* The Rebel: An Essay on Man in Revolt *(1954), for which he received the Nobel Prize for Literature (1957). Other books by Camus include* The Myth of Sisyphus *(1942), his first collection of philosophical essays, and the novels* The Stranger *(1942),* The Plague *(1947),* The Fall *(1956), and* Exile and the Kingdom *(1957). In this story, Camus analyzes the meaning and impact of the fate of Sisyphus—a symbol of the human condition.*

1 The gods had condemned Sisyphus to ceaselessly rolling a rock to the top of a mountain, whence the stone would fall back of its own weight. They had thought with some reason that there is no more dreadful punishment than futile and hopeless labor. 1

If one believes Homer, Sisyphus was the wisest and most prudent of mortals. According to another tradition, however, he was disposed to practice the profession of highwayman. I see no contradiction in this. Opinions differ as to the reasons why he became the futile laborer of the underworld. To begin with, he is accused of a certain levity in regard to the gods. He stole their secrets. Aegina, the daughter of

Aesopus, was carried off by Jupiter. The father was shocked by that disappearance and complained to Sisyphus. He, who knew of the abduction, offered to tell about it on condition that Aesopus would give water to the citadel of Corinth. To the celestial thunderbolts he preferred the benediction of water. He was punished for this in the underworld. Homer tells us also that Sisyphus had put Death in chains. Pluto could not endure the sight of his deserted, silent empire. He dispatched the god of war, who liberated Death from the hands of her conqueror.

It is said also that Sisyphus, being near to death, rashly wanted to test his wife's love. He ordered her to cast his unburied body into the middle of the public square. Sisyphus woke up in the underworld. And there, annoyed by an obedience so contrary to human love, he obtained from Pluto permission to return to earth in order to chastise his wife. But when he had seen again the face of this world, enjoyed water and sun, warm stones and the sea, he no longer wanted to go back to the infernal darkness. Recalls, signs of anger, warnings were of no avail. Many years more he lived facing the curve of the gulf, the sparkling sea, and the smiles of earth. A decree of the gods was necessary. Mercury came and seized the impudent man by the collar and, snatching him from his joys, led him forcibly back to the underworld, where his rock was ready for him.

You have already grasped that Sisyphus is the absurd hero. He *is,* as much through his passions as through his torture. His scorn of the gods, his hatred of death, and his passion for life won him that unspeakable penalty in which the whole being is exerted toward accomplishing nothing. This is the price that must be paid for the passions of this earth. Nothing is told us about Sisyphus in the underworld. Myths are made for the imagination to breathe life into them. As for this myth, one sees merely the whole effort of a body straining to raise the huge stone, to roll it and push it up a slope a hundred times over; one sees the face screwed up, the cheek tight against the stone, the shoulder bracing the clay-covered mass, the foot wedging it, the fresh start with arms outstretched, the wholly human security of two earth-clotted hands. At the very end of his long effort measured by skyless space and time without depth, the purpose is achieved. Then Sisyphus watches the stone rush down in a few moments toward that lower world whence he will have to push it up again toward the summit. He goes back down to the plain.

5 It is during that return, that pause, that Sisyphus interests me. A face that toils so close to stones is already stone itself! I see that man going back down with a heavy yet measured step toward the torment of which he will never know the end. That hour like a breathing-space which returns as surely as his suffering, that is the hour of consciousness. At each of those moments when he leaves the heights and gradually sinks toward the lairs of the gods, he is superior to his fate. He is stronger than his rock.

If this myth is tragic, that is because its hero is conscious. Where would his torture be, indeed, if at every step the hope of succeeding upheld him? The workman of today works every day in his life at the same tasks, and his fate is no less absurd. But it is tragic only at the rare moments when it becomes conscious. Sisyphus, proletarian of the gods, powerless and rebellious, knows the whole extent of his wretched condition: it is what he thinks of during his descent. The lucidity that was to constitute his torture at the same time crowns his victory. There is no fate that cannot be surmounted by scorn.

If the descent is thus sometimes performed in sorrow, it can also take place in joy. This word is not too much. Again I fancy Sisyphus returning toward his rock, and the sorrow was in the beginning. When the images of earth cling too tightly to memory, when the call of happiness becomes too insistent, it happens that melancholy rises in man's heart: this is the rock's victory, this is the rock itself. The boundless grief is too heavy to bear. These are our nights of Gethsemane. But crushing truths perish from being acknowledged. Thus, Oedipus at the outset obeys fate without knowing it. But from the moment he knows, his tragedy begins. Yet at the same moment, blind and desperate, he realizes that the only bond linking him to the world is the cool hand of a girl. Then a tremendous remark rings out: "Despite so many ordeals, my advanced age and the nobility of my soul make me conclude that all is well." Sophocles' Oedipus, like Dostoevsky's Kirilov, thus gives the recipe for the absurd victory. Ancient wisdom confirms modern heroism.

One does not discover the absurd without being tempted to write a manual of happiness. "What! by such narrow ways—?" There is but one world, however. Happiness and the absurd are two sons of the same earth. They are inseparable. It would be a mistake to say that happiness necessarily springs from the absurd discovery. It happens as well that the feeling of the absurd springs from happiness. "I conclude that all is well," says Oedipus, and that remark is sacred. It echoes in the wild and limited universe of man. It teaches that all is not, has not been, exhausted. It drives out of this world a god who had come into it with dissatisfaction and a preference for futile sufferings. It makes of fate a human matter, which must be settled among men.

All Sisyphus' silent joy is contained therein. His fate belongs to him. His rock is his thing. Likewise, the absurd man, when he contemplates his torment, silences all the idols. In the universe suddenly restored to its silence, the myriad wondering little voices of the earth rise up. Unconscious, secret calls, invitations from all the faces, they are the necessary reverse and price of victory. There is no sun without shadow, and it is essential to know the night. The absurd man says yes and his effort will henceforth be unceasing. If there is a personal fate, there is no higher destiny, or at least there is but one which he concludes is inevitable and despicable. For the rest, he knows himself to be the master of his days. At that subtle moment when man glances backward over his life, Sisyphus returning toward his rock, in that slight pivoting he contemplates that series of unrelated actions which becomes his fate, created by him, combined under his memory's eye and soon sealed by his death. Thus, convinced of the wholly human origin of all that is human, a blind man eager to see who knows that the night has no end, he is still on the go. The rock is still rolling.

10 I leave Sisyphus at the foot of the mountain! One always finds 10
one's burden again. But Sisyphus teaches the higher fidelity that negates the gods and raises rocks. He too concludes that all is well. This universe henceforth without a master seems to him neither sterile nor futile. Each atom of that stone, each mineral flake of that night-filled mountain, in itself forms a world. The struggle itself toward the heights is enough to fill a man's heart. One must imagine Sisyphus happy.

## Questions on Meaning

1. What is Camus' thesis for the essay? Find a number of different ways in which he states it.
2. Why does Camus see no contradiction in Sisyphus's being both wise and prudent and a highwayman? What does that reflect of Camus' view of mankind?
3. Why does Camus call Sisyphus an "absurd hero"? What was Sisyphus's passion?

## Questions on Rhetorical Strategy and Style

1. Find where Camus uses a cause and effect writing strategy to explain Sisyphus's punishment.
2. Describe Camus' analysis of Sisyphus's return to the bottom of the mountain. What does Camus conclude about Sisyphus at the end of his return trip?
3. How does Camus compare and contrast absurdity and happiness? Explain why you agree or disagree that they are "sons of the same earth."

## Writing Assignments

1. Consider an endless task that you have faced—a chore, a school assignment, a summer job—in which you were able to overcome absurdity with happiness. At what point did you come face-to-face with the absurdity of your toil? How did that recognition change your perspective?
2. How does Camus relate Sisyphus's fate to the human condition? Do you "imagine Sisyphus happy"? How does this essay make you feel about your lot in life?
3. Write an essay describing one of your "nights of Gethsemane." Explain what led you into despair and the agony you felt. Describe how it resolved. Were you able to put aside the "crushing truths"? If so, how?

# WHY WE DON'T NEED ANIMAL EXPERIMENTATION

## Peggy Carlson

*Peggy Carlson, a physician, has served as research director of the Physician's Committee for Responsible Medicine. This essay, published as a rebuttal letter to the* Wall Street Journal *in 1995, argues that real breakthroughs in medicine result from research on human subjects.*

1 The issue of animal experimentation has become so polarized 1
that rational thinking seems to have taken a back seat. Heloisa Sabin's October 18 editorial-page article "Animal Research Saves Lives" serves only to further misinform and polarize. She does a great disservice to science to incorrectly portray the debate about animal experimentation as occurring between "animal rights activists" and scientists. The truth is, the value of animal experimentation is being questioned by many scientists.

Mrs. Sabin uses the example of the polio vaccine developed by her husband to justify animal experimentation. However, in the case of the polio vaccine, misleading animal experiments detoured scientists away from reliable clinical studies thereby, according to Dr. Sabin himself, delaying the initial work on polio prevention. It was also unfortunate that the original polio vaccine was produced using monkey cells instead of available human cells as can be done today. The use of monkey cells resulted in viruses with the potential to cause serious disease being transferred to humans when the polio vaccine was administered.

The polio vaccine example cannot logically be used to justify the current level of animal experimentation—several billion dollars and about 30 million animals yearly. Although most people would prefer to believe that the death and suffering of all these animals is justified, the facts do not support that conclusion.

Nearly everything that medicine has learned about what substances cause human cancer and birth defects has come from human clinical and epidemiological studies because animal experiments do not accurately predict what occurs in humans. Dr. Bross, the former Director of Biostatistics at the Roswell Institute for Cancer Research states, "While conflicting animal results have often delayed and hampered advances in the war on cancer, they have never produced a single substantial advance either in the prevention or treatment of cancer." A 1990 editorial in *Stroke* notes that none of the twenty-five compounds "proven" efficacious for treating stroke in animal experiments over the preceding ten years had been effective for use in humans. From human studies alone we have learned how to lessen the risk of heart attacks. Warnings to the public that smoking cigarettes leads to an increased risk of cancer were delayed as researchers sought, unsuccessfully, to confirm the risk by using animals.

5 Animal tests for drug safety, cancer-causing potential, and toxicity are unreliable, and science is leading us to more accurate methods that will offer greater protection. But if we refuse to acknowledge the inadequacies of animal tests we put a stranglehold on the very progress that will help us. Billions of precious health-care dollars have been spent to fund animal experiments that are repetitious or that have no human relevance.

An uncritical acceptance of the value of animal experiments leads to its overfunding, which, in turn, leads to the underfunding of other more beneficial areas.

## Questions on Meaning

1. State Carlson's thesis in your own words. Why does she believe that irrational thinking has incorrectly portrayed the animal experimentation debate as being between scientists and animal rights activists?
2. What was the annual level of animal experimentation in dollars and numbers of animals when this letter was written?
3. Carlson states that most of what has been learned about the causes of human cancers and birth defects has come from human studies. Why is this?

## Questions on Rhetorical Strategy and Style

1. Carlson cites polio research in her argument against animal experimentation, stating that "misleading animal experiments detoured scientists away from reliable clinical studies." She does not back up this statement with facts, but rather attributes it to polio vaccine developer Sabin. Explain why you think she did or did not make a convincing argument without providing additional information.
2. How does Carlson use a cause and effect writing strategy to explain how the use of monkey cells in polio vaccine created a risk for human users? Discuss the impact of this statement on her argument.
3. Carlson argues that the facts don't justify the death and suffering of animals used in medical experiments. What facts does she present to support this statement? How persuasive do you find this information?

## Writing Assignments

1. How does this essay affect your feelings about animal experimentation? When do you feel it is justified, and when should it not be used? Explain why you would or would not need to have more information on the subject before forming an opinion.
2. Research the current debate over animal experimentation. Who are the opponents and proponents? Where do pharmaceutical companies stand on the issue? Who do you feel are the most credible and least credible individuals or groups in the debate, and why?

3. Find a letter-to-the editor on any topic that you disagree with (check the campus newspaper, a local newspaper, the *New York Times* or *Wall Street Journal,* or a national magazine, for example) and write a short essay in opposition. Research the issue, if necessary, to find data that will help make your argument persuasive. Summarize your thesis in your conclusion to help readers remember your message.

# MY FATHER'S LIFE

## Raymond Carver

*Raymond Carver (1938–1988) was born in Chatskanie, Oregon. He received a B.A. from Humboldt State College (1963) and studied creative writing at the University of Iowa and (with the late novelist John Gardner) at Chico State College. A dedicated writer with a worldwide following, Carver is one of the better known short-story writers of the late 20th century. His books include the short story collections* Will You Please Be Quiet, Please *(1976) (a National Book Award nominee),* What We Talk About When We Talk About Love *(1981),* Cathedral *(1983), and* Where I'm Calling From *(1988); the miscellaneous collection* Fires: Essays, Poems, Stories *(1983); and the poetry collections* In a Marine Light *(1987) and—posthumously—*A New Path to the Waterfall *(1989). In addition, he published stories in* The Atlantic Monthly, Esquire, *and* The New Yorker. *Carver's stories are often sparse and seldom without the poignancy of the dark side of life—such as depression, unemployment, alcoholism, and divorce. This essay—originally published in* Esquire *in 1984—exhibits Carver's sensitivity for human relationships. Notice how he reveals his own pain as he describes his father's charm and weaknesses.*

1 My dad's name was Clevie Raymond Carver. His family called 1
him Raymond and friends called him C.R. I was named Raymond Clevie Carver Jr. I hated the "Junior" part. When I was little my dad called me Frog, which was okay. But later, like everybody else in the family, he began calling me Junior. He went on calling me this until I was thirteen or fourteen and announced that I

---

From *Fires: Essays, Poems, Stories.* Originally appeared in *Esquire* (September, 1994).

wouldn't answer to that name any longer. So he began calling me Doc. From then until his death, on June 17, 1967, he called me Doc, or else Son.

When he died, my mother telephoned my wife with the news. I was away from my family at the time, between lives, trying to enroll in the School of Library Science at the University of Iowa. When my wife answered the phone, my mother blurted out, "Raymond's dead!" For a moment, my wife thought my mother was telling her that I was dead. Then my mother made it clear *which* Raymond she was talking about and my wife said, "Thank God. I thought you meant *my* Raymond."

My dad walked, hitched rides, and rode in empty boxcars when he went from Arkansas to Washington State in 1934, looking for work. I don't know whether he was pursuing a dream when he went out to Washington. I doubt it. I don't think he dreamed much. I believe he was simply looking for steady work at decent pay. Steady work was meaningful work. He picked apples for a time and then landed a construction laborer's job on the Grand Coulee Dam. After he'd put aside a little money, he bought a car and drove back to Arkansas to help his folks, my grandparents, pack up for the move west. He said later that they were about to starve down there, and this wasn't meant as a figure of speech. It was during that short while in Arkansas, in a town called Leola, that my mother met my dad on the sidewalk as he came out of a tavern.

"He was drunk," she said. "I don't know why I let him talk to me. His eyes were glittery. I wish I'd had a crystal ball." They'd met once, a year or so before, at a dance. He'd had girlfriends before her, my mother told me. "Your dad always had a girlfriend, even after we married. He was my first and last. I never had another man. But I didn't miss anything."

They were married by a justice of the peace on the day they left for Washington, this big, tall country girl and a farmhand-turned-construction worker. My mother spent her wedding night with my dad and his folks, all of them camped beside the road in Arkansas.

In Omak, Washington, my dad and mother lived in a little place not much bigger than a cabin. My grandparents lived next door. My dad was still working on the dam, and later, with the huge turbines producing electricity and the water backed up for a hundred miles into Canada) he stood in the crowd and heard Franklin D. Roosevelt when he spoke at the construction site. "He never mentioned those guys who died building that dam," my dad said. Some of his friends had died there, men from Arkansas, Oklahoma, and Missouri.

He then took a job in a sawmill in Clatskanie, Oregon, a little town alongside the Columbia River. I was born there, and my mother has a picture of my dad standing in front of the gate to the mill, proudly holding me up to face the camera. My bonnet is on crooked and about to come untied. His hat is pushed back on his forehead, and he's wearing a big grin. Was he going in to work or just finishing his shift? It doesn't matter. In either case, he had a job and a family. These were his salad days.

In 1941 we moved to Yakima, Washington, where my dad went to work as a saw filer, a skilled trade he'd learned in Clatskanie. When war broke out, he was given a deferment because his work was considered necessary to the war effort. Finished lumber was in demand by the armed services, and he kept his saws so sharp they could shave the hair off your arm.

After my dad had moved us to Yakima, he moved his folks into the same neighborhood. By the mid-1940s the rest of my dad's family—his brother, his sister, and her husband, as well as uncles, cousins, nephews, and most of their extended family and friends—had come out from Arkansas. All because my dad came out first. The men went to work at Boise Cascade, where my dad worked, and the women packed apples in the canneries. And in just a little while, it seemed—according to my mother—everybody was better off than my dad. "Your dad couldn't keep money," my mother said. "Money burned a hole in his pocket. He was always doing for others."

The first house I clearly remember living in, at 1515 South Fifteenth Street, in Yakima, had an outdoor toilet. On Halloween night, or just any night, for the hell of it, neighbor kids, kids in their early teens, would carry our toilet away and leave it next to the road. My dad would have to get somebody to help him bring it home. Or these kids would take the toilet and stand it in somebody else's backyard. Once they actually set it on fire, but ours wasn't the only house that had an outdoor toilet. When I was old enough to know what I was doing, I threw rocks at the other toilets when I'd see someone go inside. This was called bombing the toilets. After a while, though, everyone went to indoor plumbing until, suddenly, our toilet was the last outdoor one in the neighborhood. I remember the shame I felt when my third-grade teacher, Mr. Wise, drove me home from school one day. I asked him to stop at the house just before ours, claiming I lived there.

I can recall what happened one night when my dad came home late to find that my mother had locked all the doors on him from the inside. He was drunk, and we could feel the house shudder as he rattled the door. When he'd managed to force open a window, she hit him between the eyes with a colander and knocked him out. We could see him down there on the grass. For years afterward, I used to pick up this colander—it was as heavy as a rolling pin—and imagine what it would feel like to be hit in the head with something like that.

It was during this period that I remember my dad taking me into the bedroom, sitting me down on the bed, and telling me that I might have to go live with my Aunt LaVon for a while. I couldn't understand what I'd done that meant I'd have to go away from home to live. But this, too—whatever prompted it—must have blown over, more or less, anyway, because we stayed together, and I didn't have to go live with her or anyone else.

I remember my mother pouring his whiskey down the sink. Sometimes she'd pour it all out and sometimes, if she was afraid of getting caught, she'd only pour half of it out and then add water to the rest. I tasted some of his whiskey once myself. It was terrible stuff, and I don't see how anybody could drink it.

After a long time without one, we finally got a car, in 1949 or 1950, a 1938 Ford. But it threw a rod the first week we had it, and my dad had to have the motor rebuilt.

15 "We drove the oldest car in town," my mother said. "We could have had a Cadillac for all he spent on car repairs." One time she found someone else's tube of lipstick on the floorboard, along with a lacy handkerchief. "See this?" she said to me. "Some floozy left this in the car."

Once I saw her take a pan of warm water into the bedroom where my dad was sleeping. She took his hand from under the covers and held it in the water. I stood in the doorway and watched. I wanted to know what was going on. This would make him talk in his sleep, she told me. There were things she needed to know, things she was sure he was keeping from her.

Every year or so, when I was little, we would take the North Coast Limited across the Cascade Range from Yakima to Seattle and stay in the Vance Hotel and eat, I remember, at a place called the Dinner Bell Cafe. Once we went to Ivar's Acres of Clams and drank glasses of warm clam broth.

In 1956, the year I was to graduate from high school, my dad quit his job at the mill in Yakima and took a job in Chester, a little sawmill town in northern California. The reasons given at the time for his taking the job had to do with a higher hourly wage and the vague promise that he might, in a few years' time, succeed to the job of head filer in this new mill. But I think, in the main, that my dad had grown restless and simply wanted to try his luck elsewhere. Things had gotten a little too predictable for him in Yakima. Also, the year before, there had been the deaths, within six months of each other, of both his parents.

But just a few days after graduation, when my mother and I were packed to move to Chester, my dad penciled a letter to say he'd been sick for a while. He didn't want us to worry, he said, but he'd cut himself on a saw. Maybe he'd got a tiny sliver of steel in his blood. Anyway, something had happened and he'd had to miss work, he said. In the same mail was an unsigned postcard from somebody down there telling my mother that my dad was about to die and that he was drinking "raw whiskey."

When we arrived in Chester, my dad was living in a trailer that belonged to the company. I didn't recognize him immediately. I guess for a moment I didn't want to recognize him. He was skinny and pale and looked bewildered. His pants wouldn't stay up. He didn't look like my dad. My mother began to cry. My dad put his arm around her and patted her shoulder vaguely, like he didn't know what this was all about, either. The three of us took up life together in the trailer, and we looked after him as best we could. But my dad was sick, and he couldn't get any better. I worked with him in the mill that summer and part of the fall. We'd get up in the mornings and eat eggs and toast while we listened to the radio, and then go out the door with our lunch pails. We'd pass through the gate together at eight in the morning, and I wouldn't see him again until quitting time. In November I went back to Yakima to be closer to my girlfriend, the girl I'd made up my mind I was going to marry.

He worked at the mill in Chester until the following February, when he collapsed on the job and was taken to the hospital. My mother asked if I would come down there and help. I caught a bus from Yakima to Chester, intending to drive them back to Yakima. But now, in addition to being physically sick, my dad was in the midst of a nervous breakdown, though none of us knew to call it that at the time. During the entire trip back to Yakima, he didn't speak, not even when asked a direct question. ("How do you feel, Raymond?" "You okay, Dad?") He'd communicate if he communicated at all, by moving his head or by turning his palms up as if to say he didn't know or care. The only time he said anything on the trip, and for nearly a month afterward, was when I was speeding down a gravel road in Oregon and the car muffler came loose. "You were going too fast," he said.

Back in Yakima a doctor saw to it that my dad went to a psychiatrist. My mother and dad had to go on relief, as it was called, and the county paid for the psychiatrist. The psychiatrist asked my dad, "Who is the President?" He'd had a question put to him that he could answer. "Ike," my dad said. Nevertheless, they put him on the fifth floor of Valley Memorial Hospital and began giving him electroshock treatments. I was married by then and about to start my own family. My dad was still locked up when my wife went into this same hospital, just one floor down, to have our first baby. After she had delivered, I went upstairs to give my dad the news. They let me in through a steel door and showed me where I could find him. He was sitting on a couch with a blanket over his lap. *Hey,* I thought. *What in hell is happening to my dad?* I sat down next to him and told him he was a grandfather. He waited a minute and then said, "I feel like a grandfather." That's all he said. He didn't smile or move. He was in a big room with a lot of other people. Then I hugged him, and he began to cry.

Somehow he got out of there. But now came the years when he couldn't work and just sat around the house trying to figure what next and what he'd done wrong in his life that he'd wound up like this. My mother went from job to crummy job. Much later she referred to that time he was in the hospital, and those years just afterward, as "when Raymond was sick." The word *sick* was never the same for me again.

In 1964, through the help of a friend, he was lucky enough to be hired on at a mill in Klamath, California. He moved down there by himself to see if he could hack it. He lived not far from the mill, in a one-room cabin not much different from the place he and my mother had started out living in when they went west. He scrawled letters to my mother, and if I called she'd read them aloud to me over the phone. In the letters, he said it was touch and go. Every day that he went to work, he felt like it was the most important day of his life. But every day, he told her, made the next day that much easier. He said for her to tell me he said hello. If he couldn't sleep at night, he said, he thought about me and the good times we used to have. Finally, after a couple of months, he regained some of his confidence. He could do the work and didn't think he had to worry that he'd let anybody down ever again. When he was sure, he sent for my mother.

He'd been off from work for six years and had lost everything in that time—home, car, furniture, and appliances, including the big freezer that had been my mother's pride and joy. He'd lost his good name too—Raymond Carver was someone who couldn't pay his bills—and his self-respect was gone. He'd even lost his virility. My mother told my wife, "All during that time Raymond was sick we slept together in the same bed, but we didn't have relations. He wanted to a few times, but nothing happened. I didn't miss it, but I think he wanted to, you know."

During those years I was trying to raise my own family and earn a living. But, one thing and another, we found ourselves having to move a lot. I couldn't keep track of what was going down in my dad's life. But I did have a chance one Christmas to tell him I wanted to be a writer. I might as well have told him I wanted to become a plastic surgeon. "What are you going to write about?" he wanted to know. Then, as if to help me out, he said, "Write about stuff you know about. Write about some of those fishing trips we took." I said I would, but I knew I wouldn't. "Send me what you write," he said. I said I'd do that, but then I didn't. I wasn't writing anything about fishing, and I didn't think he'd particularly care about, or even necessarily understand, what I was writing in those days. Besides, he wasn't a reader. Not the sort, anyway, I imagined I was writing for.

Then he died. I was a long way off, in Iowa City, with things still to say to him. I didn't have the chance to tell him goodbye, or that I thought he was doing great at his new job. That I was proud of him for making a comeback.

My mother said he came in from work that night and ate a big supper. Then he sat at the table by himself and finished what was left of a bottle of whiskey, a bottle she found hidden in the bottom of the garbage under some coffee grounds a day or so later. Then he got up and went to bed, where my mother joined him a little later. But in the night she had to get up and make a bed for herself on the couch. "He was snoring so loud I couldn't sleep," she said. The next morning when she looked in on him, he was on his back with his mouth open, his cheeks caved in. *Graylooking,* she said. She knew he was dead—she didn't need a doctor to tell her that. But she called one anyway, and then she called my wife.

Among the pictures my mother kept of my dad and herself during those early days in Washington was a photograph of him standing in front of a car, holding a beer and a stringer of fish. In the photograph he is wearing his hat back on his forehead and has this awkward grin on his face. I asked her for it and she gave it to me, along with some others. I put it up on my wall, and each time we moved, I took the picture along and put it up on another wall. I looked at it carefully from time to time, trying to figure out some things about my dad, and maybe myself in the process. But I couldn't. My dad just kept moving further and further away from me and back into time. Finally, in the course of another move, I lost the photograph. It was then that I tried to recall it, and at the same time make an attempt to say something about my dad, and how I thought that in some important ways we might be alike. I wrote the poem when I was living in an apartment house in an urban area south of San Francisco, at a time when I found myself, like my dad, having trouble with alcohol. The poem was a way of trying to connect up with him.

## *Photograph of My Father in His Twenty-Second Year*

*October.* Here in this dank, unfamiliar kitchen
I study my father's embarrassed young man's face.
Sheepish grin, he holds in one hand a string
of spiny yellow perch, in the other
a bottle of Carlsberg beer.

In jeans and flannel shirt, he leans
against the front fender of a 1934 Ford.
He would like to pose brave and hearty for his posterity,
wear his old hat cocked over his ear.
All his life my father wanted to be bold.

But the eyes give him away, and the hands
that limply offer the string of dead perch
and the bottle of beer. Father, I love you,
yet how can I say thank you, I who can't hold my liquor either
and don't even know the places to fish.

30 The poem is true in its particulars, except that my dad died in 30 June and not October, as the first word of the poem says. I wanted a word with more than one syllable to it to make it linger a little. But more than that, I wanted a month appropriate to what I felt at the time I wrote the poem—a month of short days and failing light, smoke in the air, things perishing. June was summer nights and days, graduations, my wedding anniversary, the birthday of one of my children. June wasn't a month your father died in.

After the service at the funeral home, after we had moved outside, a woman I didn't know came over to me and said, "He's happier where he is now." I stared at this woman until she moved away. I still remember the little knob of a hat she was wearing. Then one of my dad's cousins—I didn't know the man's name—reached out and took my hand, "We all miss him," he said, and I knew he wasn't saying it just to be polite.

I began to weep for the first time since receiving the news. I hadn't been able to before. I hadn't had the time, for one thing. Now, suddenly, I couldn't stop. I held my wife and wept while she said and did what she could do to comfort me there in the middle of that summer afternoon.

I listened to people say consoling things to my mother, and I was glad that my dad's family had turned up, had come to where he was. I thought I'd remember everything that was said and done that day and maybe find a way to tell it sometime. But I didn't. I forgot it all, or nearly. What I do remember is that I heard our name used a lot that afternoon, my dad's name and mine. But I knew they were talking about my dad. *Raymond,* these people kept saying in their beautiful voices out of my childhood. *Raymond.*

## Questions on Meaning

1. How were Carver and his father similar? Although Carver was a college graduate and a writer, and his father was a laborer, describe how their lifestyles were similar.
2. What does Carver mean when he describes his father as being in "his salad days"? What job characteristics were important to his father?
3. What roles do women play in Carver's father's life—his wife and his girlfriends? How would you describe Carver's own relationship with women from the faint glimpses he gives us of his life?

## Questions on Rhetorical Strategy and Style

1. Find where the narration would begin if it were written in strict chronological order. Why do you think Carver begins his essay with a flashback to his father's death? How would it affect the essay to place the discussion of the call from his mother at the end of the essay?
2. What mood does Carver create when he writes about the period "when Raymond was sick," beginning with his graduation from high school in 1956 and ending in 1964, when his father went back to work? How does the mood compare and contrast with the narrative leading up to it and the narrative after it?
3. Why does Carver insert his poem to his father into the essay? What is he trying to say in the poem? What does he mean by the line, "how can I say thank you"?

## Writing Assignments

1. "My dad," Carver writes, "just kept moving further and further away from me and back into time." Identify someone in your life who meant a lot to you when he or she was alive but who you now have difficulty remembering. Why are your memories fading? What do you do to keep the memories alive? What do you do to connect with the person?
2. Carver struggled with alcoholism for much of his short life; he finally was able to quit drinking in 1977, when he was nearly 40. Learn more about Carver's life and how it was affected by alcohol. How did drinking affect his writing, his relationship with his wife, and his health? How did he change after he stopped drinking?

3. Find a familiar old photograph of a deceased family member—such as the photograph of Carver's father with the string of perch and a bottle of Carlsberg. Write an essay about what the photograph says to you—whom you really see in the photo, what the person's life was like, and whether the photograph truly reflects what you know about the person. How has the meaning of the photograph changed for you over the years? In what ways do you see yourself in the photograph?

# MARRYING ABSURD

## Joan Didion

*Joan Didion (1934– ) was born in Sacramento, California. She received a B.A. at the University of California at Berkeley in 1956, and then moved to New York City, where she spent 7 years working as an associate editor at* Vogue *and as a contributor to* Esquire, The National Review, *and* The Saturday Evening Post. *In 1964, Didion married writer John Gregory Dunne and returned to California, where she began to write the essays and fiction that became her genre: personal commentaries on contemporary events that expose social disintegration. Her published works include the collections of essays* Slouching Towards Bethlehem *(1968),* The White Album *(1970), and* After Henry *(1992); the novels* Run River *(1963),* Play It As It Lays *(1970),* A Book of Common Prayer *(1977), and* Democracy *(1984); and the nonfiction books* Salvador *(1983) and* Miami *(1987). She also has collaborated on screenplays with her husband. Didion is known for her concise, yet often barbed, delivery, a style you should easily recognize in this 1967 essay on the paradoxes of Las Vegas weddings, taken from* Slouching Towards Bethlehem.

1 To be married in Las Vegas, Clark County, Nevada, a bride 1
must swear that she is eighteen or has parental permission and a bridegroom that he is twenty-one or has parental permission. Someone must put up five dollars for the license. (On Sundays and holidays, fifteen dollars. The Clark County Courthouse issues marriage licenses at any time of the day or night except between noon and one in the afternoon, between eight and nine in the evening, and between four and five in the morning.) Nothing else is required. The

---

State of Nevada, alone among these United States, demands neither a premarital blood test nor a waiting period before or after the issuance of a marriage license. Driving in across the Mojave from Los Angeles, one sees the signs way out on the desert, looming up from that moonscape of rattlesnakes and mesquite, even before the Las Vegas lights appear like a mirage on the horizon: "GETTING MARRIED? Free License Information First Strip Exit." Perhaps the Las Vegas wedding industry achieved its peak operational efficiency between 9:00 p.m. and midnight of August 26, 1965, an otherwise unremarkable Thursday which happened to be, by Presidential order, the last day on which anyone could improve his draft status merely by getting married. One hundred and seventy-one couples were pronounced man and wife in the name of Clark County and the State of Nevada that night, sixty-seven of them by a single justice of the peace, Mr. James A. Brennan. Mr. Brennan did one wedding at the Dunes and the other sixty-six in his office, and charged each couple eight dollars. One bride lent her veil to six others. "I got it down from five to three minutes," Mr. Brennan said later of his feat. "I could've married them *en masse,* but they're people, not cattle. People expect more when they get married."

What people who get married in Las Vegas actually do expect—what, in the largest sense, their "expectations" are—strikes one as a curious and self-contradictory business. Las Vegas is the most extreme and allegorical of American settlements, bizarre and beautiful in its venality and in its devotion to immediate gratification, a place the tone of which is set by mobsters and call girls and ladies' room attendants with amyl nitrite poppers in their uniform pockets. Almost everyone notes that there is no "time" in Las Vegas, no night and no day and no past and no future (no Las Vegas casino, however, has taken the obliteration of the ordinary time sense quite so far as Harold's Club in Reno, which for a while issued, at odd intervals in the day and night, mimeographed "bulletins" carrying news from the world outside); neither is there any logical sense of where one is. One is standing on a highway in the middle of a vast hostile desert looking at an eighty-foot sign which blinks "STARDUST" or "CAESAR'S PALACE." Yes, but what does that explain? This geographical implausibility reinforces the sense that what happens there has no connection with "real" life; Nevada cities like Reno and Carson are ranch towns, Western towns, places behind which there is some historical imperative. But Las Vegas seems to exist only in the eye of the beholder. All of which makes it an extraordinarily stimulating and interesting place, but an odd one in which to want to wear a candlelight satin Priscilla of Boston wedding dress with Chantilly lace insets, tapered sleeves and a detachable modified train.

And yet the Las Vegas wedding business seems to appeal to precisely that impulse. "Sincere and Dignified Since 1954," one wedding chapel advertises. There are nineteen such wedding chapels in Las Vegas, intensely competitive, each offering better, faster, and, by implication, more sincere services than the next: Our Photos Best Anywhere, Your Wedding on a Phonograph Record, Candlelight with Your Ceremony, Honeymoon Accommodations, Free Transportation from Your Motel to Courthouse to Chapel and Return to Motel, Religious or Civil Ceremonies, Dressing Rooms, Flowers, Rings, Announcements, Witnesses Available, and Ample Parking. All of these services, like most others in Las Vegas (sauna baths, payroll-check cashing, chinchilla coats for sale or rent) are offered twenty-four hours a day, seven days a week, presumably on the premise that marriage, like craps, is a game to be played when the table seems hot.

But what strikes one most about the Strip chapels, with their wishing wells and stained-glass paper windows and their artificial bouvardia, is that so much of their business is by no means a matter of simple convenience, of late-night liaisons between show girls and baby Crosbys. Of course there is some of that. (One night about eleven o'-clock in Las Vegas I watched a bride in an orange minidress and masses of flame-colored hair stumble from a Strip chapel on the arm of her bridegroom, who looked the part of the expendable nephew in movies like *Miami Syndicate.* "I gotta get the kids," the bride whimpered. "I gotta pick up the sitter, I gotta get to the midnight show." "What you gotta get," the bridegroom said, opening the door of a Cadillac Coupe de Ville and watching her crumple on the seat, "is sober.") But Las Vegas seems to offer something other than "convenience"; it is merchandising "niceness," the facsimile of proper ritual, to children who do not know how else to find it, how to make the arrangements, how to do it "right." All day and evening long on the Strip, one sees actual wedding parties, waiting under the harsh lights at a crosswalk, standing uneasily in the parking lot of the Frontier while the photographer hired by The Little Church of the West ("Wedding Place of the Stars") certifies the occasion, takes the picture: the bride in a veil and white satin pumps, the bridegroom usually in a white dinner jacket, and even an attendant or two, a sister or a best friend in hot-pink *peau de soie,* a flirtation veil, a carnation nosegay. "When I Fall in Love It Will Be Forever," the organist plays, and then a few bars of Lohengrin. The mother cries; the stepfather, awkward in his role, invites the chapel hostess to join them for a drink at the Sands. The hostess declines with a professional smile; she has already transferred her interest to the group waiting outside. One bride out, another in, and again the sign goes up on the chapel door: "One moment please—Wedding."

5 I sat next to one such wedding party in a Strip restaurant the last time I was in Las Vegas. The marriage had just taken place; the bride still wore her dress, the mother her corsage. A bored waiter poured out a few swallows of pink champagne ("on the house") for everyone but the bride, who was too young to be served. "You'll need something with more kick than that," the bride's father said with heavy jocularity to his new son-in-law; the ritual jokes about the wedding night had a certain Panglossian character, since the bride was clearly several months pregnant. Another round of pink champagne, this time not on the house, and the bride began to cry. "It was just as nice," she sobbed, "as I hoped and dreamed it would be."

## Questions on Meaning

1. The requirements for marriage in Las Vegas sound absurd, as Didion reflects in her title for this essay. Why? Find out what the marriage requirements are where you live, and consider the major differences. What makes Didion's lead so dramatic?
2. Didion calls Las Vegas "the most extreme and allegorical of American settlements." How does she support this statement in the essay? How does her use of the word "settlement" contribute to the effectiveness of this statement?

## Questions on Rhetorical Strategy and Style

1. This brief essay exhibits a mixture of rhetorical styles. Find examples of description, comparison and contrast, and classification and division, and analyze how these are used
2. Absurdity often lends itself to satire. Although there may be black humor in Didion's words, she is not a humorist. Read back through the essay and note passages that another author might have written as satire. How do you think the satire would have affected Didion's biting commentary?

## Writing Assignments

1. Many years have passed and times have changed since Didion wrote this essay. Are her reflections of marriage in Las Vegas (which continues as it was when she published this essay) as paradoxical today as they were in the 1960s? Write an essay in which you discuss your reactions to the Las Vegas style wedding in today's world.
2. What was the reason that 175 couples were married in Las Vegas between 9 p.m. and midnight on August 26, 1965? Learn something about draft dodging in the sixties to appreciate the significance of these eleventh-hour nuptials.
3. Absurdity abounds in life. Write an essay about some absurd institution or activity you are familiar with, mirroring Didion's dry, descriptive style. Try to avoid slipping into satire; use definition, description, startling truths, and dramatic contrasts to engage your reader.

# SO THIS WAS ADOLESCENCE

## Annie Dillard

*Annie Dillard (1945) was born in Pittsburgh, Pennsylvania. She received a B.A. (1967) and an M.A. (1968) from Hollins College and then embarked on a career as a writer and teacher. Dillard has worked as a columnist for* The Living Wilderness *and a contributing editor for Harper's and has taught at Western Washington University and Wesleyan University in Connecticut. Fascinated with the intricacies of the natural world and blessed with an introspective, poetic mind, Dillard has earned a reputation for insightful descriptions of the relationships between humans and nature, physically and spiritually. She has been compared to Henry David Thoreau, and her work has been compared to his* Walden. *An accomplished writer, Dillard has published non-fiction, poetry, literary criticism, essays, autobiographies, and a novel. Her published work includes* Pilgrim at Tinker Creek *(1974), observations about nature for which she received a Pulitzer Prize;* Tickets for a Prayer Wheel *(1974), a volume of poetry;* Living By Fiction *(1982), a collection of literary criticism;* Teaching a Stone to Talk *(1982), a collection of essays;* An American Childhood *(1987), an account of her youth in Pittsburgh;* The Writing Life *(1983), reflections on the process of writing; and* The Living *(1992), a novel. This essay, taken from* An American Childhood, *is a lively and passionate description of Dillard's sensations of adolescence.*

---

1 When I was fifteen, I felt it coming; now I was sixteen, and it hit.

My feet had imperceptibly been set on a new path, a fast path into a long tunnel like those many turnpike tunnels near Pittsburgh, turnpike tunnels whose entrances bear on brass plaques a roll call of those men who died blasting them. I wandered witlessly for-ward and found myself going down, and saw the light dimming; I adjusted to the slant and dimness, traveled further down, adjusted to greater dimness, and so on. There wasn't a whole lot I could do about it, or about anything. I was going to hell on a handcart, that was all, and I knew it and everyone around me knew it, and there it was.

I was growing and thinning, as if pulled. I was getting angry, as if pushed. I morally disapproved most things in North America, and blamed my innocent parents for them. My feelings deepened and lingered. The swift moods of early childhood—each formed by and suited to its occasion—vanished. Now feelings lasted so long they left stains. They arose from nowhere, like winds or waves, and battered at me or engulfed me.

When I was angry, I felt myself coiled and longing to kill someone or bomb something big. Trying to appease myself, during one winter I whipped my bed every afternoon with my uniform belt. I despised the spectacle I made in my own eyes—whipping the bed with a belt, like a creature demented!—and I often began halfheartedly, but I did it daily after school as a desperate discipline, trying to rid myself and the innocent world of my wildness. It was like trying to beat back the ocean.

Sometimes in class I couldn't stop laughing; things were too funny
5 to be borne. It began then, my surprise that no one else saw what was so funny.

I read some few books with such reverence I didn't close them at the finish, but only moved the pile of pages back to the start, without breathing, and began again. I read one such book, an enormous novel, six times that way—closing the binding between sessions, but not between readings.

On the piano in the basement I played the maniacal "Poet and Peasant Overture" so loudly, for so many hours, night after night, I damaged the piano's keys and strings. When I wasn't playing this crashing overture, I played boogie-woogie, or something else, anything else, in octaves—otherwise, it wasn't loud enough. My fingers were so strong I could do push-ups with them. I played one piece with my fists. I banged on a steel-stringed guitar till I bled, and once on a particularly piercing rock-and-roll downbeat I broke straight through one of Father's snare drums.

I loved my boyfriend so tenderly, I thought I must transmogrify into vapor. It would take spectroscopic analysis to locate my molecules in thin air. No possible way of holding him was close enough. Nothing could cure this bad case of gentleness except, perhaps, violence: maybe if he swung me by the legs and split my skull on a tree? Would that ease this insane wish to kiss too much his eyelids' outer corners and his temples, as if I could love up his brain?

I envied people in books who swooned. For two years I felt myself continuously swooning and continuously unable to swoon; the blood drained from my face and eyes and flooded my heart; my hands emptied, my knees unstrung, I bit at the air for something worth breathing—but I failed to fall, and I couldn't find the way to black out. I had to live on the lip of a waterfall, exhausted.

When I was bored I was first hungry, then nauseated, then furious
10 and weak. "Calm yourself," people had been saying to me all my life.
Since early childhood I had tried one thing and then another to calm myself, on those few occasions when I truly wanted to. Eating helped; singing helped. Now sometimes I truly wanted to calm myself. I couldn't lower my shoulders; they seemed to wrap around my ears. I couldn't lower my voice although I could see the people around me flinch. I waved my arm in class till the very teachers wanted to kill me.

I was what they called a live wire. I was shooting out sparks that were digging a pit around me, and I was sinking into that pit. Laughing with Ellin at school recess, or driving around after school with Judy in her jeep, exultant, or dancing with my boyfriend to Louis Armstrong across a polished diningroom floor, I got so excited I looked around wildly for aid; I didn't know where I should go or what I should do with myself. People in books split wood.

When rage or boredom reappeared, each seemed never to have left. Each so filled me with so many years' intolerable accumulation it jammed the space behind my eyes, so I couldn't see. There was no room left even on my surface to live. My rib cage was so taut I couldn't breathe. Every cubic centimeter of atmosphere above my shoulders and head was heaped with last straws. Black hatred clogged my very blood. I couldn't peep, I couldn't wiggle or blink; my blood was too mad to flow.

For as long as I could remember, I had been transparent to myself, unselfconscious, learning, doing, most of every day. Now I was in my own way; I myself was a dark object I could not ignore. I couldn't remember how to forget myself. I didn't want to think about myself, to reckon myself in, to deal with myself every livelong minute on top of everything else—but swerve as I might, I couldn't avoid it. I was a boulder blocking my own path. I was a dog barking between my own ears, a barking dog who wouldn't hush.

So this was adolescence. Is this how the people around me had died on their feet—inevitably, helplessly? Perhaps their own selves eclipsed the sun for so many years the world shriveled around them, and when at last their inescapable orbits had passed through these dark egoistic years it was too late, they had adjusted.

Must I then lose the world forever, that I had so loved? Was it all, Is the whole bright and various planet, where I had been so ardent about finding myself alive, only a passion peculiar to children, that I would outgrow even against my will?

## Questions on Meaning

1. In the beginning of this essay, Dillard exuberantly describes what happens as she enters adolescence. What fear is she expressing at the conclusion of the essay when she laments, "Must I then lose the world forever . . ."?
2. What are Dillard's reactions to boredom? How do they compare to your reactions?
3. What does Dillard mean by being "transparent" to herself? What has she become?

## Questions on Rhetorical Strategy and Style

1. "I was going to hell on a handcart," Dillard writes. "I was what they called a live wire." How does she support these statements? Do you think these self-assessments were only in her mind or truly reflect what others thought about her?
2. Dillard spills her emotions in this essay, with few obvious links from thought to thought, paragraph to paragraph. Reread the essay and describe the major theme of each of the three sections. Then identify linking themes that thread through the essay.

## Writing Assignments

1. Compare and contrast your ascent—or descent—into adolescence. Were you as aware of the changes you were going through as Dillard seems to have been? How would you describe yourself? How do you think others described you?
2. In some ways, we are always coming of age. If we aren't becoming an adolescent, we are becoming an adult, or a graduate, or a new employee. . . . Write an essay about a coming-of-age experience you have had that moved you permanently from one plane to another. Describe when you realized a change had occurred. Compare and contrast the old and new you.

# ADAM GOES TO SCHOOL

## Michael Dorris

*Michael Dorris (1945–1997) of the Modoc tribe, wrote both novels —*A Yellow Raft in Blue Water *(1987) and* The Crown of Columbus *(1992), and non-fiction—*The Broken Cord *(1989). In* The Broken Cord, *a National Book Critics Circle Award winner for non-fiction, Dorris details his difficulties educating his adopted son Adam (adopted with his wife, the writer Louise Erdrich), who suffers from a variety of physical and mental disabilities caused by fetal alcohol syndrome. As you read this article, note that he unflinchingly presents not only Adam's problems in school but his own attempts to deal personally with the frustration of having a disabled child.*

1 When I think back on that time, this is the scene that is con- 1
jured: at the sound of Adam's tread on the road Skahota barks eagerly, I take a sheet of steaming cookies out of the oven, and Sava pushes a chair to the table for Madeline. We always had cats living in our barn, usually named according to a prevailing theme—the most friendly were Sierra Madre, Sierra Leone, Sierra Blanca, and Sierra Nevada—and in this vision they stretch and prepare to join the party.

It is impossible that our lives were really so well ordered, so under control. On my old calendars I see the notation of many doctor visits, medical appointments in Boston. I constantly read books about learning theory and tried innovative experimental programs, searching for an approach that would be effective for Adam. My first inclination, a sort of 1960s flower child theory, was to be nonintrusive and natural, to let Adam find his own appropriate level, to allow him to be "free." I was inspired by a cartoon I had hung on the refrigerator. It showed a classroom in which all the students faced forward in

---

perfect rows of desks—except for one American Indian student who sat on the floor and looked the other way. The exasperated (insensitive) teacher berated, "Why can't you be like other people?" Well, I was not going to be *that* guy! Beneath the caption I had written: "Don't worry if Adam: 1) wets his pants; 2) disrupts a group; 3) does sloppy activities; 4) refuses to do activities; 5) does nervous hand movements, etc.; 6) is grumpy; 7) hits; 8) takes a long time." I doubt if my good intentions lasted very long.

On the "positive reenforcement" front, I mimeographed a checklist of Adam's daily home and school activities, each of which, when executed, gained him a "star." A minimal accumulation of stars at the end of the day produced a "certificate" and a designated number of certificates could be spent, like money, for toys, fast food, or anything else he desired. The sheets, titled "Adam's Day," included such categories as "Sat Still at Breakfast," "Stayed Dry in the Morning," "Was Cheerful at __________," and "Got Undressed by Self."

The concept of saving, however, was lost on Adam, and still is. He is a living embodiment of the Roman poet Horace's adage *"Carpe diem"* ("Seize the day"). Tomorrow, as a concept, is no competition for *now,* and after a month or so of mixed results the lists were put aside. Denial of privilege was no more effective. There was nothing Adam wanted enough that the threat of its loss would alter his spontaneous behavior. If I said, "Adam, if you don't stay dry, you'll have to wear a diaper to school," he would, without embarrassment, wear a diaper. If I threatened to banish him to his room unless he sat still during an activity, he would accept the consequence without complaint—and *I* would feel like a rotten bully. Not that there weren't bursts of progress, whole weeks of operation on a new plateau in some area or another.

5 With total concentration, occasional hysteria, and insistent instruction, I could coerce, encourage, or manipulate Adam into modifying unacceptable behavior. But the moment I stopped pushing, ceased to monitor, he reverted to old habits. Nothing seemed "automatic" with him. There was no branching curiosity, no internal motivation to be more grown up, no quick building on previous experience, no secure gain. Regardless of how much energy I, or his teachers, expended, Adam, for the first hundred or so repetitions, always eventually wound up back at Go. His maturation was a pitched battle between our exhortation and his indifference, yet outwardly he remained serene, forgiving of adult frustration, content with and impervious to whatever new method we might employ.

Sweet disposition was Adam's talent, and it was so striking that it often obscured his lack of progress. In recent years I've wondered how I could have closed my eyes for so long to the fact that Adam had enduring disabilities—three years after his adoption I wrote a psychologist that I was "convinced that there is nothing permanently wrong with Adam. I'm sure you hear that from every parent with whom you work, but I think I've been open in making a judgment. . . . While it is obvious that he is developmentally young for his chronological age in certain areas, his improvements have been dramatic, erratic, and far more rapid than I would have predicted." I concluded my five single-spaced pages by noting: "I guess if I could wish one thing for him it would be for him to be more vulnerable—for disapproval and approval to matter more than they do—for him to get his kicks out of other people more. He has this insulation, and a good thing he did, of course, in his past, but it's time for it to come down a bit, and I need to know how to help him to trust. He is a sweet, loving, affectionate, and gentle boy—as nice a person as I've ever met."

A succession of teachers reacted the same way, as evidenced by the observations they sent home at the end of every school year. "Adam is a delightful boy and a real pleasure to have in my class," commented his third-grade teacher. "Adam is a very loving child. I enjoy working with him," said his fourth-grade instructor. "He's doing *so well* this year! It's hard to believe it's the same youngster," wrote the school principal at the beginning of the fifth grade. All these good men and women were determinedly optimistic. They praised Adam's "progress" in things like map making and social studies, his fondness for reading books, his great interest in art, the leaps he was making in friendships and self-control. They proclaimed his mastery of basic arithmetic ("He understands the process of addition and subtraction and has computed problems with the use of counters and the number line. . . . He has demonstrated good ability and understanding with regard to our unit on geometry"), vocabulary, telling time.

I saved these encomia in a scrapbook as an antidote to discouragement. They testified to what I wanted to believe, and I quoted them to psychologists and doctors and new homeroom teachers as proofs. It is only now, in retrospect, that I see them for what they were—collective delusion, wishful thinking. At no time in his life could Adam, by any stretch of the imagination, read a map or comprehend the principles of geometry. In eight years at the Cornish School he never once received so much as a telephone call or an invitation from a "friend." He never stayed in his seat for more than a few minutes unless he was supervised.

When Adam was young, people fell in love with him and with the idea of him. He was a living movie-of-the-week hero, an underdog who deserved a happy ending. On top of that, he had good manners, an appealing face, me to broker and block for him. He was the only full-blood Indian most people at his school had ever met. His learning problems at first appeared so marginal, so near to a solution. With just the smallest nudge they would pass over the line into the normal range. Every good teacher, every counselor, every summer camp director Adam encountered in grade school and high school viewed him as a winnable challenge and approached his education with initial gusto and determination. He teetered in his ability so close to the edge of "okay" that it seemed impossible that, with the proper impetus, he would not succeed. I understood this conviction perfectly and succumbed to it for fifteen years. I sometimes had the fantasy that if I could penetrate the fog that surrounded Adam's awareness and quickly explain what was what, he would be fine. He was just slightly out of focus.

The fact was, improvement was hard to come by and even harder to sustain once it had appeared. Reviewing those end-of-the-year teacher reports, it is now clear that in grade after grade Adam was working at the same level on exactly the same tasks. Every year he started fresh, showed promise up to a point, then couldn't take the next step. His learning curve resembled more than anything else one of those carnival strong-man games in which a platform is struck with a weighted mallet and a ball rises up a pole toward a bell. In my son's case, sometimes the bell rang, but then the ball always fell back to earth. He was the little engine that couldn't make it over the mountain, and, in frustration and disappointment, without ever actually saying so, all but a dedicated few eventually stopped thinking that his trip was worth their effort.

But what a few those were. It may sound odd to say it, but Adam has been in his life incredibly fortunate in some areas, and special education teachers are one of them. Olivia Alexion arrived at the Cornish Elementary School when Adam was in the second grade and led him through the maze of the next seven years with unflagging affection and devotion. She was very young, barely out of college, but possessed a patience and long view that perfectly equipped her for the job. Ms. Alexion was a realist who acted as though she had a short memory—that is, she had the ability to forget setbacks and to maintain steady optimism even when, year after year, she was required to repeat identical lessons for Adam. She and I formed a kind of conspiracy, an allegiance that sometimes demanded daily communication so that his victories at home or at school could be consolidated, built upon. We were the day and night shifts of the same factory, and Adam was on our assembly line, inching forward at a slow pace, but forward all the same. She wrote hundreds of notes about his activities, recorded each incremental step, celebrated each tentative advance, railed against each slippage. She believed as fiercely as I that Adam had unrealized resources. She was the antithesis of detached.

What was in it for her, I privately wondered now and then. Was it ego? Was it the will not to be defeated? She worked long hours for little pay and spent many evenings researching in the library to develop new techniques. At first I hesitated to sing her praises too loudly to other parents with children in special education—I didn't want to give away how much attention she was devoting to Adam—but it turned out that we all felt the same way about her. She concentrated on each of her students as if he or she were the only child in the world, and because of her each of them surpassed what had been regarded as maximum potential.

When Adam was halfway through the fourth grade, Ms. Alexion decided to schedule a WISC-R IQ test for him on a Saturday morning in January. She believed he had previously tested "low," and that in an ideal examination environment his scores would show significant improvement. She and I would sit in the room while Adam was questioned and this, she was sure, would alleviate his feelings of anxiety as well as mute his tendency to become easily distracted in any new situation.

The results, however, fell into the same range: a verbal IQ of 63–77; a performance IQ of 63–81; and a full-scale IQ of 64–76. As always, there was a wide scatter pattern. Adam scored best on picture completion and object assembly and lowest on block design, coding, and similarities. In other words, tasks that had to do with abstract reasoning were the most difficult for him.

This wasn't what I wanted to hear, so I all but dismissed the results in a long, rationalizing letter to Ms. Alexion. I noted that the WISC was "in significant part culture biased" in favor of "mainstream America"—as if Adam, the son of a Dartmouth professor, living in Cornish, New Hampshire, came from some exotic society. While allowing that, at age ten, such "terms as 'alike/different,' 'older/younger' " were confusing to Adam, I brought all my anthropological mumbo jumbo into play in denying the accuracy of his scores: "The sequential arrangement of pictures to form a story that 'makes sense' depends for its validity on a shared understanding of proper organization. The idea of 'ordering' a story, rather than trying to make sense out of the existing order presented, reflects a Western sense of 'controlling' the world rather than the idea of dealing with the world 'as is.' " I was really cooking.

"The test stresses some types of performance over others," I protested. "The oft-repeated direction 'work as quickly as possible' has little meaning for a child raised to emphasize process rather than strict efficiency." Was that how I raised Adam? And yet, how persuasive I sounded to myself. I could explain anything where Adam was concerned. In my defense of him, his liabilities were nothing more than pointers to the fact that, as an Indian, he conceived the world in different, preferable, terms. To read the sheaf of my letters during those years one would gather I believed that Adam was lucky not to be able to tell time, to tell a nickel from a quarter from a penny, or to consistently discriminate between large and small. The world, American Culture, individual assessors had the problems—Adam was just as he should be.

I must have been a formidable force for Adam's teachers to deal with as I tried to intellectually or culturally coerce them into sharing my views. I talked more than I listened, demanded reports of "progress," and vigorously protested any opinions that seemed to limit Adam's chances. To judge him lacking in innate ability, I darkly hinted, implied poor teaching, racism, or a defeatist attitude. My justification for pressure was rooted in my wish that Adam be all right, but it stemmed also from pride, from my arrogance, my terror.

I look back now at Adam's Cornish report cards, at all those *Satisfactory's* and *C's* in math and science and history that I had insisted appear, all those passing marks, when in truth he didn't grasp for more than a minute any of the material. To what extent was Adam's steady progress from one grade to another due to my bluster? How far did Ms. Alexion lead him by the hand? To what degree did his teachers, for liberal or self-image reasons of their own, need to believe that he should be granted the benefit of the doubt? Yet the further on paper Adam got ahead, the further he fell behind.

## Questions on Meaning

1. What teaching techniques did Dorris apply to Adam? What forms of pressure did he exert on Adam's teachers?
2. Why do you think it was important to Dorris to believe that Adam could succeed at school? What information in the essay leads you to that conclusion?
3. Do you like Dorris as a person? Why or why not? Cite passages of Dorris's descriptions that give you an indirect picture of him.
4. Are there any ways in which very bright students cause problems in the classroom similar to those that Adam caused?
5. Dorris suggests that his pressure tactics caused the teachers in the Cornish school to pass Adam along without solving his problems. What advantages and disadvantages might have resulted from requiring him to repeat one or more grades?

## Questions on Rhetorical Strategy and Style

1. When you were in school, do you remember having "mainstreamed" classmates, children who had physical or psychological problems that made them different from other students? Did you find it a problem to have such classmates? Were you a mainstreamed student? Using one of Dorris's paragraphs as a model, describe your classmate or, if you were a mainstreamed student, describe your response to your classmates.
2. What questions about Adam did Dorris leave unanswered? Can you guess why he made the choice to sketch Adam's case rather than giving the full details about any single incident?

## Writing Assignments

1. What would you have done with Adam if you had had charge of his future? Write an essay about how the educational system should deal with exceptional students.
2. Conduct some research into the various forms that intelligence can take besides mathematical and verbal IQ (e.g., musical, athletic, and social abilities). Write about the place of those other abilities in education.

# KISS ME, I'M GAY

## Barbara Ehrenreich

*Barbara Ehrenreich (1941– ) was born in Montana, earned her Ph.D. from Rockefeller University, and now lives in New York. She is known as—and speaks of herself as—an independent and outspoken feminist, liberal, and democratic socialist. Most of her nonfiction writing could be classified as social criticism, including a number of books:* The Hearts of Men *(1983),* Fear of Falling *(1989), and* The Worst Years of Our Lives *(1990). Her novel* Kipper's Game *was published in 1993. She is a regular essayist for* Time *magazine, where the essay "Kiss Me, I'm Gay" was first published in 1993. As an often controversial social critic, Ehrenreich frequently writes essays in which she tries to identify ways to correct problems or misunderstandings related to social issues. In the following essay, her real subject is not so much what it means to be gay as what society thinks about gays.*

1 A strange, unspoken assumption about human sexuality runs 1
through the current debate on gay rights. Both sides agree, without saying so explicitly, that the human race consists of two types of people: heterosexuals and—on the other side of a great sexual dividing line—homosexuals. Heterosexuals are assumed to be the majority, while gays are thought to be a "minority," analogous to African Americans, Latinos, or any other ethnic group. Thus there is "gay pride" just as there is "black pride." We have Gay Pride marches just as we have Saint Patrick's Day or Puerto Rican Day parades. Gay militants even rallied, briefly, around the idea of a "queer nation."

There are ways in which this tribalistic view of human sexuality is useful and even progressive. Before the gay rights movement,

---

From *The Snarling Citizen: Essays.* Published by Farrar Straus & Giroux, Inc. "Kiss Me, I'm Gay" first appeared in *Time* (May 10, 1993), under the title "The Gap Between Gay and Straight." 

homosexuality was conceived as a diffuse menace, attached to no particular group and potentially threatening every man, at least in its "latent" form. So, naturally, as gays came out, they insisted on a unique and prideful group identity: We're queer and we're here! How else do you get ahead in America except by banding together and hoisting a flag?

Some studies seem to indicate that homosexuality is genetically based, more or less like left-handedness or being Irish. Heterosexuals, whether out of tolerance or spite, have been only too happy to concede to gays a special and probably congenital identity of their own. It's a way of saying: We're on this side of the great sexual divide—and you're on that.

There's only one problem with the theory of gays-as-ethnic-group: it denies the true plasticity of human sexuality and, in so doing, helps heterosexuals evade that which they really fear. And what heterosexuals really fear is not that "they"—an alien subgroup with perverse tastes in bedfellows—are getting an undue share of power and attention but that "they" might well be us.

5 Yes, certainly there are people who have always felt themselves to 5
be gay—or straight—since the first unruly fifth-grade crush or tickle in the groin. But for every study suggesting that homosexuality is innate, there are plenty of others that suggest human sexuality is far more versatile—or capricious, if you like. In his pioneering study, Alfred Kinsey reported that 37 percent of the men and 19 percent of the women he surveyed acknowledged having had at least one orgasm with a partner of the same sex. William Masters and Virginia Johnson found that, among the people they studied, fantasies about sex with same-sex partners were the norm.

In some cultures, it is more or less accepted that "straight" men will nonetheless have sex with other men. The rapid spread of AIDS in Brazil, for example, is attributed to bisexual behavior on the part of ostensibly heterosexual males. In the British upper class, homosexual experience used to be a not uncommon feature of male adolescence. Young Robert Graves went off to World War I pining desperately for his schoolboy lover, but returned and eventually married. And, no, he did not spend his time in the trenches buggering his comrades-in-arms.

So being gay is not quite the same as being Irish. There are shadings; there are changes in the course of a lifetime. I know people who were once brazenly "out" and are now happily, heterosexually married—as well as people who have gone in the opposite direction. Or, to generalize beyond genital sexuality to the realm of affection and loyalty: we all know men who are militantly straight yet who reserve their deepest feelings for the male-bonded group—the team, the volunteer fire department, the men they went to war with.

The problem for the military is not that discipline will be undermined by a sudden influx of stereotypically swishy gays. The problem is that the military is still a largely unisexual institution—with all that that implies about the possibility of homosexual encounters. The traditionalists keep bringing up the "crowded showers," much like the dread unisex toilets of the ERA debate. But, from somewhere deep in the sexual imagination, the question inevitably arises: Why do they have such tiny, crowded showers anyway?

By saying that gays are a definite, distinguishable minority that can easily be excluded, the military may feel better about its own presumptive heterosexuality. But can "gays" really be excluded? Do eighteen-year-old recruits really have a firm idea what their sexuality is? The military could deal with its sexuality crisis much more simply, and justly, by ceasing to be such a unisexual institution and letting women in on an equal basis.

10 Perhaps we have all, "gays" and "straights," gotten as far as we can 10
with the metaphor of gays as a quasi-ethnic group, entitled to its own "rights." Perhaps it is time to acknowledge that the potential to fall in love with, or just be attracted to, a person of the same sex is widespread among otherwise perfectly conventional people. There would still be enormous struggle over what is right and wrong, "normal" and "abnormal." But at least this would be a struggle that everyone—gay or straight—would have a stake in: gays because of who they are; straights because of who they might be, and sometimes actually are. All men, for example, would surely be better off in a world where simple acts of affection between men occasioned no great commentary or suspicion. Where a hug would be a hug and not a "statement."

## Questions on Meaning

1. What does Ehrenreich mean when she refers to a hug as a "statement"? Why would society view it that way?
2. The word "gay" is sometimes used to refer only to men, sometimes to include both gay men and lesbian women. We can tell through her examples and pronouns that Ehrenreich is writing strictly about men, not about lesbians. What do you make of this? Do you think she would say all of her points can be made equally well about lesbians—or is there something intrinsically different about gay men in terms of the ideas she writes about in this essay?
3. Ehrenreich mentions different research into the causes of gender identity and behavioral patterns, yet she seems not to argue in a cause and effect manner. Instead, her theme is about how society views and might better view gays. Why would it be better not to understand being gay the same way we understand being left-handed or being Irish?

## Questions on Rhetorical Strategy and Style

1. Notice how the word "gay" is used in the last two paragraphs of the essay—sometimes inside quotation marks, sometimes not. Examine the pattern of word use here and explain that pattern in relation to what the essay says about what it means to be "gay."
2. Analyze how the essay develops from the first paragraph to the last. At what point does the thesis emerge clearly? Explain the advantages of having the thesis appear at that point, particularly in terms of how the essay builds to it and continues after it.
3. In much of her writing Ehrenreich interjects humor and frequently bold or outrageous figurative language. How would you characterize the tone of this piece? Comment on how the tone relates to the topic.

## Writing Assignments

1. The researchers that Ehrenreich mentions have written much about the formation of sexual identity, and it is true that no one theory of the origins of sexual preference has emerged to account for the many variations in sexual identity and behavior. These researchers also write about the personal doubts and struggles most people have in establishing their own identity and becoming

comfortable with their own sexuality. This struggle is a major theme in literature, movies, and the theater. Choose a work you have read or seen recently in which a character has this struggle. Think about that character's difficulty—does it demonstrate that sexuality is not a simple either-or, black-or-white reality?

2. Ehrenreich makes a side point in this essay with this half-joking comment: "How else do you get ahead in America except by banding together and hoisting a flag?" On college campuses one often sees such groups forming in support of their particular causes. What have you observed in your own community or campus? Using familiar examples, write an essay looking at both the benefits and the disadvantages of this collective behavior to "get ahead."
3. Women have entered the military in increasing numbers, and society seems to be becoming more accepting of such "unisexual" institutions. On college campuses, too, there are often coed dormitories where not that long ago the sexes were strictly separated by locked doors and complicated check-in arrangements. Increasingly popular also are "unisex" bathrooms in places. Write an essay in which you explore this trend in breaking down traditional barriers, using additional examples you have observed.

# THE TAPESTRY OF FRIENDSHIP

## Ellen Goodman

*Ellen Goodman (1941– ), was born in Newton, Massachusetts. A graduate of Radcliffe College (1963), Goodman worked for* Newsweek *and* The Detroit Free Press *before joining* The Boston Globe *in 1967. In addition to writing a regular column for the* Globe, *"At Large," which has been syndicated since 1976, Goodman also is a frequent radio and television commentator. The recipient of a Pulitzer Prize for distinguished commentary in 1980, Goodman has published a number of collections of her columns—including* Close to Home *(1979) and* At Large *(1981)—as well as an interview-based review of the impact of the feminist movement—*Making Sense *(1989). Goodman's essays, which often probe very personal aspects of late 20th century America, generally are a twist of irony and satire. Originally published in* The Washington Post *(1978), this short essay explores female "friends" and male "buddies," while it also probes society's changing perspective on relationships.*

1 It was, in many ways, a slight movie. Nothing actually happened. 1
There was no big-budget chase scene, no bloody shoot-out. The story ended without any cosmic conclusions.

Yet she found Claudia Weill's film *Girlfriends* gentle and affecting. Slowly, it panned across the tapestry of friendship—showing its fragility, its resiliency, its role as the connecting tissue between the lives of two young women.

When it was over, she thought about the movies she'd seen this year—*Julia, The Turning Point* and now *Girlfriends.* It seemed that the peculiar eye, the social lens of the cinema, had drastically shifted its focus. Suddenly the Male Buddy movies had been replaced by the Female Friendship flicks.

This wasn't just another binge of trendiness, but a kind of *cinéma vérité.* For once the movies were reflecting a shift, not just from men to women but from one definition of friendship to another.

5 Across millions of miles of celluloid, the ideal of friendship had always been male—a world of sidekicks and "pardners," of Butch Cassidys and Sundance Kids. There had been something almost atavistic about these visions of attachments—as if producers culled their plots from some pop anthropology book on male bonding. Movies portrayed the idea that only men, those direct descendants of hunters and Hemingways, inherited a primal capacity for friendship. In contrast, they portrayed women picking on each other, the way they once picked berries.

Well, that duality must have been mortally wounded in some shootout at the You're OK, I'm OK Corral. Now, on the screen, they were at least aware of the subtle distinction between men and women as buddies and friends.

About 150 years ago, Coleridge had written, "A woman's friendship borders more closely on love than man's. Men affect each other in the reflection of noble or friendly acts, whilst women ask fewer proofs and more signs and expressions of attachment."

Well, she thought, on the whole, men had buddies, while women had friends. Buddies bonded, but friends loved. Buddies faced adversity together, but friends faced each other. There was something palpably different in the way they spent their time. Buddies seemed to "do" things together; friends simply "were" together.

Buddies came linked, like accessories, to one activity or another. People have golf buddies and business buddies, college buddies and club buddies. Men often keep their buddies in these categories, while women keep a special category for friends.

10 A man once told her that men weren't real buddies until they'd been "through the wars" together—corporate or athletic or military. They had to soldier together, he said. Women, on the other hand, didn't count themselves as friends until they'd shared three loathsome confidences.

Buddies hang tough together; friends hang onto each other.

It probably had something to do with pride. You don't show off to a friend; you show need. Buddies try to keep the worst from each other; friends confess it.

A friend of hers once telephoned her lover, just to find out if he was home. She hung up without a hello when he picked up the phone. Later, wretched with embarrassment, the friend moaned, "Can you believe me? A thirty-five-year-old lawyer, making a chicken call?" Together they laughed and made it better.

Buddies seek approval. But friends seek acceptance.

She knew so many men who had been trained in restraint, afraid of each other's judgment or awkward with each other's affection. She wasn't sure which. Like buddies in the movies, they would die for each other, but never hug each other.

She'd reread *Babbitt* recently, that extraordinary catalogue of male grievances. The only relationship that gave meaning to the claustrophobic life of George Babbitt had been with Paul Riesling. But not once in the tragedy of their lives had one been able to say to the other: You make a difference.

Even now men shocked her at times with their description of friendship. Does this one have a best friend? "Why, of course, we see each other every February." Does that one call his most intimate pal long distance? "Why, certainly, whenever there's a real reason." Do those two old chums ever have dinner together? "You mean alone? Without our wives?"

Yet, things were changing. The ideal of intimacy wasn't this parallel playmate, this teammate, this trenchmate. Not even in Hollywood. In the double standard of friendship, for once the female version was becoming accepted as the general ideal.

After all, a buddy is a fine life-companion. But one's friends, as Santayana once wrote, "are that part of the race with which one can be human."

## Questions on Meaning

1. What does Goodman mean by the statement, "For once the movies were reflecting a shift"? This essay was published in 1978; what has happened to the "shift" she perceived?
2. What are some of the "distinctions between men and women as buddies and friends" that Goodman makes?

## Questions on Rhetorical Strategy and Style

1. Goodman relies heavily on comparison and contrast to illustrate differences in relationships between men and relationships between women. Make a two-column table, one for "men" and the other for "women," and then reread the essay and list all the characteristics of each you can find (such as buddies vs. friends, noble acts vs. love).
2. Who is the "she" in Goodman's essay? Why do you think she chose not to tell the reader any more about this person?

## Writing Assignments

1. Goodman quotes both Coleridge and Santayana to reinforce her arguments about the differences between "friends" and "buddies." Research other famous writers or philosophers to find other quotations related to friendship. Point out the distinctions they make between men and women.
2. Describe a close friendship you have with someone of the same sex. How does it parallel the friend/buddy relationships described by Goodman? Would you be comfortable in the relationship if it were more like the other gender's relationships? Would you feel comfortable discussing this essay with your friend/buddy—why or why not?
3. Goodman uses the expression *cinema verité* to indicate—rightly or wrongly—that movies were reflecting a real change in society. Write an essay about how current movies reflect American society today. Point out where you feel movies are resting on stereotypes, where you feel they reflect social trends, and where they may be pushing the envelope, depicting a fictional society. Select a cross-section of three or four movies and compare and contrast how they reflect society.

# SHAME

## Dick Gregory

*Dick Gregory (1932– ) grew up in St. Louis, Missouri. He attended Southern Illinois University and became a well-known comedian and entertainer. He was active in the civil rights movement of the 1960s and the movement against the Vietnam War. As a candidate in the Peace and Freedom Party, Gregory campaigned for president in 1968. His books include* Dick Gregory's Political Primer; From the Back of the Bus, No More Lies*; and his autobiography,* Nigger *(1964), from which the following selection is excerpted. In this episode about his early childhood, Gregory writes about one of poverty's destructive psychological effects on children.*

1 I never learned hate at home, or shame. I had to go to school for 1
that. I was about seven years old when I got my first big lesson. I was in love with a little girl named Helene Tucker, a light-complected little girl with pigtails and nice manners. She was always clean and she was smart in school. I think I went to school then mostly to look at her. I brushed my hair and even got me a little old handkerchief. It was a lady's handkerchief, but I didn't want Helene to see me wipe my nose on my hand. The pipes were frozen again, there was no water in the house, but I washed my socks and shirt every night. I'd get a pot, and go over to Mister Ben's grocery store, and stick my pot down into his soda machine. Scoop out some chopped ice. By evening the ice melted to water for washing. I got sick a lot that winter because the fire would go out at night before the clothes were dry. In the morning I'd put them on, wet or dry, because they were the only clothes I had.

---

Everybody's got a Helene Tucker, a symbol of everything you want. I loved her for her goodness, her cleanness, her popularity. She'd walk down my street and my brothers and sisters would yell, "Here comes Helene," and I'd rub my tennis sneakers on the back of my pants and wish my hair wasn't so nappy and the white folks' shirt fit me better. I'd run out on the street. If I knew my place and didn't come too close, she'd wink at me and say Hello. That was a good feeling. Sometimes I'd follow her all the way home, and shovel the snow off her walk and try to make friends with her Momma and her aunts. I'd drop money on her stoop late at night on my way back from shining shoes in the taverns. And she had a Daddy, and he had a good job. He was a paper hanger.

I guess I would have gotten over Helene by summertime, but something happened in that classroom that made her face hang in front of me for the next twenty-two years. When I played the drums in high school it was for Helene and when I broke track records in college it was for Helene and when I started standing behind microphones and heard applause I wished Helene could hear it, too. It wasn't until I was twenty-nine years old and married and making money that I finally got her out of my system. Helene was sitting in that classroom when I learned to be ashamed of myself.

It was on a Thursday. I was sitting in the back of the room, in a seat with a chalk circle drawn around it. The idiot's seat, the troublemaker's seat.

5 The teacher thought I was stupid. Couldn't spell, couldn't read, 5
couldn't do arithmetic. Just stupid. Teachers were never interested in finding out that you couldn't concentrate because you were so hungry, because you hadn't had any breakfast. All you could think about was noontime, would it ever come? Maybe you could sneak into the cloakroom and steal a bite of some kid's lunch out of a coat pocket. A bite of something. Paste. You can't really make a meal of paste, or put it on bread for a sandwich, but sometimes I'd scoop a few spoonfuls out of the paste jar in the back of the room. Pregnant people get strange tastes. I was pregnant with poverty. Pregnant with dirt and pregnant with smells that made people turn away, pregnant with cold and pregnant with shoes that were never bought for me, pregnant with five other people in my bed and no Daddy in the next room, and pregnant with hunger. Paste doesn't taste too bad when you're hungry.

The teacher thought I was a troublemaker. All she saw from the front of the room was a little black boy who squirmed in his idiot's seat and made noises and poked the kids around him. I guess she couldn't see a kid who made noises because he wanted someone to know he was there.

It was on a Thursday, the day before the Negro payday. The eagle always flew on Friday. The teacher was asking each student how much his father would give to the Community Chest. On Friday night, each kid would get the money from his father, and on Monday he would bring it to the school. I decided I was going to buy me a Daddy right then. I had money in my pocket from shining shoes and selling papers, and whatever Helene Tucker pledged for her Daddy I was going to top it. And I'd hand the money right in. I wasn't going to wait until Monday to buy me a Daddy.

I was shaking, scared to death. The teacher opened her book and started calling out names alphabetically.

"Helene Tucker?"

"My Daddy said he'd give two dollars and fifty cents."

"That's very nice, Helene. Very, very nice indeed."

That made me feel pretty good. It wouldn't take too much to top that. I had almost three dollars in dimes and quarters in my pocket. I stuck my hand in my pocket and held onto the money, waiting for her to call my name. But the teacher closed her book after she called everybody else in the class. I stood up and raised my hand.

"What is it now?"

"You forgot me."

She turned toward the blackboard. "I don't have time to be playing with you, Richard."

"My Daddy said he'd . . . "

"Sit down, Richard, you're disturbing the class."

"My Daddy said he'd give . . . fifteen dollars."

She turned around and looked mad. "We are collecting this money for you and your kind, Richard Gregory. If your Daddy can give fifteen dollars you have no business being on relief."

"I got it right now, I got it right now, my Daddy gave it to me to turn in today, my Daddy said . . . "

"And furthermore," she said, looking right at me, her nostrils getting big and her lips getting thin and her eyes opening wide, "we know you don't have a Daddy."

Helene Tucker turned around, her eyes full of tears. She felt sorry for me. Then I couldn't see her too well because I was crying, too.

"Sit down, Richard."

25 And I always thought the teacher kind of liked me. She always picked me to wash the blackboard on Friday, after school. That was a big thrill, it made me feel important. If I didn't wash it, come Monday the school might not function right.

"Where are you going, Richard?"

I walked out of school that day, and for a long time I didn't go back very often. There was shame there.

Now there was shame everywhere. It seemed like the whole world had been inside that classroom, everyone had heard what the teacher had said, everyone had turned around and felt sorry for me. There was shame in going to the Worthy Boys Annual Christmas Dinner for you and your kind, because everybody knew what a worthy boy was. Why couldn't they just call it the Boys Annual Dinner, why'd they have to give it a name? There was shame in wearing the brown and orange and white plaid mackinaw the welfare gave to 3,000 boys. Why'd it have to be the same for everybody so when you walked down the street the people could see you were on relief? It was a nice warm mackinaw and it had a hood , and my Momma beat me and called me a little rat when she found out I stuffed it in the bottom of a pail full of garbage way over on Cottage Street. There was shame in running over to Mister Ben's at the end of the day and asking for his rotten peaches, there was shame in asking Mrs. Simmons for a spoonful of sugar, there was shame in running out to meet the relief truck. I hated that truck, full of food for you and your kind. I ran into the house and hid when it came. And then I started to sneak through alleys, to take the long way home so the people going into White's Eat Shop wouldn't see me. Yeah, the whole world heard the teacher that day, we all know you don't have a Daddy.

It lasted for a while, this kind of numbness. I spent a lot of time feeling sorry for myself. And then one day I met this wino in a restaurant. I'd been out hustling all day, shining shoes, selling newspapers, and I had goo-gobs of money in my pocket. Bought me a bowl of chili for fifteen cents, and a cheeseburger for fifteen cents, and a Pepsi for five cents, and a piece of chocolate cake for ten cents. That was a good meal. I was eating when this old wino came in. I love winos because they never hurt anyone but themselves.

30 The old wino sat down at the counter and ordered twenty-six cents worth of food. He ate it like he really enjoyed it. When the

owner, Mister Williams, asked him to pay the check, the old wino didn't lie or go through his pocket like he suddenly found a hole.

He just said: "Don't have no money."

The owner yelled: "Why in hell you come in here and eat my food if you don't have no money? That food cost me money."

Mister Williams jumped over the counter and knocked the wino off his stool and beat him over the head with a pop bottle. Then he stepped back and watched the wino bleed. Then he kicked him. And he kicked him again.

I looked at the wino with blood all over his face and I went over. "Leave him alone, Mister Williams. I'll pay the twenty-six cents."

The wino got up, slowly, pulling himself up to the stool, then up to the counter, holding on for a minute until his legs stopped shaking so bad. He looked at me with pure hate. "Keep your twenty-six cents. You don't have to pay, not now. I just finished paying for it."

He started to walk out, and as he passed me, he reached down and touched my shoulder. "Thanks, sonny, but it's too late now. Why didn't you pay it before?"

I was pretty sick about that. I waited too long to help another man.

## Questions on Meaning

1. Why does the child Richard feel no shame before the incident with the teacher, but then feels shame for a long time afterwards? How is shame tied up with his feelings for Helene?
2. Gregory does not explicitly explain how the later incident with the wino led to his overcoming some of his shame, but we can sense the effect of that incident. Describe how you think Richard changes as a result of the interaction with the wino.
3. What does the essay reveal about issues of education and poverty?

## Questions on Rhetorical Strategy and Style

1. Reread the first five paragraphs of the essay, taking note of Gregory's use of descriptive detail. Which details in particular make an impression on you about the kind of poverty in which he grew up?
2. Analyze the structure of the essay—how the two narratives are put together to develop his theme about shame. How does Gregory use introductory and transitional statements about shame to prepare us for and guide us through the narratives?
3. Gregory uses dialogue as a key part of the narration. Reread the scene in which the teacher and Richard talk about his "daddy's" contribution to the Community Chest, which is written almost entirely in dialogue. Which phrases spoken by the teacher reveal her personality? Which phrases spoken by Richard reveal his emotions at the moment?

## Writing Assignments

1. The young Dick Gregory was ashamed of his poverty and not having a father, although neither of these was his own fault—he felt shame when he discovered that others were judging him by these facts. In what other ways do people, or society as a whole, judge individuals? By what they look like? what clothes they wear? how they act, etc.? Make a list of factors that contribute to how people are judged by others. Then sort your list into those things that are beyond a person's control, and those things that result from the person's own choices. Does society pay more attention to one kind of factor than another? Which individual factors

*should* you pay more attention to when forming an opinion about someone else?

2. Although most of us have not experienced the kind of poverty that Gregory describes, we all remember unpleasant or embarrassing moments in our childhood that we'd probably rather forget. Choose some childhood incident that sticks in your memory, and think about why you've never forgotten it. Write a narrative essay about that incident, introducing it in a way that helps the reader grasp its meaning. Use detail to make your narrative vivid.

# DON'T LET STEREOTYPES WARP YOUR JUDGMENTS

**Robert Heilbroner**

*Robert Heilbroner (1919– ) attended Harvard University and the New School for Social Research, where he has taught economics since 1972. His books include* the Future as History *(1960),* A Primer of Government Spending: Between Capitalism and Socialism *(1970), and* An Inquiry into the Human Prospect *(1974). This essay, published in* Reader's Digest, *highlights dangers of stereotyping—both to others as well as to ourselves—and suggests how we can correct this tendency.*

1 Is a girl called Gloria apt to be better-looking than one called 1
Bertha? Are criminals more likely to be dark than blond? Can you tell a good deal about someone's personality from hearing his voice briefly over the phone? Can a person's nationality be pretty accurately guessed from his photograph? Does the fact that someone wears glasses imply that he is intelligent?

The answer to all these questions is obviously, "No."

Yet, from all the evidence at hand, most of us believe these things. Ask any college boy if he'd rather take his chances with a Gloria or a Bertha, or ask a college girl if she'd rather blind-date a Richard or a Cuthbert. In fact, you don't have to ask: college students in questionnaires have revealed that names conjure up the same images in their minds as they do in yours—and for as little reason.

Look into the favorite suspects of persons who report "suspicious characters" and you will find a large percentage of them to be "swarthy" or "dark and foreign-looking"—despite the testimony of criminologists that criminals do not tend to be dark, foreign or "wild-eyed." Delve into the main asset of a telephone stock swindler and you will find it to be a marvelously confidence-inspiring telephone

---

From *Reader's Digest.*

"personality." And whereas we all think we know what an Italian or a Swede looks like, it is the sad fact that when a group of Nebraska students sought to match faces and nationalities of 15 European countries, they were scored wrong in 93 percent of their identifications. Finally, for all the fact that horn-rimmed glasses have now become the standard television sign of an "intellectual," optometrists know that the main thing that distinguishes people with glasses is just bad eyes.

5 Stereotypes are a kind of gossip about the world, a gossip that makes us pre-judge people before we ever lay eyes on them. Hence it is not surprising that stereotypes have something to do with the dark world of prejudice. Explore most prejudices (note that the word means prejudgment) and you will find a cruel stereotype at the core of each one.

For it is the extraordinary fact that once we have typecast the world, we tend to see people in terms of our standardized pictures. In another demonstration of the power of stereotypes to affect our vision, a number of Columbia and Barnard students were shown 30 photographs of pretty but unidentified girls, and asked to rate each in terms of "general liking," "intelligence," "beauty" and so on. Two months later, the same group were shown the same photographs, this time with fictitious Irish, Italian, Jewish and "American" names attached to the pictures. Right away the ratings changed. Faces which were now seen as representing a national group went down in looks and still farther down in likability, while the "American" girls suddenly looked decidedly prettier and nicer.

Why is it that we stereotype the world in such irrational and harmful fashion? In part, we begin to typecast people in our childhood years. Early in life, as every parent whose child has watched a TV Western knows, we learn to spot the Good Guys from the Bad Guys. Some years ago, a social psychologist showed very clearly how powerful these stereotypes of childhood vision are. He secretly asked the most popular youngsters in an elementary school to make errors in their morning gym exercises. Afterwards, he asked the class if anyone had noticed any mistakes during gym period. Oh, yes, said the children. But it was the *unpopular* members of the class—the "bad guys"—they remembered as being out of step.

We not only grow up with standardized pictures forming inside of us, but as grown-ups we are constantly having them thrust upon us. Some of them, like the half-joking, half-serious stereotypes of mothers-in-law, or country yokels, or psychiatrists, are dinned into us by the stock jokes we hear and repeat. In fact, without such stereotypes, there would be a lot fewer jokes. Still other stereotypes are perpetuated by the advertisements we read, the movies we see, the books we read.

And finally, we tend to stereotype because it helps us make sense out of a highly confusing world, a world which William James once described as "one great, blooming, buzzing confusion." It is a curious fact that if we don't *know* what we're looking at, we are often quite literally unable to *see* what we're looking at. People who recover their sight after a lifetime of blindness actually cannot at first tell a triangle from a square. A visitor to a factory sees only noisy chaos where the superintendent sees a perfectly synchronized flow of work. As Walter Lippmann has said, "For the most part we do not first see, and then define; we define first, and then we see."

10 Stereotypes are one way in which we "define" the world in order to see it. They classify the infinite variety of human beings into a convenient handful of "types" towards whom we learn to act in stereotyped fashion. Life would be a wearing process if we had to start from scratch with each and every human contact. Stereotypes economize on our mental effort by covering up the blooming, buzzing confusion with big recognizable cut-outs. They save us the "trouble" of finding out what the world is like—they give it its accustomed look.

Thus the trouble is that stereotypes make us mentally lazy. As S. I. Hayakawa, the authority on semantics, has written: "The danger of stereotypes lies not in their existence, but in the fact that they become for all people some of the time, and for some people all the time, *substitutes for observation.*" Worse yet, stereotypes get in the way of our judgment, even when we do observe the world. Someone who has formed rigid preconceptions of all Latins as "excitable," or all teenagers as "wild," doesn't alter his point of view when he meets a calm and deliberate Genoese, or a serious-minded high school student. He brushes them aside as "exceptions that prove the rule." And, of course, if he meets someone true to type, he stands triumphantly vindicated. "They're all like that," he proclaims, having encountered an excited Latin, an ill-behaved adolescent.

Hence, quite aside from the injustice which stereotypes do to others, they impoverish ourselves. A person who lumps the world into simple categories, who type-casts all labor leaders as "racketeers," all businessmen as "reactionaries," all Harvard men as "snobs," and all Frenchmen as "sexy," is in danger of becoming a stereotype himself. He loses his capacity to be himself—which is to say, to see the world in his own absolutely unique, inimitable and independent fashion.

Instead, he votes for the man who fits his standardized picture of what a candidate "should" look like or sound like, buys the goods that someone in his "situation" in life "should" own, lives the life that others define for him. The mark of the stereotype person is that he never surprises us, that we do indeed have him "typed." And no one fits this straitjacket so perfectly as someone whose opinions about *other people* are fixed and inflexible.

Impoverishing as they are, stereotypes are not easy to get rid of. The world we type-cast may be no better than a Grade B movie, but at least we know what to expect of our stock characters. When we let them act for themselves in the strangely unpredictable way that people do act, who knows but that many of our fondest convictions will be proved wrong?

15 Nor do we suddenly drop our standardized pictures for a blinding vision of the Truth. Sharp swings of ideas about people often just substitute one stereotype for another. The true process of change is a slow one that adds bits and pieces of reality to the pictures in our heads, until gradually they take on some of the blurriness of life itself. Little by little, we learn not that Jews and Negroes and Catholics and Puerto Ricans are "just like everybody else"—for that, too, is a stereotype—but that each and every one of them is unique, special, different and individual. Often we do not even know that we have let a stereotype lapse until we hear someone saying, "all so-and-so's are like such-and-such, and we hear ourselves saying, "Well-maybe."

Can we speed the process along? Of course we can.

First, we can become *aware* of the standardized pictures in our heads, in other peoples' heads, in the world around us.

Second, we can become suspicious of all judgments that we allow exceptions to "prove." There is no more chastening thought than that in the vast intellectual adventure of science, it takes but one tiny exception to topple a whole edifice of ideas.

Third, we can learn to be chary of generalizations about people. As F. Scott Fitzgerald once wrote: "Begin with an individual, and before you know it you have created a type; begin with a type, and you find you have created—nothing."

20 Most of the time, when we type-cast the world, we are not in fact generalizing about people at all. We are only revealing the embarrassing facts about the pictures that hang in the gallery of stereotypes in our own heads.

## Questions on Meaning

1. What are some of the common sources of prejudice that Heilbroner identifies?
2. List the negative effects of stereotyping that Heilbroner describes in this essay. What other negatives would you add to this list?
3. Heilbroner says it is not easy to rid ourselves of stereotypes, but that it can be done. What is his three-step process?

## Questions on Rhetorical Strategy and Style

1. Find where Heilbroner uses a cause and effect writing strategy to illustrate the impact of ethnicity on such perceived personal characteristics as intelligence and beauty.
2. How does Heilbroner define "stereotypes" and "prejudice"? How are these two terms related?
3. How does Heilbroner use irony to explain that stereotyping not only affects how we see other people but also affects how people see us? Think of ways that you may have inadvertently stereotyped yourself.

## Writing Assignments

1. Heilbroner explains that stereotyping is a form of classification that helps us "make sense of a highly confusing world"? List some common "types" of individuals based on visual characteristics (i.e., ethnic group, occupation, attitude, hygiene, etc.), then go to a busy public place—such as the student union, a downtown street corner, or a mass transit stop—and classify people for a few minutes. Next, observe another set of strangers, but his time write descriptions of each person without stereotyping him or her. How do your images of the second group compare with the first group?
2. Research Hayakawa and the study of "general semantics," in particular, theories of observation. Write an essay in which you explain what "general semantics" is and describe how it can affect how we observe people, places, and things.

# THAT WORD *BLACK*

## Langston Hughes

*Langston Hughes (1902–1967), a poet, short-story writer, essayist, and playwright, was born in Joplin, Missouri, and grew up in Kansas and Ohio. After graduating from high school (where he began writing poetry), Hughes spent 15 months in Mexico with his father, attended Columbia University for a year, worked as a seaman on cargo ships bound to Africa and Europe, and bused tables at a hotel in New York City. Later, he returned to school and graduated from Lincoln University (1929). Part of the "Harlem Renaissance" or "New Negro Renaissance"—and fiercely proud of his African-American heritage—Hughes often drew from Negro spirituals and blues and jazz in his literary work. Hughes was published in* Amsterdam News, Crisis, The New Negro, *and other periodicals. His books include the novel* Not Without Laughter *(1930); the short story collection* The Ways of White Folks *(1934); the play* The Mulatto *(1935); his autobiography* The Big Sea *(1940); and his poetry collections* The Weary Blues *(1926),* Shakespeare of Harlem *(1942),* Montage of a Dream Deferred *(1951), and* Ask Your Mama *(1961). In this essay, through his character "Simple," Hughes shows how the word "black" has acquired many negative connotations.*

1 "This evening," said Simple, "I feel like talking about the word black." 1

"Nobody's stopping you, so go ahead. But what you really ought to have is a soap-box out on the corner of 126th and Lenox where the rest of the orators hang out."

"They expresses some good ideas on that corner," said Simple, "but for my ideas I do not need a crowd. Now, as I were saying, the word *black,* white folks have done used that word to mean something bad so often until now when the N.A.A.C.P asks for civil rights for the black man, they think they must be bad. Looking back into history, I reckon it all started with a *black* cat meaning bad luck. Don't let one cross your path!

"Next, somebody got up a *blacklist* on which you get if you don't vote right. Then when lodges come into being, the folks they didn't want in them got *blackballed.* If you kept a skeleton in your closet, you might get *blackmailed.* And everything bad was *black.* When it came down to the unlucky ball on the pool table, the eight-rock, they made it the *black* ball. So no wonder there ain't no equal rights for the *black* man."

5 "All you say is true about the odium attached to the word *black,*" I said. "You've even forgotten a few. For example, during the war if you bought something under the table, illegally, they said you were trading on the *black* market. In Chicago, if you're a gangster, the *Black Hand Society* may take you for a ride. And certainly if you don't behave yourself, your family will say you're a *black* sheep. Then, if your mama burns a *black* candle to change the family luck, they call it *black* magic."

"My mama never did believe in voodoo so she did not burn no black candles," said Simple.

"If she had, that would have been a *black* mark against her."

"Stop talking about my mama. What I want to know is, where do white folks get off calling everything bad *black*? If it is a dark night, they say it's *black* as hell. If you are mean and evil, they say you got a *black* heart. I would like to change all that around and say that the people who Jim Crow me have got a *white* heart. People who sell dope to children have got a *white* mark against them. And all the white gamblers who were behind the basketball fix are the *white* sheep of the sports world. God knows there was few, if any, Negroes selling stuff on the black market during the war, so why didn't they call it the *white* market? No, they got to take me and my color and turn it into everything bad. According to white folks, black is bad.

"Wait till my day comes! In my language, bad will be *white.* Blackmail will be *white*mail. Black cats will be good luck, and *white* cats will be bad. If a *white* cat crosses your path, look out! I will take the black ball for the cue ball and let the *white* ball be the unlucky eight-rock. And on my blacklist—which will be a *white*list then—I will put everybody who ever Jim Crowed me from Rankin to Hitler, Talmadge to Malan, South Carolina to South Africa.

10 "I am black. When I look in the mirror, I see myself, daddy-o, but 10 I am not ashamed. God made me. He also made F.D., dark as he is. He did not make us no badder than the rest of the folks. The earth is black and all kinds of good things comes out of the earth. Trees and flowers and fruit and sweet potatoes and corn and all that keeps mens alive comes right up out of the earth—good old black earth. Coal is black and it warms your house and cooks your food. The night is black, which has a moon, and a million stars, and is beautiful. Sleep is black which gives you rest, so you wake up feeling good. I am black. I feel very good this evening.

"What is wrong with black?"

## Questions on Meaning

1. Why does Simple declare that "civil rights" mean something "bad" to white people?
2. How does Simple intend to reverse the negative connotations attached to the word *black*?
3. What is Hughes' thesis in this piece? Is it explicitly stated?

## Questions on Rhetorical Strategy and Style

1. Hughes wrote this piece entirely in dialogue. Describe the effect on his delivery—and message—if he had used a narrative form, without dialogue. How does the interaction between the speakers help strengthen his arguments?
2. What examples does Hughes give of negative word forms incorporating *black*? What positive uses of *black* does he give?
3. In addition to *two* speakers and *two* colors, how else does Hughes use duality in this essay?
4. Choose five of the negative word forms using *black* and use each in a sentence. Next, rewrite the sentence, replacing the offensive word form with another expression. How difficult is it to eliminate these words? Explain how the revised sentences differ in meaning from the original sentence.

## Writing Assignments

1. Write an essay on the use of politically correct speech—such as using "chairperson" rather than "chairman" or using contractions, such as "s/he." Explain why you feel these more sensitive word choices are necessary or not. Provide recommendations for acceptable writing today.
2. Look up the word *black* in the Oxford English Dictionary. Report the changes in meaning the word has undergone since its first recorded use in English.

# THE AMERICANIZATION IDEAL

## Barbara Jordan

*Barbara Jordan (1937–1996), the first African-American woman from the South to serve in the U.S. House of Representatives since Reconstruction, chaired the U.S. Commission on Immigration Reform. In this 1995* New York Times *article, Jordan argues that the United States should maintain its immigration policies.*

1 Congress is considering legislation to curb illegal immigration 1
and set priorities for legal admissions. Several presidential candidates have made immigration a keystone of their campaigns. Newspapers carry immigration-related articles almost daily, in contrast to just a few years ago when hardly any appeared.

This attention is not misplaced. Reform is needed in policies that permit the continued entry of hundreds of thousands of illegal aliens and blur distinctions between what is legal and beneficial and what is illegal and harmful. The Commission on Immigration Reform issued a report last year on illegal immigration and will release its second report, on legal migrants, tomorrow. These two reports outline a rational set of principles that will restore credibility to our policies while setting priorities for the future.

Legitimate concern about weaknesses in our immigration policy should not, however, obfuscate what remains the essential point: The United States has been and should continue to be a nation of immigrants. A well-regulated system of legal immigration is in our national interest.

There have always been those who despised the newcomers. The history of American immigration policy is full of racism and ethnic prejudice. The Know-Nothings. The Chinese Exclusion Acts. Even before the Revolution, as eminent a person as Benjamin Franklin feared that Germans coming to Pennsylvania would not become English.

5 Of course, German immigrants to Pennsylvania did not become English, nor did they make Pennsylvanians into Germans. Instead, they became *Americans.* So did the Chinese, Japanese, and Koreans who came, despite prejudice. So do the Mexicans, Cubans, and Haitians who come today.

The United States has united immigrants and their descendants around a commitment to democratic ideals and constitutional principles. People from an extraordinary range of ethnic and religious backgrounds have embraced these ideals.

There is a word for this process: Americanization. That word earned a bad reputation when it was stolen by racists and xenophobes in the 1920s. But it is our word, and we are taking it back. Americanization means becoming a part of the polity—becoming one of us. But that does not mean conformity. We are more than a melting pot; we are a kaleidoscope, where every turn of history refracts new light on the old promise.

Immigration imposes mutual obligations. Those who choose to come here must embrace the common core of American civic culture. We must assist them in learning our common language: American English. We must renew civic education in the teaching of American history for all Americans. We must vigorously enforce the laws against hate crimes and discrimination. We must remind ourselves, as we illustrate for newcomers, what makes us America.

Naturalization is a vital step in this process. Interest in naturalization has never been greater; applications for citizenship exceed in number and proportion any previous period in our history. But would-be citizens must wait too long to be processed, as much as two years in some cities. The Immigration and Naturalization Service must make timely naturalization a strategic goal while maintaining rigorous standards.

10 Reforming our immigration policy is the best way to revitalize our commitment to immigration and to immigrants. It is literally a matter of who we are as a nation, and who we become as a people.

## Questions on Meaning

1. What is Jordan's thesis? Restate her position in your own words.
2. Why does Jordan feel that America must reform its immigration policy? What does Jordan believe that the U.S. Immigration and Naturalization Service must make its goal?
3. What does Jordan mean when she describes America as a "kaleidoscope"?

## Questions on Rhetorical Strategy and Style

1. Jordan uses the writing strategy of definition to introduce the concept of Americanization. How has was that concept altered in the 1920s? Why does she say, "We are taking it back"?
2. What examples does Jordan give of the "racism and ethnic prejudice" that have marred American immigration policy? If you are not familiar with the specific incidents she mentions, look them up.
3. Jordan was lauded for her oratorical abilities. Read the essay aloud and mark passages that reflect the rhythm and timing of a skilled public speaker.

## Writing Assignments

1. Jordan comments in this 1995 essay that immigration policy had been a "keystone" of some presidential campaigns. Research the role of immigration policy during the campaigns of the most recent presidential election. Describe why you feel the tone of campaign rhetoric reflects a trend toward or away from isolationism.
2. Research immigration policy and determine when a newcomer is considered to be an "illegal alien." What action must one take to become "legal"? Explain why you feel these requirements are too restrictive or too permissive.
3. Write an essay about how immigration has affected the place you lived while you were in high school. What ethnic groups are increasing in number? What impact have their cultures had on the community? What have you learned about prejudice and tolerance from the way long-time residents responded? Describe what can be done to help immigrants become part of the community.

# A CASE OF ASSISTED SUICIDE

## Jack Kevorkian

*Jack Kevorkian (1928– ) was born in Pontiac, Michigan. A graduate of the University of Michigan medical school with a specialty in pathology (1952), Kevorkian has become one of the most well-known proponents of euthanasia because of the many "assisted suicides" he has attended. Kevorkian's active involvement in euthanasia began in 1990, when a 54-year-old woman diagnosed with Alzheimer's disease died after using his home-built "suicide machine" or "death machine." Since that time, Kevorkian—also called "Dr. Death" by some in the media—has facilitated numerous euthanasia deaths, all the while fighting court injunctions, murder charges, legislative bans on assisted suicide, and the loss of his license to practice medicine in California and Michigan. Kevorkian's publications include the article "The Last Fearsome Taboo: Medical Aspects of Planned Death" in* Medicine and Law *(1988) and the book* Prescription: Medicide *(1991). In this excerpt from* Prescription: Medicide, *Kevorkian describes the first use of his so-called "death machine" and advances his reasons for using it.*

1 Amid the flurry of telephone calls in the fall of 1989 was one 1
from a man in Portland, Oregon, who learned of my campaign from an item in *Newsweek* (November 13, 1989). Ron Adkins's rich, baritone, matter-of-fact voice was tinged with a bit of expectant anxiety as he calmly explained the tragic situation of his beloved wife. Janet Adkins was a remarkable, accomplished, active

From *Prescription: Medicide* by Dr. Jack Kevorkian. Published by Prometheus Books.

woman—wife, mother, grandmother, revered friend, teacher, musician, mountain climber, and outdoorsperson—who, for some time, had noticed (as did her husband) subtle and gradually progressive impairment of her memory. The shock of hearing the diagnosis of Alzheimer's disease four months earlier was magnified by the abrupt and somewhat callous way her doctor announced it. The intelligent woman knew what the diagnosis portended, and at that instant decided she would not live to experience the horror of such a death.

Knowing that Janet was a courageous fighter, Ron and their three sons pleaded with her to reconsider and at least give a promising new therapy regimen a try. Ron explained to me that Janet was eligible to take part in an experimental trial using the newly developed drug Tacrine® or THA at the University of Washington in Seattle. I concurred that Janet should enroll in the program because any candidate for the Mercitron must have exhausted every potentially beneficial medical intervention, no matter how remotely promising.

I heard nothing more from the Adkinses until April 1990. Ron called again, after Janet and he saw me and my device on a nationally televised talk show. Janet had entered the experimental program in January, but it had been stopped early because the new drug was ineffective. In fact, her condition got worse; and she was more determined than ever to end her life. Even though from a physical standpoint Janet was not imminently terminal, there seemed little doubt that mentally she was—and, after all, it is one's mental status that determines the essence of one's existence. I asked Ron to forward to me copies of Janet's clinical records, and they corroborated what Ron had said.

I then telephoned Janet's doctor in Seattle. He opposed her planned action and the concept of assisted suicide in general. It was his firm opinion that Janet would remain mentally competent for at least a year (but from Ron's narrative I concluded that her doctor's opinion was wrong and that time was of the essence). Because Janet's condition was deteriorating and there was nothing else that might help arrest it, I decided to accept her as the first candidate—a qualified, justifiable candidate if not "ideal"—and well aware of the vulnerability to criticism of picayune and overly emotional critics.

A major obstacle was finding a place to do it. Because I consider medicide to be necessary, ethical, and legal, there should be nothing furtive about it. Another reason to pursue the practice above-board is to avert the harrassment or vindictiveness of litigation. Consequently, when searching for a suitable site I always explained that I planned to assist a suffering patient to commit suicide. That posed no problem for helping a Michigan resident in his or her own residence. But it was a different matter for an out-of-state guest who must rent temporary quarters.

And I soon found out how difficult a matter it could be. My own apartment could not be used because of lease constraints, and the same was true of my sister's apartment. I inquired at countless motels, funeral homes, churches of various denominations, rental office buildings, clinics, doctors' offices for lease, and even considered the futile hope of renting an emergency life-support ambulance. Many owners, proprietors, and landlords were quite sympathetic but fearful and envisioned the negative public reaction that could seriously damage and even destroy their business enterprises. In short, they deemed it bad for public relations. More dismaying yet was the refusal of people who are known supporters and active campaigners for euthanasia to allow Janet and me the use of their homes.

Finally, a friend agreed to avail us of his modest home in Detroit; I immediately contacted Ron to finalize plans. My initial proposal was to carry out the procedure at the end of May 1990, but Ron and Janet preferred to avoid the surge of travel associated with the Memorial Day weekend. The date was postponed to Monday, June 4th.

In the meantime, my friend was warned by a doctor, in whom he confided, not to make his home available for such a purpose. Soon thereafter the offer was quickly withdrawn. With the date set and airline tickets having been purchased by Janet, Ron, and a close friend of Janet's, I had to scamper to find another site. The device required an electrical outlet, which limited the possibilities.

I had made a Herculean effort to provide a desirable, clinical setting. Literally and sadly, there was "no room at the inn." Now, having been refused everywhere I applied, the *only alternative* remaining was my 1968 camper and a suitable campground.

10 As expected, the owners of a commercial site refused permission, 10
even though they were sympathetic to the proposed scheme. They then suggested the solution by recommending that I rent space at a public camping site not too far away. The setting was pleasant and idyllic.

As with many other aspects of this extraordinary event, I was aware of the harsh criticism that would be leveled at the use of a "rusty old van." In the first place, the twenty-two-year-old body may have been rusting on the outside, but its interior was very clean, orderly, and comfortable. I have slept in it often and not felt degraded. But carping critics missed the point: the essence and significance of the event are far more important than the splendor of the site where it takes place. If critics are thus deluded into denouncing the exit from existence under these circumstances, then why not the same delusional denunciation of entrance into existence when a baby is, of necessity, born in an old taxicab? On the contrary, the latter identical scenario seems to arouse only feelings of sentimental reverence and quaint joy.

But the dishonesty doesn't stop there. I have been repeatedly criticized for having assisted a patient after a short personal acquaintance of two days. Overlooked or ignored is my open avowal to be the first practitioner in this country of a new and as yet officially unrecognized specialty. Because of shameful stonewalling by her own doctors, Janet was forced to refer herself to me. And acting as a unique specialist, of necessity self-proclaimed, solitary, and independent, I was obligated to scrutinize Janet's clinical records and to consult with her personal doctor. The latter's uncooperative attitude (tacitly excused by otherwise harsh critics) impaired but did not thwart fulfillment of my duties to a suffering patient and to my profession.

It is absurd even to imply, let alone to protest outright, that a medical specialist's competence and ethical behavior are contingent upon some sort of time interval, imposed arbitrarily or by fiat. When a doctor refers a patient for surgery, in many cases the surgical specialist performs his *ultimate* duty after personal acquaintance with the patient from a mere hour or two of prior consultation (in contrast to my having spent at least twelve hours in personal contact with Janet). In a few instances the surgeon operates on a patient seen for the first time on the operating table—and anesthetized to unconsciousness.

Moreover, in sharp contrast to the timorous, secretive, and even deceitful intention and actions of other medical euthanasists on whom our so-called bioethicists now shower praise, I acted openly, ethically, legally, with complete and uncompromising honesty, and—even more important—I remained in personal attendance during the second most meaningful medical event in a patient's earthly existence. Were he alive today, it's not hard to guess what Hippocrates would say about all this.

My two sisters, Margo and Flora, and I met with Ron, Janet, and Janet's close friend Carroll Rehmke in their motel room on Saturday afternoon, 2 June 1990. After getting acquainted through a few minutes of conversation, the purpose of the trip was thoroughly discussed. I had already prepared authorization forms signifying Janet's intent, determination, and freedom of choice, which she readily agreed to sign. Here again, while she was resolute in her decision, and absolutely mentally competent, her impaired memory was apparent when she needed her husband's assistance in forming the cursive letter "A." She could print the letter but not write it, and the consent forms required that her signature be written. So her husband showed her on another piece of paper how to form the cursive "A," and Janet complied. At this time, Ron and Carroll also signed a statement attesting to Janet's mental competence. Following this signing session, I had Flora videotape my interview with Janet and Ron. The forty-five-minute taping reinforced my own conviction that Janet was mentally competent but that her memory had failed badly. However, the degree of memory failure led me to surmise that within four to six months she would be too incompetent to qualify as a candidate. It should be pointed out that in medical terms loss of memory does not automatically signify mental incompetence. Any rational critic would concede that a mentally sound individual can be afflicted with even total amnesia.

Around 5:30 P.M. that same day all six of us had dinner at a well-known local restaurant. Seated around the same table for many hours, our conversation covered many subjects, including the telling of jokes. Without appearing too obvious, I constantly observed Janet's behavior and assessed her moods as well as the content and quality of her thoughts. There was absolutely no doubt that her mentality was intact and that she was not the least depressed over her impending death. On the contrary, the only detectable anxiety or disquieting demeanor was among the rest of us to a greater or lesser degree. Even in response to jokes, Janet's appropriately timed and modulated laughter indicated clear and coherent comprehension. The only uneasiness or distress she exhibited was due to her embarrassment at being unable to recall aspects of the topic under discussion at the time. And that is to be expected of intelligent, sensitive, and diligent individuals.

We left the restaurant at 12:30 A.M. Sunday. Janet and Ron enjoyed their last full day by themselves.

At 8:30 A.M. the next day, Monday, 4 June 1990, I drove into a rented space at Groveland Park in north Oakland County, Michigan. At the same time, my sisters drove to the motel to fetch Janet, who had composed (and submitted to my sister) a brief and clear note reiterating her genuine desire to end her life and exonerating all others in this desire and the actual event. For the last time, Janet took tearful leave of her grieving husband and Carroll, both of whom were inconsolable. It was Janet's wish that they not accompany her to the park.

The day began cold, damp, and overcast. I took a lot of time in setting up the Mercitron and giving it a few test runs. In turning to get a pair of pliers in the cramped space within the van, I accidentally knocked over the container of thiopental solution, losing a little over half of it. I was fairly sure that the remainder was enough to induce and maintain adequate unconsciousness, but I chose not to take the risk. I drove the forty-five miles home and got some more.

In the meantime, at about 9:30 A.M. my sisters and Janet had arrived at the park. They were dismayed to learn of the accidental spill and opted to accompany me on the extra round trip, which required two and one-half hours. We reentered the park at approximately noontime. Janet remained in the car with Margo while Flora helped me with minor tasks in the van as I very carefully prepared and tested the Mercitron. Everything was ready by about 2:00 P.M., and Janet was summoned.

She entered the van alone through the open sliding side door and lay fully clothed on the built-in bed covered with freshly laundered sheets. Her head rested comfortably on a clean pillow. The windows were covered with new draperies. With Janet's permission I cut small holes in her nylon stockings at the ankles, attached ECG electrodes to her ankles and wrists, and covered her body with a light blanket. Our conversation was minimal. In accordance with Janet's wish, Flora read to her a brief note from her friend Carroll, followed by a reading of the Lord's prayer. I then repeated my earlier instructions to Janet about how the device was to be activated, and asked her to go through the motions. In contrast to my sister and me, Janet was calm and outwardly relaxed.

I used a syringe with attached needle to pierce a vein near the frontal elbow area of her left arm. Unfortunately, her veins were delicate and fragile; even slight movement of the restrained arm caused the needle to penetrate through the wall of the vein resulting in leakage. Two more attempts also failed, as did a fourth attempt on the right side. Finally an adequate puncture was obtained on the right arm. (It was reassuring to me to learn later that doctors in Seattle had had similar difficulty with her veins.)

The moment had come. With a nod from Janet I turned on the ECG and said, "Now." Janet hit the Mercitron's switch with the outer edge of her palm. In about ten seconds her eyelids began to flicker and droop. She looked up at me and said, "Thank you, thank you." I replied at once as her eyelids closed, "Have a nice trip." She was unconscious and perfectly still except for two widely spaced and mild coughs several minutes later. Agonal complexes in the ECG tracing indicated death due to complete cessation of blood circulation in six minutes.

It was 2:30 P.M. Suddenly—for the first time that cold, dank day—warm sunshine bathed the park.

## Questions on Meaning

1. What is Kevorkian's thesis? Explain why you agree or disagree.
2. Why was Kevorkian forced to perform his first assisted suicide in his 20-year-old camper? What does this experience reflect about the perceptions and legal uncertainty of euthanasia in the late 1980s? What do you think the responses would be today if he attempted to find a hospital or clinic in which to perform an assisted suicide?
3. What does Kevorkian believe "determines the essence of one's existence"? Explain why you agree or disagree.

## Questions on Rhetorical Strategy and Style

1. Describe your emotions as you read Kevorkian's narrative. Reread the essay and write adjectives that express your feelings—such as relieved, sad, uneasy, tense—next to each paragraph. Also, indicate the passages in which you feel he was convincing and the passages in which you did not agree with him.
2. Identify how Kevorkian uses description to reveal the irony of his critics' reaction to the physical surroundings of Adkins' death versus the common reaction to a birth in a similar environment. Why does he feel the physical surroundings are quite secondary to the event?

## Writing Assignments

1. What is your feeling about euthanasia? Explain why you believe euthanasia should be monitored or controlled by the government, or not. If you think euthanasia should be regulated, what do you believe are the circumstances in which it is appropriate? Under what circumstances do you feel you *might* choose euthanasia?
2. What is the legal status of euthanasia today? Does it vary from state to state? How is it regulated? Ask your librarian to show you how to research a legal question.
3. In defense of the relatively brief period that he had known Adkins, Kevorkian notes that many physicians have very little if any personal contact with their patients. Write an essay about your experiences with medical personnel. If you believe there is a personal element lacking, explain why. What suggestions would you give for making patient treatment more personal and meaningful?

# LEARNING THE LANGUAGE

## Perri Klass

*Perri Klass (1958– ) was born to American parents in Trinidad and earned her M. D. from Harvard in 1986, going on to become a pediatrician. She has been writing and publishing widely while pursuing her medical career. Her fiction includes two novels,* Recombinations *(1985) and* Other Women's Children *(1990), and a collection of short stories,* I Am Having an Adventure *(1986). She published a collection of autobiographical essays,* A Not Entirely Benign Procedure *(1987) about her experience in medical school. The following selection, "Learning the Language," is excerpted from that book. Klass is sensitive to uses of language and understands how language affects thinking. As you read this essay, think about other special groups who also use language in unique ways.*

1 "Mrs. Tolstoy is your basic LOL in NAD, admitted for a soft rule-out MI," the intern announces. I scribble that on my patient list. In other words, Mrs. Tolstoy is a Little Old Lady in No Apparent Distress who is in the hospital to make sure she hasn't had a heart attack (rule out a Myocardial Infarction). And we think it's unlikely that she has had a heart attack (a *soft* rule-out).

If I learned nothing else during my first three months of working in the hospital as a medical student, I learned endless jargon and abbreviations. I started out in a state of primeval innocence, in which I didn't even know that "s̄ CP, SOB, N/V" meant "without chest pain, shortness of breath, or nausea and vomiting." By the end I took the abbreviations so much for granted that I would complain to my

---

mother the English professor, "And can you believe I had to put down three NG tubes last night?"

"You'll have to tell me what an NG tube is if you want me to sympathize properly," my mother said. NG, nasogastric—isn't it obvious?

I picked up not only the specific expressions but also the patterns of speech and the grammatical conventions; for example, you never say that a patient's blood pressure fell or that his cardiac enzymes rose. Instead, the patient is always the subject of the verb: "He dropped his pressure." "He bumped his enzymes." This sort of construction probably reflects the profound irritation of the intern when the nurses come in the middle of the night to say that Mr. Dickinson has disturbingly low blood pressure. "Oh, he's gonna hurt me bad tonight," the intern might say, inevitably angry at Mr. Dickinson for dropping his pressure and creating a problem.

5 When chemotherapy fails to cure Mrs. Bacon's cancer, what we say is, "Mrs. Bacon failed chemotherapy."

"Well, we've already had one hit today, and we're up next, but at least we've got mostly stable players on our team." This means that our team (group of doctors and medical students) has already gotten one new admission today, and it is our turn again, so we'll get whoever is admitted next in emergency, but at least most of the patients we already have are fairly stable, that is, unlikely to drop their pressures or in any other way get suddenly sicker and hurt us bad. Baseball metaphor is pervasive. A no-hitter is a night without any new admissions. A player is always a patient—a nitrate player is a patient on nitrates, a unit player is a patient in the intensive care unit, and so on, until you reach the terminal player.

It is interesting to consider what it means to be winning, or doing well, in this perennial baseball game. When the intern hangs up the phone and announces, "I got a hit," that is not cause for congratulations. The team is not scoring points; rather, it is getting hit, being bombarded with new patients. The object of the game from the point of view of the doctors, considering the players for whom they are already responsible, is to get as few new hits as possible.

This special language contributes to a sense of closeness and professional spirit among people who are under a great deal of stress. As a medical student, I found it exciting to discover that I'd finally cracked the code, that I could understand what doctors said and wrote, and could use the same formulations myself. Some people seem to become enamored of the jargon for its own sake, perhaps because they are so deeply thrilled with the idea of medicine, with the idea of themselves as doctors.

I knew a medical student who was referred to by the interns on the team as Mr. Eponym because he was so infatuated with eponymous terminology, the more obscure the better. He never said "capillary pulsations" if he could say "Quincke's pulses." He would lovingly tell over the multinamed syndromes—Wolff-Parkinson-White, Lown-Ganong-Levine, Schönlein-Henoch—until the temptation to suggest Schleswig-Holstein or Stevenson-Kefauver or
10 Baskin-Robbins became irresistible to his less reverent colleagues.

And there is the jargon that you don't ever want to hear yourself using. You know that your training is changing you, but there are certain changes you think would be going a little too far.

The resident was describing a man with devastating terminal pancreatic cancer. "Basically he's CTD," the resident concluded. I reminded myself that I had resolved not to be shy about asking when I didn't understand things. "CTD?" I asked timidly.

The resident smirked at me. "Circling The Drain."

The images are vivid and terrible. "What happened to Mrs. Melville?"

15 "Oh, she boxed last night." To box is to die, of course.

Then there are the more pompous locutions that can make the beginning medical student nervous about the effects of medical training. A friend of mine was told by his resident, "A pregnant woman with sickle-cell represents a failure of genetic counseling."

Mr. Eponym, who tried hard to talk like the doctors, once explained to me, "An infant is basically a brainstem preparation." The term "brainstem preparation," as used in neurological research, refers to an animal whose higher brain functions have been destroyed so that only the most primitive reflexes remain, like the sucking reflex, the startle reflex, and the rooting reflex.

And yet at other times the harshness dissipates into a strangely elusive euphemism. "As you know, this is a not entirely benign procedure," some doctor will say, and that will be understood to imply agony, risk of complications, and maybe even a significant mortality rate.

The more extreme forms aside, one most important function of medical jargon is to help doctors maintain some distance from their patients. By reformulating a patient's pain and problems into a language that the patient doesn't even speak, I suppose we are in some sense taking those pains and problems under our jurisdiction and also reducing their emotional impact. This linguistic separation between doctors and patients allows conversations to go on at the bedside that are unintelligible to the patient. "Naturally, we're worried about adeno-CA," the intern can say to the medical student, and lung cancer need never be mentioned.

I learned a new language this past summer. At times it thrills me to hear myself using it. It enables me to understand my colleagues, to communicate effectively in the hospital. Yet I am uncomfortably aware that I will never again notice the peculiarities and even atrocities of medical language as keenly as I did this summer. There may be specific expressions I manage to avoid, but even as I remark them, promising myself I will never use them, I find that this language is becoming my professional speech. It no longer sounds strange in my ears—or coming from my mouth. And I am afraid that as with any new language, to use it properly you must absorb not only the vocabulary but also the structure, the logic, the attitudes. At first you may notice these new and alien assumptions every time you put together a sentence, but with time and increased fluency you stop being aware of them at all. And as you lose that awareness, for better or for worse, you move closer and closer to being a doctor instead of just talking like one.

## Questions on Meaning

1. Reread the opening paragraph in which the doctors discuss the patient at her bedside. What is the advantage of the medical jargon and abbreviations they use?
2. Klass describes how the syntax of medicine always makes the patient the subject of the sentence; for example, "he dropped his pressure." Klass leaves it to us, however, to think out the implications of talking about patients in that way. What do you think are the implications? Might this affect how doctors think about their patients? Is this good or bad? Why would doctors talk this way—what gain is there for the doctor?
3. At the close of the essay Klass states that in learning this new language she is also absorbing "the logic, the attitudes." Give some examples of doctor's attitudes that you see in the essay. Why does this disturb her?

## Questions on Rhetorical Strategy and Style

1. Klass weaves in examples of all the points she makes about how doctors use language. Analyze five or six instances of her examples, with particular attention to her use of transitions among examples.
2. This is an example of a personal essay—an essay that is as much about the person who is writing it as it is about the subject. Reread the essay, focusing not on what she has to say about doctors and language but what she writes about her own changes and growing awareness. Explain how these two dimensions of the essay work together to develop one overall thesis.

## Writing Assignments

1. Imagine that a close friend or family member is in the hospital and you are visiting this very ill patient when two doctors come into the room. As they look at the bedside chart, you hear one of them say, "Basically the patient is CTD." Having read Klass's essay, you know what this phrase means. How would you feel? What would you want to say to that doctor? How would you feel about the quality of medical care that doctor is giving a patient he or she has already labeled CTD?

2. Many other professions and activities also have special vocabulary and way of speaking. Choose an activity you know well and analyze its special uses of language. Pay attention not only to the terms of that activity, the vocabulary, but also to *how* the people in that activity speak or write. Do patterns emerge? What attitudes are expressed through this use of language? Write an essay describing your conclusions.

# ARE THE HOMELESS CRAZY?


## Jonathan Kozol


*Jonathan Kozol (1936– ) was born in Boston and graduated from Harvard University. He has taught at Yale University, Trinity College, and the University of Massachusetts at Amherst as well as several public schools. He is well known for his writing on social and educational issues, often calling for educational reform and more realistic examination of societal problems. His books include* Death at an Early Age *(1967),* Free Schools *(1972),* On Being a Teacher *(1981),* Illiterate America *(1985),* Rachel and Her Children: Homeless Families in American *(1986), and* Savage Inequalities: Children in America's Schools *(1991). The essay "Are the Homeless Crazy?" was published in* Harper's *in 1988. In it Kozol analyzes the complex causes of homelessness in America. As you read this essay, pay close attention to how Kozol builds his argument, using specific evidence to counter the incorrect myths that have been put forward by politicians and others.*

1 It is commonly believed by many journalists and politicians that 1
the homeless of America are, in large part, former patients of large mental hospitals who were deinstitutionalized in the 1970s—the consequence, it is sometimes said, of misguided liberal opinion that favored the treatment of such persons in community-based centers. It is argued that this policy, and the subsequent failure of society to build such centers or to provide them in sufficient number, is the primary cause of homelessness in the United States.

---

Those who work among the homeless do not find that explanation satisfactory. While conceding that a certain number of the homeless are or have been mentally unwell, they believe that, in the case of most unsheltered people, the primary reason is economic rather than clinical. The cause of homelessness, they say with disarming logic, is the lack of homes and of income with which to rent or acquire them.

They point to the loss of traditional jobs in industry (two million every year since 1980) and to the fact that half of those who are laid off end up in work that pays a poverty-level wage. They point out that since 1968 the number of children living in poverty has grown by three million, while welfare benefits to families with children have declined by 35 percent.

And they note, too, that these developments have occurred during a time in which the shortage of low-income housing has intensified as the gentrification of our major cities has accelerated. Half a million units of low-income housing are lost each year to condominium conversion as well as to arson, demolition, or abandonment. Between 1978 and 1980, median rents climbed 30 percent for people in the lowest income sector, driving many of these families into the streets. Since 1980, rents have risen at even faster rates.

5 Hard numbers, in this instance, would appear to be of greater 5
help than psychiatric labels in telling us why so many people become homeless. Eight million American families now use half or more of their income to pay their rent or mortgage. At the same time, federal support for low-income housing dropped from $30 billion (1980) to $7.5 billion (1988). Under Presidents Ford and Carter, 500,000 subsidized private housing units were constructed. By President Reagan's second term, the number had dropped to 25,000.

In our rush to explain the homeless as a psychiatric problem even the words of medical practitioners who care for homeless people have been curiously ignored. A study published by the Massachusetts Medical Society, for instance, has noted that, with the exceptions of alcohol and drug use, the most frequent illnesses among a sample of the homeless population were trauma (31 percent), upper-respiratory disorders (28 percent), limb disorders (19 percent), mental illness (16 percent), skin diseases (15 percent), hypertension (14 percent), and neurological illnesses (12 percent). Why, we may ask, of all these calamities, does mental illness command so much political and press attention? The answer may be that the label of mental illness places the destitute outside the sphere of ordinary life. It personalizes an anguish that is public in its genesis; it individualizes a misery that is both general in cause and general in application.

There is another reason to assign labels to the destitute and single out mental illness from among their many afflictions. All these other problems—tuberculosis, asthma, scabies, diarrhea, bleeding gums, impacted teeth, etc.—bear no stigma, and mental illness does. It conveys a stigma in the United States. It conveys a stigma in the [former] Soviet Union as well. In both nations the label is used, whether as a matter of deliberate policy or not, to isolate and treat as special cases those who, by deed or word or by sheer presence, represent a threat to national complacence. The two situations are obviously not identical, but they are enough alike to give Americans reason for concern.

The notion that the homeless are largely psychotics who belong in institutions, rather than victims of displacement at the hands of enterprising realtors, spares us from the need to offer realistic solutions to the deep and widening extremes of wealth and poverty in the United States. It also enables us to tell ourselves that the despair of homeless people bears no intimate connection to the privileged existence we enjoy—when, for example, we rent or purchase one of those restored town houses that once provided shelter for people now huddled in the street.

What is to be made, then, of the supposition that the homeless are primarily the former residents of mental hospitals, persons who were carelessly released during the 1970s? Many of them are, to be sure. Among the older men and women in the streets and shelters, as many as one-third (some believe as many as one-half) may be chronically disturbed, and a number of these people were deinstitutionalized during the 1970s. But to operate on that assumption in a city such as New York—where nearly half the homeless are small children whose average age is six—makes no sense. Their parents, with an average age of twenty-seven, are not likely to have been hospitalized in the 1970s, either.

10 A frequently cited set of figures tells us that in 1955 the average 10
daily census of non-federal psychiatric institutions was 677,000, and that by 1984 the number had dropped to 151,000. But these people didn't go directly from a hospital room to the street. The bulk of those who had been psychiatric patients and were released from hospitals

during the 1960s and early 1970s had been living in low-income housing, many in skid-row hotels or boardinghouses. Such housing—commonly known as SRO (single-room occupancy) units—was drastically diminished by the gentrification of our cities that began in the early '70s. Almost 50 percent of SRO housing was replaced by luxury apartments or office buildings between 1970 and 1980, and the remaining units have been disappearing even more rapidly.

Even for those persons who are ill and were deinstitutionalized during the decades before 1980, the precipitating cause of homelessness in 1987 is not illness but loss of housing. SRO housing offered low-cost sanctuaries for the homeless, providing a degree of safety and mutual support for those who lived within them. They were a demeaning version of the community health centers that society had promised; they were the de facto "halfway houses" of the 1970s. For these people too—at most half of the homeless single persons in America—the cause of homelessness is lack of housing.

Even in those cases where mental instability is apparent, homelessness itself is often the precipitating factor. For example, many pregnant women without homes are denied prenatal care because they constantly travel from one shelter to another. Many are anemic. Many are denied essential dietary supplements by recent federal cuts. As a consequence, some of their children do not live to see their second year of life. Do these mothers sometimes show signs of stress? Do they appear disorganized, depressed, disordered? Frequently. They are immobilized by pain, traumatized by fear. So it is no surprise that when researchers enter the scene to ask them how they "feel," the resulting reports tell us that the homeless are emotionally unwell. The reports do not tell us that we have *made* these people ill. They do not tell us that illness is a natural response to intolerable conditions. Nor do they tell us of the strength and the resilience that so many of these people retain despite the miseries they must endure.

A writer in the *New York Times* describes a homeless woman standing on a traffic island in Manhattan. "She was evicted from her small room in the hotel just across the street," and she is determined to get revenge. Until she does, "nothing will move her from that spot. . . . Her argumentativeness and her angry fixation on revenge, along with the apparent absence of hallucinations, mark her as a paranoid." Most physicians, I imagine, would be more reserved in passing judgment with so little evidence, but this reporter makes his diagnosis without hesitation. "The paranoids of the street," he says, "are among the most difficult to help."

Perhaps so. But does it depend on who is offering the help? Is anyone offering to help this woman get back her home? Is it crazy to seek vengeance for being thrown into the street? The absence of anger, some psychiatrists believe, might indicate much greater illness.

"No one will be turned away," says the mayor of New York City, as hundreds of young mothers with their infants are turned from the doors of shelters season after season. That may sound to some like a denial of reality. "Now you're hearing all kinds of horror stories," says the president of the United States as he denies that anyone is cold or hungry or unhoused. On another occasion he says that the unsheltered "are homeless, you might say, by choice." That sounds every bit as self-deceiving.

The woman standing on the traffic island screaming for revenge until her room has been restored to her sounds relatively healthy by comparison. If three million homeless people did the same, and all at the same time, we might finally be forced to listen.

## Questions on Meaning

1. What does Kozol say is the root cause for most homelessness, if it is not mental illness? Why does it matter, according to Kozol, what the cause is?
2. Is Kozol arguing that people who live in condos or luxury apartments built on the site of low-income housing should feel guilty for displacing low-income residents? How would you (or do you) feel if you yourself lived in a building that had displaced such residents?
3. Does Kozol argue for a particular solution for homelessness? If so, what is it? If not, what does he argue for instead?

## Questions on Rhetorical Strategy and Style

1. An argument's effectiveness depends on both the quantity and quality of the evidence offered in support of the argument. Evaluate Kozol's evidence. How convincing is his argument?
2. Kozol uses a cause and effect rhetorical strategy to develop the essay. Reread the essay and analyze the specific causes described, including how each is linked to the effect of homelessness.

## Writing Assignments

1. One aspect of the debate about homelessness is the issue of responsibility. Some people say homelessness is caused by society's actions, and therefore society must solve the problem. Others say the homeless themselves are mostly responsible for their situation, and therefore society has only a limited responsibility to help solve the problem. Examine your own thoughts on this debate and talk with others to learn their ideas. Then write an essay in which you explore this issue of responsibility and explain your own position.
2. Homelessness and poverty also tend to be very emotional issues. How do you feel when you see a homeless person on the street? How do you react when a panhandler asks you for money? Someone once said, half jokingly, that it would be a lot easier to help the homeless if they were clean and dressed better—another emotional aspect of how we interact with people different from ourselves. Write an essay in which you explore the role of emotions, for both individuals and society as a whole, when dealing with problems such as homelessness and poverty.

3. Choose another problem in our society and analyze it, as Kozol does, in a cause and effect manner. (Examples of such problems are crime, domestic violence, underfunded public schools in some areas, drug use among teenagers, driving while intoxicated, corrupt politicians, and so on.) Write an essay in which you use cause and effect rhetorical strategies to explain your ideas about the problem you choose.

# THE SCHEME OF COLOR

## Mary Mebane

*Mary Mebane (1933– ) was born into and reared in the poverty of rural Durham County in North Carolina, where she pursued an education culminating in a Ph.D. at the University of North Carolina. She has taught at the college level and wrote* Mary: An Autobiography, *from which the following essay is taken. As you read the essay, note the calm and reasoned way she develops a description of a particularly hateful form of racism.*

1 I don't know whether African men recently transported to the New 1
World considered themselves handsome or, more important, whether they considered African women beautiful in comparison with Native American Indian women or immigrant European women. It is a question that I have never heard raised or seen research on. If African men considered African women beautiful, just when their shift in interest away from black black women occurred might prove to be an interesting topic for researchers. But one thing I know for sure: by the twentieth century, really black skin on a woman was considered ugly in this country. This was particularly true among those who were exposed to college.

Hazel, who was light brown, used to say to me, "You are *dark,* but not *too* dark." The saved commiserating with the damned. I had the feeling that if nature had painted one more brushstroke on me, I'd have had to kill myself.

Black skin was to be disguised at all costs. Since a black face is rather hard to disguise, many women took refuge in ludicrous makeup. Mrs. Burry, one of my teachers in elementary school, used white face powder. But she neglected to powder her neck and arms, and even the black on her face gleamed through the white, giving her an eerie appearance. But she did the best she could.

I observed all through elementary and high school that for various entertainments the girls were placed on the stage in order of color. And very black ones didn't get into the front row. If they were past caramel-brown, to the back row they would go. And nobody questioned the justice of these decisions—neither the students nor the teachers.

5 One of the teachers at Wildwood School, who was from the Deep South and was just as black as she could be, had been a strict enforcer of these standards. That was another irony—that someone who had been judged outside the realm of beauty herself because of her skin tones should have adopted them so wholeheartedly and applied them herself without question.

One girl stymied that teacher, though. Ruby, a black cherry of a girl, not only got off the back row but off the front row as well, to stand alone at stage center. She could outsing, outdance, and outdeclaim everyone else, and talent proved triumphant over pigmentation. But the May Queen and her Court (and in high school, Miss Wildwood) were always chosen from among the lighter ones.

When I was a freshman in high school, it became clear that a light-skinned sophomore girl named Rose was going to get the "best girl scholar" prize for the next three years, and there was nothing I could do about it, even though I knew I was the better. Rose was caramel-colored and had shoulder-length hair. She was highly favored by the science and math teacher, who figured the averages. I wasn't. There was only one prize. Therefore, Rose would get it until she graduated. I was one year behind her, and I would not get it until after she graduated.

To be held in such low esteem was painful. It was difficult not to feel that I had been cheated out of the medal, which I felt that, in a fair competition, I perhaps would have won. Being unable to protest or do anything about it was a traumatic experience for me. From then on I instinctively tended to avoid the college-exposed dark-skinned male, knowing that when he looked at me he saw himself and, most of the time, his mother and sister as well, and since he had rejected his blackness, he had rejected theirs and mine.

Oddly enough, the lighter-skinned black male did not seem to feel so much prejudice toward the black black woman. It was no accident, I felt, that Mr. Harrison, the eighth-grade teacher, who was reddish-yellow himself, once protested to the science and math teacher about the fact that he always assigned sweeping duties to Doris and Ruby Lee, two black black girls. Mr. Harrison said to them one day, right in the other teacher's presence, "You must be some bad girls. Every day I come down here ya'll are sweeping." The science and math teacher got the point and didn't ask them to sweep anymore.

Uneducated black males, too, sometimes related very well to the black black woman. They had been less firmly indoctrinated by the white society around them and were more securely rooted in their own culture.

Because of the stigma attached to having dark skin, a black black woman had to do many things to find a place for herself. One possibility was to attach herself to a light-skinned woman, hoping that some of the magic would rub off on her. A second was to make herself sexually available, hoping to attract a mate. Third, she could resign herself to a more chaste life-style either (for the professional woman) teaching and work in established churches or (for the uneducated woman) domestic work and zealous service in the Holy and Sanctified churches.

Even as a young girl, Lucy had chosen the first route. Lucy was short, skinny, short-haired, and black black, and thus unacceptable. So she made her choice. She selected Patricia, the lightest-skinned girl in the school, as her friend, and followed her around. Patricia and her friends barely tolerated Lucy, but Lucy smiled and doggedly hung on, hoping that some who noticed Patricia might notice her, too. Though I felt shame for her behavior, even then I understood.

As is often the case of the victim agreeing with and adopting the attitudes of the oppressor, so I have seen it with black black women. I have seen them adopt the oppressor's attitude that they are nothing but "sex machines," and their supposedly superior sexual performance becomes their sole reason for being and for esteeming themselves. Such women learn early that in order to make themselves attractive to men they have somehow to shift the emphasis from physical beauty to some other area—usually sexual performance. Their constant talk is of their desirability and their ability to gratify a man sexually.

I knew two such women well—both of them black black. To hear their endless talk of sexual conquests was very sad. I have never seen the category that these women fall into described anywhere. It is not that of promiscuity or nymphomania. It is the category of total self-rejection: "Since I am black, I am ugly, I am nobody. I will perform on the level that they have assigned to me." Such women are the pitiful results of what not only white America but also, and more important, black America has done to them.

Some, not taking the sexuality route but still accepting black society's view of their worthlessness, swing all the way across to intense religiosity. Some are staunch, fervent workers in the more traditional Southern churches—Baptist and Methodist—and others are leaders and ministers in the lower-status, more evangelical Holiness sects.

Another avenue open to the black black woman is excellence in a career. Since in the South the field most accessible to such women is education, a great many of them prepared to become teachers. But here, too, the black black woman had problems. Grades weren't given to her lightly in school, nor were promotions on the job. Consequently, she had to prepare especially well. She had to pass examinations with flying colors or be left behind; she knew that she would receive no special consideration. She had to be overqualified for a job because otherwise she didn't stand a chance of getting it—and she was competing only with other blacks. She had to have something to back her up: not charm, not personality—but training.

The black black woman's training would pay off in the 1970s. With the arrival of integration the black black woman would find, paradoxically enough, that her skin color in an integrated situation was not the handicap it had been in an all-black situation. But it wasn't until the middle and late 1960s, when the post-1945 generation of black males arrived on college campuses, that I noticed any change in the situation at all. *He* wore an afro and *she* wore an afro, and sometimes the only way you could tell them apart was when his afro was taller than hers. Black had become beautiful, and the really black girl was often selected as queen of various campus activities. It was then that the dread I felt at dealing with the college-educated black male began to ease. Even now, though, when I have occasion to engage in any type of transaction with a college-educated black man, I gauge his age. If I guess he was born after 1945, I feel confident that the transaction will turn out all right. If he probably was born before 1945, my stomach tightens, I find myself taking shallow breaths, and I try to state my business and escape as soon as possible.

## Questions on Meaning

1. Compile a list of the qualities of the "black black" woman.
2. Explain how white and black attitudes on race interact to create the specific form of racism directed at black black women.

## Questions on Rhetorical Strategy and Style

1. Mebane writes with the scholar's detached tone, even though she is describing her personal experience. Locate a passage in which she describes a personal injustice. Which of the words she chooses have the most emotional overtones? Would you characterize her tone as angry or hurt? Why or why not?
2. By implication, Mebane suggests the definition of a form of racism practiced by black people against other black people. Create an explicit definition of this black on black racism.

## Writing Assignments

1. Write an essay in which you describe a form of in-group bigotry that you have experienced. It might relate to your race, or your gender, or your status in a family, or school, or job.
2. Conduct a research study among members of a minority group on your campus. Develop a questionnaire that focuses on discriminatory practices within the group, as opposed to those practiced against the group from without. Report your results in an essay.

# RELIGION MAKES A COMEBACK. (BELIEF TO FOLLOW)


## Jack Miles


*Jack Miles (1942- ) received a Ph.D. from Harvard University in Near Eastern Languages in 1971 and has been an editor for the book publishers Doubleday and the University of California Press. He also has been an editor for the* Los Angeles Times *and* The Atlantic Monthly, *for whom he is currently a contributing editor. He has taught theology at Loyola University and is the Mellon Visiting Professor of Humanities at the California Institute of Technology, as well as the director of the Humanities Center at the Claremont Graduate School. In 1995, he won a Pulitzer Prize for his book* God: A Biography. *In this selection from the December 7, 1997 issue of* The New York Times Magazine, *Miles talks about recent developments in attitudes about God and religion.*

1 Is America in the grip of a religious revival? Hundreds of thousands 1
of Christian Promise Keepers rally in Washington, and hundreds of thousands of black men gather, at a Muslim's call, to make "atonement." Religion comes to life on television in series like "Seventh Heaven," "Touched by an Angel" and "Nothing Sacred." Religious books, once ghettoized by the publishing trade, are promoted heavily by the biggest chains, reviewed in major newspapers and monitored closely by Publishers Weekly. The Pope, of all people, writes a runaway best seller. Time and Newsweek seem virtually obsessed with religion: everything from the Infant Jesus to the Baby Dalai Lama.

---

"Religion Makes a Comeback. (Belief to Follow.)" by Jack Miles, published in *The New York Times*, December 7, 1997.

Or is religion continuing the slow fade perennially lamented by religious leaders? Jews worry about the high rate of inter-marriage. Catholics worry that too few young people seem willing to serve as nuns or priests. Mainstream Protestants worry that parish rolls are shrinking, with national budgets shrinking apace. And then there is unbelief, the ever popular default option. On a head count of purest honesty, would not these unbelievers constitute the biggest "church" in America?

One key to making sense of these contradictory indicators is the unique functioning of individualism in American religious culture. As long ago as 1840, Alexis de Tocqueville wrote of the pervasiveness in American life of "a calm and considered feeling which disposes each citizen to isolate himself from the mass of his fellows and withdraw into the circle of family and friends; with this little society formed to his taste, he gladly leaves the greater society to look after itself."

What this "calm and considered feeling" produces in the realm of religion is an institutionalized anti-institutionalism. Americans are particularly at ease with forms of religious expression that require little in the way of organizational commitment and impose little in the way of group identity. Religious books, television shows and one-time events like marches and revivals all meet those criteria. Less in the individualist American grain is church or synagogue or mosque membership, which does indeed impose a group identity and which, even more important, demands regular attendance, steady financial support and religious education of the young. In general, classic organized religion functions more as a corrective to American individualism than as an expression of it; for that very reason, it is both prized and resisted.

5 Collective religious identity is further weakened and individual 5
religious autonomy further strengthened by the separation of religion and nationality in American culture—the fact that an American may be of any religion or none and still be fully an American. In Bosnia, if you are a Catholic, you are a Croat, and vice versa, to the point that if you change your religion from Catholicism to Orthodoxy or Islam, you will feel as if you have also changed your nationality to Serb or "Turk." In this country, by sharpest contrast, your American identity remains unchanged when you change your religion, a fact that makes such a change considerably easier to undertake, even repeatedly.

But if American religious individualism smoothes the path to conversion, it also smoothes the path to apostasy. Until recently, this may be what happened most often. Even though conversion in the U.S. was easy by European standards, it was easier still to drop out of religion totally. The complications facing a back-slid Protestant, a lapsed Catholic or a nonobservant Jew were simple compared with those facing a Southern Baptist converting to Catholicism or a Catholic converting to Judaism or a Jew converting to any form of Christianity. By condemning the turncoat so much more harshly than the deserter, organized religion may have actually fostered desertion.

By the same token, if Americans now take conversion more casually, the result may be an aggregate *increase* in religious participation. Two years ago I attended the wedding of a Catholic and a Jew, blessed jointly by a priest and a rabbi. Forty years ago, the marriage itself could doubtless have taken place one way or another, but not the doubly sanctified wedding. Instead, quite probably, the young wedding partners would have become dropouts from their respective traditions. In one way, the joint wedding ceremony represents the confounding of two proud and ancient traditions by the youthful spirit of American religious individualism. In another, it represents a victory for both over the tendency of American religious individualism to make each man and woman a happy sect of one.

That tendency is scarcely to be counted out. Unbelief remains omnipresent in American life, the position one takes by taking no position. Is there any reason to believe that fewer Americans are defaulting to this position and that, as a result, religion in the United States is experiencing a net gain at the expense of irreligion?

A recurring experience that I had as the author of "God: A Biography" suggests to me that there has been such a gain. In that book, I wrote about God as—and only as—the literary protagonist of the Old Testament, but my very abstention from theology seemed to embolden people to tell me what they thought about God. Over time, what struck me most about these conversations was a note of defiance, the defiant rejection of the widespread assumption that doubt and religion are incompatible. "Take it (belief) or leave it (religion)"—this was the dilemma I heard brusquely rejected in favor of a third alternative: *If I may doubt the practice of medicine from the operating table, if I may doubt the political system from the voting booth, if I may doubt the institution of marriage from the conjugal bed, why may I not doubt religion from the pew?*

Why this mood of challenge or dare? Because this was a novel attitude for the people expressing it. Some were newcomers to the expression of doubt, but others were newcomers to the pew. They were excited and a bit combative, as people tend to be when they are doing something they have been told they may not do. But *why* were they doing it? Why not just vacate the pew (or never enter it) if you have doubts about God?

In answering that question, it matters greatly where one imagines the doubting to originate. Is religion in question? Are the doubts mainly doubts about God? Or is society in question and religion one of the proposed answers, notwithstanding the difficulty of belief?

It may well be true that organized religion has functioned as a corrective to American individualism. But religion has not been the only corrective available. Innumerable secular forms of association have also tried to deliver the psychological and moral counterbalance that American individualism requires. There are Americans for whom knowledge or politics or career or therapy provides sanctuary, collective purpose and a measure of personal transcendence. There are even those for whom, as we say, body-building is a religion. The question that must now be asked is whether the society that has relied so heavily on such alternatives to religion is succeeding or failing. Have its own citizens lost confidence in it? Are they suffering a secular loss of faith?

One who believes they are is the Mexican poet-philosopher Octavio Paz. In his recent memoirs, "In Light of India," Paz maintains that capitalist democracy has turned us all into "hermits," replacing "fraternity with a perpetual struggle among individuals." An admirer of Tocqueville, Paz finds the Frenchman's worst fears about the corrosive effect of individualism "utterly fulfilled in our time" and in a rather violent reaction, manages a degree of sympathy for India's religiously grounded caste system. (Paz was once Mexico's ambassador to India.) That system is full of disgraceful abuses, Paz admits, and yet, he insists, it at least brings an entire population into a stable and understood relationship.

Paz does not endorse a systematic rejection of capitalist democracy. He simply looks at what it has become and recoils. Though he cannot be said to proclaim his faith in religion, he confesses a loss of faith in the viability of Western society *without* religion. If Americans of some indeterminate number are finding themselves where Paz finds himself, we should not wonder that a religious revival may be under way. These would be Americans who, like Paz, have looked at what their society has become and recoiled, who are weary of being hermits, who want to place some collective check on their relentless competitiveness. Like Paz, these Americans have not so much recovered their faith in religion as lost their faith in the alternatives.

15 Several months ago, I came across a recent anthology of essays titled "Outside the Law: Narratives on Justice in America." One scathingly brilliant contribution, "The Myth of Justice," announces that "religion isn't the opiate of the people, the conception of justice is." Mere atheism, the essay explains, is for beginners. Real unbelief requires flushing out and crushing delusions like "As you reap, so will you sow" and "Whatever goes around comes around." "In your dreams, sucker," the writer sneers, and the empirical evidence for his view is undeniably enormous. Still, what his lacerating bitterness most bespeaks is the personal cost to him of his own conclusion. I read his statement with sadness, for I knew him, and I knew that shortly after writing it, he committed suicide.

Neither Octavio Paz's social despair nor this kind of personal despair leads infallibly to religion, much less to suicide, yet the alternatives can seem almost that stark. It thereby follows that, though many people who turn up in church or synagogue are not truly believers, they are not hypocrites either. What appeals to them in the first instance may be the social and esthetic refuge provided by religion, but they arrive with open minds regarding belief. This openness is the defiance I noticed in my book-tour conversations. It is the defiance of the doubter in the pew.

Organized religion typically provides for the seasons of life: for birth, childhood and coming-of-age; for marriage and other forms of life companionship; for old age and death, bereavement and remembrance; and even for a harmonious division of the calendar year into seasons of mourning and joy, repentance and triumph. Though some will always find this rigmarole repellent, more find it calming and attractive. To make their attraction intellectually acceptable, they do not require that an irrefragable case for belief be established. They require only that the case for unbelief be somewhat neutralized.

This may be little to ask, but that little is indispensable. Accordingly, even if few people have the patience or the intellectual preparation for theology, those few are disproportionately important. If the social viability of religion for the many depends significantly on the intellectual viability of religion for the few, then the question becomes: Can a post-modern path be opened for the few to a form of religion they can honestly practice?

If the answer is yes, I suspect that the first step on that path will be a religious reflection on secular uncertainty—a reversal of the familiar phenomenon of secular reflection on religious uncertainty. The question "Does God really exist?" takes on a different coloring when and if the reality of other things now confidently thought to exist also comes into question. Take mathematics, for example, the paradigm of clear answers to clear questions. Reuben Hersh, in a new book titled "What Is Mathematics, Really?" writes that "mathematics is like money, war or religion—not physical, not mental, but social." There is no mathematical reality "out there," he maintains, and his mathematical agnosticism would seem rather clearly to have implications for the reality behind any theory that depends on mathematics.

Most mathematicians do not share Hersh's agnosticism, but none can deny that, despite it, he is a practicing mathematician. This state of affairs—a theory standoff between agnostics and believers that leaves practice surprisingly untouched—can be documented in many other disciplines. Why may it not be so in theology as well? Some who come to worship believing in the old way might find this stance strange, just as some mathematicians find Hersh's stance strange, but would they bar the door?

Religion has always been, among other things, a response to the intellectual inadequacy of the human species: neither individually nor collectively can we know all that we need to know, much less all that we might wonder about. Recalling that fact and taking full note of the current state of secular dubiety at the highest intellectual levels, a man or woman who decides to practice a religion may do so not to acknowledge the mystery *of* religion but to acknowledge, first, the mystery *in response to which* religion has come into being and, second, the felt necessity—somewhat mysterious in itself—to live a moral life even when the grounds of morality cannot be known.

In short, to ask "Does God really exist, yes or no?" may not be the right question. It might be better to ask, "Is the word 'existence' really just another word, yes or no?" When the latter question is in the air (and it increasingly is), an intellectual decision pro or con religious affiliation need not wait on a final verdict about whether God (or anything else) "really exists."

"Two things fill the mind with ever-increasing admiration and awe, the oftener and the more steadily we reflect on them," Immanuel Kant wrote 200 years ago, "the starry heaven above and the moral law within." Judeo-Christian morality has linked these two sources of wonder through God, the creator and guarantor of the physical as well as the moral order:

> *Thy steadfast love, O Lord, extends to the heavens,*
> *thy faithfulness to the clouds.*
> *Thy righteousness is like the mountains of God,*
> *thy judgments are like the great deep.* (Psalm 36: 5–6)

Even when silence is maintained about God, the fact that existence can be predicated of cosmos and conscience alike creates a link between the two. If, however, we begin to entertain doubts about existence as such, than all links become dubious, not just the link between the heavens above and the moral law within. Once the philosophical glue is gone, everything comes unstuck. Our various intellectual enterprises, call them what we will, may go forward unchecked, but they will go forward under an enormous question mark.

The armed-and-dangerous ignorance of religious fanaticism deserves to be quarantined. Let's be clear about that. I dread it as much as any atheist does. All the same, the trouble in which secular ideology finds itself—and it does find itself in some kind of trouble—does not seem to me to be generated wholly from without. During the cold war, Americans dared not consider the erosion of our interlocking secular beliefs any more than we dared consider the nuclear contamination of our landscape. Now, like a jury summons that can be put off no longer, the long-postponed questions are being taken up. At the deepest level, nothing else can explain the recent resurgence of interest in religion. Alas, there is a vast difference between taking the questions up and answering them.

Despair, according to a study published in the American Heart Association's journal, is as bad for the human heart as a pack-a-day smoking habit. "Steps should be taken," writes one doctor in the study, "to try to change" the cardiac patients' situation "so they gain hope or become more optimistic."

Steps should be taken by whom? In our day, religion often begins in despair—in personal despair that hardens the arteries, in cultural despair that darkens the heart, in intellectual despair that humbles the mind—and moves from there to hope, not through argument but through affiliation. (I hesitate to use the word love.) Just how anyone makes the decision to affiliate—to go it, but not alone, to be (gag) a joiner—is difficult to describe and impossible to recover, but it happens, this decision, and many such decisions can accrue to a movement. A movement toward hope? Perhaps. A refusal, at least, to despair.

## Questions on Meaning

1. Why, according to Miles, are Americans returning to religion? How does he explain this phenomenon?
2. What does Miles mean when he says, "if American religious individualism smoothes the path to conversion, it also smoothes the path to apostasy"?
3. What is the significance of the term *individualism* in this article? What, in the author's opinion, is the problem with it?

## Questions on Rhetorical Strategy and Style

1. How would you describe Miles's attitude toward his subject?
2. What kind of evidence does Miles use to convince us that America is experiencing a "religious revival"?

## Writing Assignments

1. How would you explain the current interest in religion as it is reflected in television and the movies? Pick a few contemporary examples and analyze their religious aspects. How would Miles explain these examples? Do you agree with him? Explain your position in a short essay.
2. Do you have a friend or family member who has recently taken on a new commitment to religion? What has prompted this person to make this move? Interview them about their beliefs and write about their experience.

# GAY TEACHERS, GAY STUDENTS

## Neil Miller

*Neil Miller (1945– ) has written on gay and lesbian issues in two books,* In Search of Gay America *(1990) and* Out in the World: Gay and Lesbian Life from Buenos Aires to Bangkok *(1992). The essay you will read was published in 1992 in* The Boston Globe Magazine. *Miller reports on his study of gay life at exclusive boarding schools, which are among the first to confront the issue of openly gay students and teachers.*

1 It is a warm spring night, and the young man with the ponytail is going to a gay dance—his first—and he is delighted and nervous. For most of his time at school, the Phillips Exeter senior couldn't imagine "coming out" in a dorm populated by varsity football and lacrosse players. But last year, he joined the New Hampshire boarding school's gay/straight alliance, established to educate the campus on homosexual issues. At gay/straight alliance meetings, you don't have to state your sexual orientation; you can just come to terms with yourself at your own pace in a supportive atmosphere. Today, on the way to the dance, the young man says, "I guess I'm gay," astonished at his own forthrightness. A few months earlier, he didn't feel comfortable uttering the words.

The dance is part of a weekend "retreat" of prep school gay/straight alliances taking place at America's oldest and richest private school, Phillips Andover. With its ancient elms and tradition-bound quadrangles, the alma mater of George Bush seems an unlikely spot for the unfolding of the latest chapter of the sexual revolution. In fact, Andover has been a pioneer in such matters; 4 1/2 years ago, it approved the formation of the first gay/straight alliance at an East Coast prep school.

---

Downstairs at Graham House, where the gathering is being held, some 40 or so students are quizzing undergraduates from Tufts and the Massachusetts Institute of Technology about what it's like to be gay and in college. Upstairs, their faculty advisers are comparing notes: At Choate, everything is "warm and fuzzy—homosexuality is a feel-good issue," a teacher reports; at Andover, where the gay/straight alliance has been around for much longer, being a member isn't as "cool" as it once was; at one posh New England boarding school, the headmaster is said to have refused to permit the formation of a gay/straight alliance.

Following dinner at the Commons, there is a performance of the musical *In Trousers*, the first of the *Falsettos* trilogy, about a gay married man and his relationships. Directed by the student president of Andover's gay/straight alliance, the musical serves as campus-wide entertainment on a Saturday night and receives an enthusiastic response. Then comes the dance, in the social hall of a nearby Unitarian church. It's the first gay and lesbian dance for most of the students, and the enterprise has a slightly awkward air. The students dance in groups, still reluctant to pair off with someone of the same sex.

"I can't wait till I go off to college next year," says the senior with the ponytail. "Someplace where being gay is kind of, well, normal."

High schools are one area in which little has changed: Gay and lesbian teachers overwhelmingly remain in the closet, fearful of the personal and professional consequences of coming out. Gay teenagers are isolated, facing rejection both at home and at school. A 1989 study by the US Department of Health and Human Services found that gay and lesbian adolescents make up almost a third of all teenage suicides. The situation is particularly acute in public schools. There, antigay comments are common currency long after ethnic and racial slurs have been deemed unacceptable; cautious administrators and school boards often discourage open discussion that might create a more accepting atmosphere.

One teacher in a white-collar Boston suburb described attitudes prevailing at her school this way: "We counsel gay students not to come out. They'd get killed. At our school, male students get harassed just for being in drama or chorus."

Today, students and teachers around New England are trying to change those attitudes, with much of the momentum coming from elite boarding and day schools. A year and a half ago, among private schools, only Andover and Concord Academy had campus gay/straight alliances. Since then, such organizations have sprung up at Exeter, Milton Academy, Choate Rosemary Hall, Northfield Mount Hermon, Buckingham Browne & Nichols, The Winsor School, The Putney School, and Brewster Academy. A gay/straight alliance was established at Newton South High School last spring. Cambridge Rindge and Latin has a similar organization, called Project Ten East. Few students in these groups identify themselves as gay or lesbian; in a world of teen-age macho and peer pressure, coming out is still a bold step, even in ostensibly tolerant surroundings.

Concord Academy and Milton Academy now have three openly gay teachers; Andover boasts two, and Cambridge Rindge and Latin and Newton South one each. An organization called GLISTEN—Gay and Lesbian Independent School Teacher Network—was created in December 1991 to serve as a vehicle for raising the issue in the prep school world. A GLISTEN conference held at Milton Academy this past April was attended by almost 300 people, and the keynote speaker was Milton headmaster Edward P. Fredie. Milton seniors spend two to three weeks learning about the gay movement as part of a civil rights course; a unit on gay and lesbian history, designed by Arthur Lipkin, a research associate at the Harvard Graduate School of Education, was given a test run at Cambridge Rindge and Latin last year. In an effort to promote a more diverse faculty, Concord Academy advertises job openings in gay newspapers.

Most of the teachers crusading for a more accepting attitude toward homosexuality in secondary schools are young; many came out while in college and refuse to go back into the closet. "Part of what is happening is due to the new militancy within the gay movement and a refusal to be intimidated," says Kevin Jennings, an openly gay history teacher at Concord Academy and founder and cochairman of GLISTEN. "In addition, the AIDS crisis has forced educators to see the consequences of refusing to deal with sexuality. It has forced them to listen."

Progress does not necessarily come easily. Prep schools worry about what effect the presence of gay teachers and gay-friendly groups will have on admissions and endowments. Incidents such as the recent L. Lane Bateman case, in which the head of the Exeter drama department was convicted of possession and distribution of pornography, exacerbate such concerns. (Bateman was closeted and not involved with the school's gay/straight alliance.)

When a lesbian physical education teacher at a Boston-area day school announced she wanted to come out, she was told she could not do so, and she resigned. At the St. Paul's School, in Concord, New Hampshire, "We want to move carefully," says vice president John Burton, concerned that too much attention to the issue could be divisive. Even at supportive Milton Academy, the gay/straight alliance was left off a list of student organizations in the catalog, an omission that officials ascribe to an oversight.

While some parents applaud the new openness, others are uneasy. "You hear both sides," says Clinton J. Kendrick, a New York investment manager who has two children at Andover. "There are some parents who say it's wonderful. There are others who say it makes them very nervous and it's not acceptable."

Kendrick, who also serves on the Andover school's board of trustees, believes that the presence of a gay/straight alliance on campus could prove confusing to students unsure about their sexual orientation. But the overriding issue, in his view, is that of individual rights. "I am trying to emerge from the '50s," he says. "I believe very strongly that people have civil rights. The important thing is to have effective teachers, straight or gay."

When hundreds of Cambridge Rindge and Latin students and teachers marked National Coming Out Day in October last year by wearing pink triangles (the symbol gays were forced to wear in Nazi death camps), Rev. Earl W Jackson, a staunch opponent of gay rights, came to the school to protest. In his view, the only reason a gay teacher would want to be open with his students is "to push the agenda for homosexuality."

Rev. Jackson, who is the pastor of the New Cornerstone Exodus Church, in Mattapan, advocates the firing of openly gay teachers and believes that gay/straight alliance-type organizations have no place in public schools. "We are not going to let anyone stand up and say, 'I'm a lesbian,'" he says. "In fact, we don't want anyone to stand up and say, I'm a heterosexual,' either. I don't see the point."

Openly gay and lesbian faculty offer a variety of responses as to why it is important for teachers to come out in school: to provide role models to both gay and straight students, to fight prejudice, to be honest with their students. At boarding schools, relationships between teachers and pupils extend beyond classroom hours, to the playing field, dining room, and dormitory. For a teacher to keep such a crucial part of his or her private life hidden becomes difficult—and demoralizing. As Concord Academy's Jennings puts it, "I came out because I had to. I couldn't stay in teaching if I didn't. It was too damaging to my self-esteem. The constant energy I was putting into hiding was draining my ability to interact with students. And it was also making me feel I was a bad person."

Some administrators are sympathetic. "In an ideal world, I really don't believe that one's sexuality is a matter of anyone's concern," says Milton Academy headmaster Fredie. "But until we deal with the range of homophobia, then it becomes absolutely necessary for students and teachers who are ready to take that courageous step [to come out of the closet]." Fredie believes that chapel, where ethical issues are traditionally discussed, is an appropriate forum for teachers to discuss their sexual orientation.

Andover headmaster Donald W. McNemar contends that the school must make sure that all students have someone to look up to. "Some of our students are going to lead a gay or lesbian life," he says. "We would want them to have some role models in the faculty, as well."

The role-model issue, combined with the alarming rate of suicide among gay teenagers, is a compelling impetus for many homosexual teachers to make their sexuality known. Some are determined to spare another generation the same experience they themselves had as high school students. Concord Academy's Jennings describes how, wracked by guilt after his first teen-age homosexual experience, he washed down 140 aspirins with a glass of gin. Milton Academy's Todd Fry, an openly gay English teacher, also planned to kill himself while he was in high school. "Obviously, every teenager who is gay isn't suicidal, but a lot of kids feel so alone and so isolated," says Fry. "In speaking at various schools, I can certainly pluck those kids out of the audience. They are the ones who come up to speak to me afterward. I could give you the names of four suicidal kids right now in western Massachusetts I happen to know."

Despite this sense of urgency, most openly gay and lesbian teachers maintain they don't want their reputation as educators to rest with a single issue. Milton Academy's Fry, for instance, has gained high marks for his stewardship of a series of Youth Outreach weekends during which 150 students from private schools work at Boston-area homeless shelters. In a November 1989 letter to the school newspaper, in which he revealed his homosexuality, Fry wrote, "Please bear in mind that most of the time I am not thinking about gay and lesbian issues. When you see me talking with someone, we're probably talking about something else." At Andover, meanwhile, the school's openly lesbian assistant athletic director, Kathy Henderson, says, "The way I want to be remembered is as a great coach."

At the Andover athletic office, Lisa Hamilton, the captain of the girls' lacrosse team, is talking about homosexuality at Andover and, in particular, about coach Henderson. "When everyone first gets here, they are really amazed," says Hamilton. "Most of the kids haven't been comfortable with homosexuality. They come from Greenwich, Connecticut, or from snotty parts of New York. They are really surprised that no one here has a problem with it. By their last two years—I guess it has something to do with maturity—they realize it isn't a big deal."

When Hamilton first tried out for lacrosse, other students asked her, "Do you know?" about coach Henderson. "They really didn't take it beyond that," she says. "But there was some weird feeling that people thought they had to tell me. It wasn't that they wanted to sit there and make fun of her."

In a school where most of her female classmates look as if they stepped out of the J. Crew catalog, Hamilton is determined to dress in her own style. "I'm not your usual little preppy girl. You get a lot of hassle for not shaving your legs or not dressing and wearing your hair like everyone else. What Kathy told me was to 'be yourself,'" Hamilton says. "That really meant a lot to me. A lot of teachers at this school would say, 'do your best,' but they wouldn't necessarily encourage you to be an individual. From Kathy I got a different message."

When Kathy Henderson came to Andover eight years ago, at age 28, she was still struggling with her homosexuality. On her first day on the job, someone walked into her office and saw her picture of the University of New Hampshire women's lacrosse team on the wall and said, 'Any dykes in that picture? I hate dykes." Henderson stayed in the closet for two years. From the moment she arrived, though, she was constantly hearing about Andover's commitment to diversity, honesty, and integrity. She felt that by concealing an important part of herself she wasn't living up to the values the school espoused. Finally, she stood up at a faculty meeting and announced she was a lesbian. "I tell my classes," she says. "I don't really talk to my team unless they want to talk about it. When we are out there, we only have an hour-and-a-half practice, and we practice."

Since coming out of the closet, Henderson has felt much more welcome at Andover. Last spring, she co-taught an English class, with the proviso that she be allowed to teach Fannie Flagg's novel *Fried Green Tomatoes at the Whistle Stop Cafe.* In the book, she explains, the relationship between the two central female characters is more explicitly lesbian than in the film adaptation. "The kids loved it," she says. 'They got to look at sex roles in a new way. And it was a change from Faulkner!"

Henderson is one of four faculty advisers, two homosexual and two heterosexual, of Andover's gay/straight alliance. The organization was started by a lesbian student who came out in a letter to the school newspaper, *The Phillipan.* Today, headmaster McNemar praises the "real courage" exhibited by that founding student. The gay/straight alliance, he says, "is important as a statement in a community that all students, regardless of race, class, and sexual orientation, are respected and are part of the place."

Still, gay/straight alliance advisers estimate that there are nearly 20 gay faculty members at the school, but only two are out of the closet. Last year, four students were openly gay or lesbian in a student body of more than 1,200. Posters advertising gay/straight alliance events are routinely torn down. Much of the campus is "scared to death" of the issue, according to Steven Sultan, who headed the group until he graduated in June.

Controversy erupted last year over a longstanding school policy that permits only legally married couples to reside in nondormitory campus housing. The gay/straight alliance proposed extending the privilege to partners of gay and lesbian faculty, but the school balked. Trustees say they have no objections to single, openly gay teachers living in dormitories. But they are unwilling to liberalize the rules to put gay and lesbian relationships on the same footing as that of married, heterosexual ones.

The school's reluctance to implement policy changes has been disillusioning. As Kathy Henderson puts it, "When you first start your gay/straight alliance and get initial approval, it is similar to when you first come out and find that the majority of people in your life still love you and care about you. That's wonderful. But over time, you begin to look for an existence as equally fulfilling as that of heterosexuals. That is when it gets tougher. And that is where we are right now."

The complaints of gay faculty and students at Andover may appear trivial compared with the situation prevailing in the public schools. At Newton North High School, for example, in one of Boston's most liberal suburbs, there are no openly gay students or faculty, no alliance, just brochures in the library entitled, "I Think I Might Be Gay..." and "I Think I Might Be Lesbian..."

The only time one closeted senior at Newton North heard anything positive about homosexuality was in his honors English class, when the teacher noted that Walt Whitman was gay. "At North, the word 'faggot' is a totally common thing," the student says. "We've already had a racial incident this year. If they don't accept black people, they are never going to accept gay people."

Midway through his senior year, this student became depressed. He talked with his mother, who suggested he go to the Boston Alliance for Gay and Lesbian Youth, which meets twice weekly in the basement of a Beacon Hill church. "I've made a lot of friends through BAGLY," he says. "If I hadn't found BAGLY, if I had been going on like I was, I would have really been in bad shape." He says that had there been an openly gay teacher at North, he might have confided in him.

One closeted teacher at the school believes that it is important for gay teachers to be open about their homosexuality but is convinced such candor would have severely negative consequences. "People wouldn't and couldn't be held accountable," the teacher fears. "I'm afraid they would smash my car. This isn't *Blackboard Jungle.* But it is a school with a mixed population and strong feelings."

Last year, however, at neighboring Newton South High School, Matt Flynn came out of the closet at the beginning of his senior year. A Vietnamese who was adopted as an infant by a Newton couple, Flynn is personable and popular. He is also a star gymnast. When he told his friends he was gay, they were shocked at first but were eventually "cool and accepting." His straight friends now give him advice about his love life. Coming out was a "boulder being lifted off my back," Flynn says. "But you have to be strong. You know that bad things will be said, and you have to anticipate the worst."

After he came out, Flynn helped lead a petition drive to persuade the Newton School Committee to approve the distribution of condoms at both high schools. Seven hundred signatures were garnered from students at South and North, and a third of the faculty and some 30 parents were persuaded to support the drive. In the end, the School Committee approved the proposal by a 7-1 vote.

His activism and openness about his sexuality won Flynn a good deal of respect in Newton. Linda Shapiro, director of counseling at Newton North, says, "Just seeing him is a help to all the kids at Newton South. He does them a favor." At South's graduation ceremonies, the valedictorian praised Flynn for helping the entire class to grow.

A week after Flynn told his friends about his sexuality, Bob Parlin came out to his history classes at Newton South, making him only one of a handful of teachers in the public schools around Boston to declare their homosexuality. (Parlin, who has been teaching at South for more than five years, is the lover of Concord Academy teacher Kevin Jennings.) "The kids were fantastic," Parlin recalls. "They came up and hugged me afterwards." An exception was one student who began to withdraw from class discussions and stopped doing his homework. After a couple of weeks, though, the student began to participate in class again as if nothing had happened.

As a result of Parlinis announcement, things have changed significantly at Newton South. A series of educational programs on homosexuality has taken place, including skits performed in freshman homerooms by members of the drama club. Last spring, at Parlin's prodding, Newton South established a gay/straight alliance. Ten to 12 students attended the first meetings. Except for Mart Flynn, all identify themselves as heterosexual.

At Newton North, the administration has tried to be supportive, but without an openly gay teacher like Parlin to push the issue, that support has not amounted to much. Principal James Marini concedes that the school hasn't been as active on the subject as Newton South. "Whenever opportunities arise for us to affirm the respect and dignity for all races, ethnic groups, gender issues, and sexual preference issues, we do so," he says.

The principal's comments aside, at Newton North's senior prom this past spring, the gay student interviewed for this article showed up with a female friend as his date. At South's prom, Mart Flynn went with his boyfriend. Bob Parlin brought Kevin Jennings. At one point during the evening, both male couples were slow-dancing across the floor, in the midst of a crowd of heterosexual couples. No one seemed to pay any attention. "That," says Parlin, "is progress."

## Questions on Meaning

1. Does this article seem to be pro-gay rights to you? Anti-gay rights? Relatively impartial? Point out a couple of passages that support your opinion and explain.
2. Evaluate the reasons openly gay faculty offer for teachers' coming out in school.
3. Why does Miller focus on prep schools? Is the process of education different in prep schools, many of which require students to live on campus, than in public schools?

## Questions on Rhetorical Strategy and Style

1. This article develops its point through interviews of individuals. Why do you think Miller chose this form of development? What other kinds of information might he have chosen? How would the article have changed?
2. Read through the essay looking for a paragraph or group of paragraphs (other than the present introduction) that might serve as the introduction to this essay. Explain why they would work and outline the revisions that would be required if you used them as the introduction.

## Writing Assignments

1. Miller seems to suggest gays can expect better treatment in expensive private prep schools than in public schools. Does your school experience corroborate Miller's descriptions?
2. Write an essay that describes the language of homosexuality. Research the history of words like gay, straight, lesbian and other terms used to refer to homosexuals and the homosexual lifestyle. You may find it useful to consult an encyclopedia, a recent college dictionary, or the *Oxford English Dictionary* to get started before branching out to articles and books on the subject.
3. Describe the positive and negative consequences of "coming out."

# THE WAY TO RAINY MOUNTAIN

## N. Scott Momaday

*N. Scott Momaday (1934– ) was born in Lawton, Oklahoma, and grew up on Indian reservations. He has a B.A. from the University of New Mexico and an M.A. and Ph.D. from Stanford University. He has taught literature and writing at the University of California, Stanford, and the University of Arizona. His first novel,* House Made of Dawn *(1968), won a Pulitzer Prize.* The Way to Rainy Mountain *(1969), from which the following selection is excerpted, is a collection of Kiowa folk tales and legends. His other works include an autobiographical book* The Names: A Memoir *(1976); two collections of poetry,* Angle of Geese and Other Poems *(1974) and* The Gourd Dance *(1976); and another novel,* The Ancient Child *(1989). In addition, Momaday's drawings and paintings are shown in a number of museums and galleries. You will see his artist's eye combined with the writer's hand in the following description of his grandmother and the Kiowa people.*

1 A single knoll rises out of the plain in Oklahoma, north and west of the Wichita range. For my people, the Kiowas, it is an old landmark, and they gave it the name Rainy Mountain. The hardest weather in the world is there. Winter brings blizzards, hot tornadic winds arise in the spring, and in summer the prairie is an anvil's edge. The grass turns brittle and brown, and it cracks beneath your feet. There are green belts along the rivers and creeks, linear groves of hickory and pecan, willow, and witch hazel. At a distance in July or August the steaming foliage seems almost to writhe in fire.

---

First published in *The Reporter,* 26 January 1967. Reprinted from *The Way to Rainy Mountain.* 

Great green-and-yellow grasshoppers are everywhere in the tall grass, popping up like corn to sting the flesh, and tortoises crawl about on the red earth, going nowhere in the plenty of time. Loneliness is an aspect of the land. All things in the plain are isolate; there is no confusion of objects in the eye, but *one* hill or *one* tree or *one* man. To look upon that landscape in the early morning, with the sun at your back, is to lose the sense of proportion. Your imagination comes to life, and this, you think, is where Creation was begun.

I returned to Rainy Mountain in July. My grandmother had died in the spring, and I wanted to be at her grave. She had lived to be very old and at last infirm. Her only living daughter was with her when she died, and I was told that in death her face was that of a child.

I like to think of her as a child. When she was born, the Kiowas were living the last great moment of their history. For more than a hundred years they had controlled the open range from the Smoky Hill River to the Red, from the headwaters of the Canadian to the fork of the Arkansas and Cimarron. In alliance with the Comanches, they had ruled the whole of the southern Plains. War was their sacred business, and they were among the finest horsemen the world has ever known. But warfare for the Kiowas was pre-eminently a matter of disposition rather than of survival, and they never understood the grim, unrelenting advance of the U.S. Cavalry. When at last, divided and ill provisioned, they were driven onto the Staked Plains in the cold rains of autumn, they fell into panic. In Palo Duro Canyon they abandoned their crucial stores to pillage and had nothing then but their lives. In order to save themselves, they surrendered to the soldiers at Fort Sill and were imprisoned in the old stone corral that now stands as a military museum. My grandmother was spared the humiliation of those high gray walls by eight or ten years, but she must have known from birth the affliction of defeat, the dark brooding of old warriors.

Her name was Aho, and she belonged to the last culture to evolve in North America. Her forebears came down from the high country in western Montana nearly three centuries ago. They were a mountain people, a mysterious tribe of hunters whose language has never been positively classified in any major group. In the late seventeenth century they began a long migration to the south and east. It was a long journey toward the dawn, and it led to a golden age. Along the way the Kiowas were befriended by the Crows, who gave them the culture and religion of the Plains. They acquired horses, and their ancient

nomadic spirit was suddenly free of the ground. They acquired Tai-me, the sacred Sun Dance doll, from that moment the object and symbol of their worship, and so shared in the divinity of the sun. Not least, they acquired the sense of destiny, therefore courage and pride. When they entered upon the southern Plains they had been transformed. No longer were they slaves to the simple necessity of survival; they were a lordly and dangerous society of fighters and thieves, hunters and priests of the sun. According to their origin myth, they entered the world through a hollow log. From one point of view, their migration was the fruit of an old prophecy, for indeed they emerged from a sun-
5 less world. 5

Although my grandmother lived out her long life in the shadow of Rainy Mountain, the immense landscape of the continental interior lay like memory in her blood. She could tell of the Crows, whom she had never seen, and of the Black Hills, where she had never been. I wanted to see in reality what she had seen more perfectly in the mind's eye, and drove fifteen hundred miles to begin my pilgrimage.

Yellowstone, it seemed to me, was the top of the world, a region of deep lakes and dark timber, canyons and waterfalls. But, beautiful as it is, one might have the sense of confinement there. The skyline in all directions is close at hand, the high wall of the woods and deep cleavages of shade. There is a perfect freedom in the mountains, but it belongs to the eagle and the elk, the badger and the bear. The Kiowas reckoned their stature by the distance they could see, and they were bent and blind in the wilderness.

Descending eastward, the highland meadows are a stairway to the plain. In July the inland slope of the Rockies is luxuriant with flax and buckwheat, stonecrop and larkspur. The earth unfolds and the limit of the land recedes. Clusters of trees and animals grazing far in the distance cause the vision to reach away and wonder to build upon the mind. The sun follows a longer course in the day, and the sky is immense beyond all comparison. The great billowing clouds that sail upon it are shadows that move upon the grain like water, dividing light. Farther down, in the land of the Crows and Blackfeet, the plain is yellow. Sweet clover takes hold of the hills and bends upon itself to cover and seal the soil. There the Kiowas paused on their way; they had come to the place where they must change their lives. The sun is at home on the plains. Precisely there does it have the certain character of a god. When the Kiowas came to the land of the Crows, they could see the dark lees of the hills at dawn across the Bighorn River, the profusion of light on the grain shelves, the oldest deity ranging after the solstices. Not yet would they veer southward to the caldron of the land that lay below; they must wean their blood from the northern winter and hold the mountains a while longer in their view. They bore Tai-me in procession to the east.

A dark mist lay over the Black Hills, and the land was like iron. At the top of a ridge I caught sight of Devil's Tower upthrust against the gray sky as if in the birth of time the core of the earth had broken through its crust and the motion of the world was begun. There are things in nature that engender an awful quiet in the heart of man; Devil's Tower is one of them. Two centuries ago, because they could not do otherwise, the Kiowas made a legend at the base of the rock. My grandmother said:

"Eight children were there at play, seven sisters and their brother. Suddenly the boy was struck dumb; he trembled and began to run upon his hands and feet. His fingers became claws, and his body was covered with fur. Directly there was a bear where the boy had been. The sisters were terrified; they ran, and the bear after them. They came to the stump of a great tree, and the tree spoke to them. It bade them climb upon it, and as they did so, it began to rise into the air. The bear came to kill them, but they were just beyond its reach. It reared against the tree and scored the bark all around with its claws. The seven sisters were borne into the sky, and they became the stars of the Big Dipper."

From that moment, and so long as the legend lives, the Kiowas have kinsmen in the night sky. Whatever they were in the mountains, they could be no more. However tenuous their well-being, however much they had suffered and would suffer again, they had found a way out of the wilderness.

My grandmother had a reverence for the sun, a holy regard that now is all but gone out of mankind. There was a wariness in her and an ancient awe. She was a Christian in her later years, but she had come a long way about, and she never forgot her birthright. As a child she had been to the Sun Dances; she had taken part in those annual rites, and by them she had learned the restoration of her people in the presence of Tai-me. She was about seven when the last Kiowa Sun Dance was held in 1887 on the Washita River above Rainy Mountain Creek. The buffalo were gone. In order to consummate the ancient sacrifice—to impale the head of a buffalo bull upon the medicine tree—a delegation of old men journeyed into Texas, there to beg and barter for an animal from the Goodnight herd. She was ten when the Kiowas came together for the last time as a living Sun Dance culture. They could find no buffalo; they had to hang an old hide from the sacred tree. Before the dance could begin, a company of soldiers rode out from Fort Sill under orders to disperse the tribe. Forbidden without cause the essential act of their faith, having seen the wild herds slaughtered and left to rot upon the ground, the Kiowas backed away forever from the medicine tree. That was July 20, 1890, at the great bend of the Washita. My grandmother was there. Without bitterness, and for as long as she lived, she bore a vision of deicide.

Now that I can have her only in memory, I see my grandmother in the several postures that were peculiar to her: standing at the wood stove on a winter morning and turning meat in a great iron skillet; sitting at the south window, bent above her beadwork, and afterwards, when her vision failed, looking down for a long time into the fold of her hands; going out upon a cane, very slowly as she did when the weight of age came upon her; praying. I remember her most often at prayer. She made long, rambling prayers out of suffering and hope, having seen many things. I was never sure that I had the right to hear, so exclusive were they of all mere custom and company. The last time I saw her she prayed standing by the side of her bed at night, naked to the waist, the light of a kerosene lamp moving upon her dark skin. Her long, black hair, always drawn and braided in the day, lay upon her shoulders and against her breasts like a shawl. I do not speak Kiowa, and I never understood her prayers, but there was something inherently sad in the sound, some merest hesitation upon the syllables of sorrow. She began in a high and descending pitch, exhausting her breath to silence; then again and again—and always the same intensity of effort, of something that is, and is not, like urgency in the human voice. Transported so in the dancing light among the shadows of her room, she seemed beyond the reach of time. But that was illusion; I think I knew then that I should not see her again.

Houses are like sentinels in the plain, old keepers of the weather watch. There, in a very little while, wood takes on the appearance of great age. All colors wear soon away in the wind and rain, and then the wood is burned gray and the grain appears and the nails turn red with rust. The window panes are black and opaque; you imagine there is nothing within, and indeed there are many ghosts, bones given up to the land. They stand here and there against the sky, and you approach them for a longer time than you expect. They belong in the distance; it is their domain.

Once there was a lot of sound in my grandmother's house, a lot of coming and going, feasting and talk. The summers there were full of excitement and reunion. The Kiowas are a summer people; they abide the cold and keep to themselves; but when the season turns and the land becomes warm and vital, they cannot hold still; an old love of going returns upon them. The aged visitors who came to my grandmother's house when I was a child were made of lean and leather, and they bore themselves upright. They wore great black hats and bright ample shirts that shook in the wind. They rubbed fat upon their hair and wound their braids with strips of colored cloth. Some of them painted their faces and carried the scars of old and cherished enmities. They were an old council of warlords, come to remind and be reminded of who they were. Their wives and daughters served them well. The women might indulge themselves; gossip was at once the mark and compensation of their servitude. They made loud and elaborate talk among themselves, full of jest and gesture, fright and false alarm. They went abroad in fringed and flowered shawls, bright beadwork, and German silver. They were at home in the kitchen, and they prepared meals that were banquets.

There were frequent prayer meetings, and nocturnal feasts. When I was a child, I played with my cousins outside, where the lamplight fell upon the ground and the singing of the old people rose up around us and carried away into the darkness. There were a lot of good things to eat, a lot of laughter and surprise. And afterwards, when the quiet returned, I lay down with my grandmother and could hear the frogs away by the river and feel the motion of the air.

Now there is a funereal silence in the rooms, the endless wake of some final word. The walls have closed in upon my grandmother's house. When I returned to it in mourning, I saw for the first time in my life how small it was. It was late at night, and there was a white moon, nearly full. I sat for a long time on the stone steps by the kitchen door. From there I could see out across the land; I could see the long row of trees by the creek, the low light upon the rolling plains, and the stars of the Big Dipper. Once I looked at the moon and caught sight of a strange thing. A cricket had perched upon the handrail, only a few inches away. My line of vision was such that the creature filled the moon like a fossil. It had gone there, I thought, to live and die, for there of all places, was its small definition made whole and eternal. A warm wind rose up and purled like the longing within me.

The next morning, I awoke at dawn and went out on the dirt road to Rainy Mountain. It was already hot, and the grasshoppers began to fill the air. Still, it was early in the morning, and the birds sang out of the shadows. The long yellow grass on the mountain shone in the bright light, and a scissortail hied above the land. There, where it ought to be, at the end of a long and legendary way, was my grandmother's grave. Here and there on the dark stones were ancestral names. Looking back once, I saw the mountain and came away.

## Questions on Meaning

1. What does Rainy Mountain symbolize to the Kiowa? How does Momaday build this meaning?
2. How does his grandmother's grave mark "the end of a long and legendary way"? What levels of meaning resonate in this phrase?
3. In writing about his grandmother's death, Momaday is also writing about the ending of his people as a separate nation. For example, when the Kiowas are driven away from the sacred tree by the soldiers, his grandmother is left with a "vision of deicide." Explain what this means. In what other ways do we see in the essay the passing away of the Kiowa as an independent people?

## Questions on Rhetorical Strategy and Style

1. Momaday uses many types of figurative language in his writing, including hyperboles (literary exaggerations) such as in these two descriptions: "The hardest weather in the world is there" and "they were the finest horsemen the world had ever known." Obviously, Momaday is not arguing for such claims—they are a stylistic device with an intended effect. What effect do these and other such figurative language have on your reading experience?
2. Momaday begins and ends with the description of going to visit his grandmother's grave. In between we learn not only about this woman but about the land, the history of the Kiowa, something about the relationship between the encroaching whites and the last of the independent Kiowa nation, and something about the author himself. How does Momaday manage all these elements in a coherent piece of writing? Choose a few paragraphs and analyze them line by line to observe his style and the flow from one element to the next.
3. Momaday's sensitivity to the natural world emerges clearly in this essay. Look at the descriptions of the land in the opening paragraph and elsewhere through the essay. What is particularly fulfilling to us as readers when reading such descriptions? How do they fit in with the essay as a whole?

## Writing Assignments

1. Momaday has a sense of community with the Kiowa through his grandmother, even though he does not speak their language and

was not alive for their "last great moment of their history." We assume he came to his understanding of the Kiowa's earlier history and culture in part through stories told by his grandmother and others. This is, indeed, one way in which we all become part of any cultural group, including the one we are born in. Examine your own life and sense of belonging in a cultural group in this context. How much do you understand about the ways of your world from what you have learned or been told by others?

2. Momaday is writing from memory about someone who means much to him. Write an essay in which you describe someone, living or dead, whom you have not seen recently. Try to capture detail in your descriptions so that the reader is able to glimpse something of that person's inner self.

# ON BOXING

## Joyce Carol Oates

*Joyce Carol Oates (1938– ) was born in Lockport, New York. Oates, who holds degrees from both Syracuse University (B. A., 1960) and the University of Wisconsin (M. A., 1961), has taught at Princeton University, the University of Detroit, and the University of Windsor (Ontario). A prolific writer who has published criticism, essays, novels, poetry, and short stories, Oates had a short story published in* Mademoiselle *magazine while still an undergraduate at Syracuse. Her publications include the books of criticism* The Edge of Impossibility *(1971),* The Poetry of D. H. Lawrence *(1973), and* New Heaven, New Earth *(1974); the novels* With Shuddering Fall *(1964), the National Book Award winner* them *(1969),* Wonderland *(1971),* Do With Me What You Will *(1973),* Childwold *(1976),* Bellefleur *(1980),* Solstice *(1985),* American Appetites *(1989),* Because It Is Bitter, and It Is My Heart *(1990), and* Foxfire: Confessions of a Girl Gang *(1993); and the short story collections* By the North Gate *(1963),* The Wheel of Love and Other Stories *(1970), and* Where is Here? *(1994). In the following essay from her nonfiction book* On Boxing *(1987), stay attuned to Oates's tone and language as she creates a different persona for the violent sport of boxing.*

1 Each boxing match is a story—a unique and highly condensed drama without words. Even when nothing sensational happens: Then the drama is "merely" psychological. Boxers are there to establish an absolute experience, a public accounting of the outermost limits of their beings; they will know, as few of us can know of

Published by Bantam, Doubleday Dell Publishing Group. Copyright © 1987 by Joyce Carol Oates.

ourselves, what physical and psychic power they possess—of how much, or how little, they are capable. To enter the ring near-naked and to risk one's life is to make of one's audience voyeurs of a kind: Boxing is so intimate. It is to ease out of sanity's consciousness and into another, difficult to name. It is to risk, and sometimes to realize, the agony of which *agon* (Greek, "contest") is the root.

In the boxing ring there are two principal players, overseen by a shadowy third. The ceremonial ringing of the bell is a summoning to full wakefulness for both boxers and spectators. It sets into motion, too, the authority of Time.

The boxers will bring to the fight everything that is themselves, and everything will be exposed—including secrets about themselves they cannot fully realize. The physical self, the maleness, one might say, underlying the "self." There are boxers possessed of such remarkable intuition, such uncanny prescience, one would think they were somehow recalling their fights, not fighting them as we watch. There are boxers who perform skillfully, but mechanically, who cannot improvise in response to another's alteration of strategy; there are boxers performing at the peak of their talent who come to realize, mid-fight, that it will not be enough; there are boxers—including great champions—whose careers end abruptly, and irrevocably, as we watch. There has been at least one boxer possessed of an extraordinary and disquieting awareness not only of his opponent's every move and anticipated move but of the audience's keenest shifts in mood as well, for which he seems to have felt personally responsible—Cassius Clay/Muhammad Ali, of course. "The Sweet Science of Bruising" celebrates the physicality of men even as it dramatizes the limitations, sometimes tragic, more often poignant, of the physical. Though male spectators identify with boxers, no boxer behaves like a "normal" man when he is in the ring and no combination of blows is "natural." All is style.

*Every talent must unfold itself in fighting.* So Nietzche speaks of the Hellenic past, the history of the "contest"—athletic, and otherwise—by which Greek youths were educated into Greek citizenry. Without the ferocity of competition, without, even "envy, jealousy, and ambition" in the contest, the Hellenic city, like the Hellenic man, degenerated. If death is a risk, death is also the prize—for the winning athlete. . . .

5 If a boxing match is a story it is an always wayward story, one in 5
which anything can happen. And in a matter of seconds. Split seconds!

(Muhammad Ali boasted that he could throw a punch faster than the eye could follow, and he may have been right.) In no other sport can so much take place in so brief a period of time, and so irrevocably.

Because a boxing match is a story without words, this doesn't mean that it has no text or no language, that it is somehow "brute," "primitive," "inarticulate," only that the text is improvised in action; the language a dialogue between the boxers of the most refined sort (one might say, as much neurological as psychological: a dialogue of split-second reflexes) in a joint response to the mysterious will of the audience, which is always that the fight be a worthy one so that the crude paraphernalia of the setting—ring, lights, ropes, stained canvas, the staring onlookers themselves—be erased, forgotten. (As in the theater or the church, settings are erased by way, ideally, of transcendent action.) Ringside announcers give to the wordless spectacle a narrative unity, yet boxing as performance is more clearly akin to dance or music than narrative.

To turn from an ordinary preliminary match to a "Fight of the Century" like those between Joe Louis and Billy Conn, Joe Frazier and Muhammad Ali, Marvin Hagler and Thomas Hearns is to turn from listening or half-listening to a guitar being idly plucked to hearing Bach's *Well-Tempered Clavier* perfectly executed, and that too is part of the story's mystery: so much happens so swiftly and with such heart-stopping subtlety you cannot absorb it except to know that something profound is happening and it is happening in a place beyond words.

## Questions on Meaning

1. Describe Oates' fascination with boxing. Why does she feel it is "so intimate," that members of the audience are "voyeurs"?
2. What are the "text" and "language" of boxing? Why does she believe that what happens in boxing is in "a place beyond words"?
3. Why does the boxing audience want the fight to be "worthy." In what other spectator events does the audience have this same desire for worthiness?

## Questions on Rhetorical Strategy and Style

1. Through much of this essay, Oates compares boxing with "a story." Locate the various common elements of boxing and a dramatic story. Describe where in your opinion this analogy works and where you feel it is weak.
2. Oates idealizes boxing, yet she does not ignore the injury and death associated with the sport. Find where she focuses on the athletic artistry, psychology, and even ancient history related to boxing to transform its violence to a "profound" experience.
3. Who is Oates' intended audience? Give examples of publications in which this essay would be well received and publications in which it would seem out of place; explain why.

## Writing Assignments

1. Boxing is a controversial sport, with many opponents decrying the violence upon which it is based and the physical harm that can come to participants. Learn about efforts to control or even prohibit boxing in the United States. Is the sport permitted in all states? What is your opinion of boxing as an Olympic sport?
2. Write an essay on the violence in another sport in which fighting is part of the game: professional hockey. Why is fighting not only condoned, but encouraged in professional hockey? Why can hockey players perform acts on the ice with impunity that would be considered assault if they took place in the stands? What effect does this double standard have on fans, on amateur hockey players (who *cannot* fight, ironically), and on society?
3. Oates speaks of the "maleness" of boxing in this 1987 essay. Write an essay on the gender of violence. What connections do you find between the male or female psyche or the gender roles in society

and violent crime? What is the significance of statistics that show a rise in violent acts by women in the United States in recent years?

# SHOOTING AN ELEPHANT

## George Orwell

*George Orwell is the pen name used by the British author Eric Blair (1903–1950). Orwell was born in the Indian village of Motihari, near Nepal, where his father was stationed in the Civil Service. India was then part of the British Empire; Orwell's grandfather too had served the Empire in the Indian Army. From 1907 to 1922 Orwell lived in England, returning to India and Burma and a position in the Imperial Police, which he held until 1927. This is the period about which he writes in "Shooting an Elephant." Thereafter he lived in England, Paris, Spain, and elsewhere, writing on a wide range of topics. He fought in the Spanish Civil War and was actively engaged in several political movements, always against totalitarianism of any kind. He is best known today for two novels of political satire:* Animal Farm *(1945) and* 1984 *(1949). He was also a prolific journalist and essayist, with his essays collected in five volumes. "Shooting an Elephant" was published in a collection of the same name in 1950. Note that Orwell is writing as an older, wiser man about events that took place when he was in his early twenties some two decades previously. This combined perspective of the young man experiencing the incident and the older man looking back on it is part of the rich reading experience.*

1 In Moulmein, in Lower Burma, I was hated by large numbers of 1
people—the only time in my life that I have been important enough for this to happen to me. I was sub-divisional police officer of the town, and in an aimless, petty, kind of way anti-European

From *Shooting an Elephant and Other Essays* by George Orwell. Published by Harcourt Brace and Company. Harcourt Brace and Company and Heath & Co., Ltd.

feeling was very bitter. No one had the guts to raise a riot, but if a European woman went through the bazaars alone somebody would probably spit betel juice over her dress. As a police officer I was an obvious target and was baited whenever it seemed safe to do so. When a nimble Burman tripped me up on the football field and the referee (another Burman) looked the other way, the crowd yelled with hideous laughter. This happened more than once. In the end the sneering yellow faces of young men that met me everywhere, the insults hooted after me when I was at a safe distance, got badly on my nerves. The young Buddhist priests were the worst of all. There were several thousands of them in the town and none of them seemed to have anything to do except stand on street corners and jeer at Europeans.

All this was perplexing and upsetting. For at that time I had already made up my mind that imperialism was an evil thing and the sooner I chucked up my job and got out of it the better. Theoretically—and secretly of course—I was all for the Burmese and all against their oppressors, the British. As for the job I was doing, I hated it more bitterly than I can perhaps make clear. In a job like that you see the dirty work of Empire at close quarters. The wretched prisoners huddling in the stinking cages of the lock-ups, the grey, cowed faces of the long-term convicts, the scarred buttocks of the men who had been flogged with bamboos—all these oppressed me with an intolerable sense of guilt. But I could get nothing into perspective. I was young and ill-educated and I had had to think out my problems in the utter silence that is imposed on every Englishman in the East. I did not even know that the British Empire is dying, still less did I know that it is a great deal better than the younger empires that are going to supplant it. All I knew was that I was stuck between my hatred of the empire I served and my rage against the evil-spirited little beasts who tried to make my job impossible. With one part of my mind I thought of the British Raj as an unbreakable tyranny, as something clamped down, in *saecula saeculorum,* upon the will of prostrate peoples; with another part I thought that the greatest joy in the world would be to drive a bayonet into a Buddhist priest's guts. Feelings like these are the normal by-products of imperialism; ask any Anglo-Indian official, if you can catch him off duty.

One day something happened which in a roundabout way was enlightening. It was a tiny incident in itself, but it gave me a better glimpse than I had had before of the real nature of imperialism—the real motives for which despotic governments act. Early one morning the sub-inspector at a police station the other end of the town rang me up on the 'phone and said that an elephant was ravaging the bazaar. Would I please come and do something about it? I did not know what I could do, but I wanted to see what was happening and I got on to a pony and started out. I took my rifle, an old .44 Winchester and much too small to kill an elephant, but I thought the noise might be useful *in terrorem.* Various Burmans stopped me on the way and told me about the elephant's doings. It was not, of course, a wild elephant, but a tame one which had gone "must." It had been chained up, as tame elephants always are when their attack of "must" is due, but on the previous night it had broken its chain and escaped. Its mahout, the only person who could manage it when it was in that state, had set out in pursuit, but had taken the wrong direction and was now twelve hours' journey away, and in the morning the elephant had suddenly reappeared in the town. The Burmese population had no weapons and were quite helpless against it. It had already destroyed somebody's bamboo hut, killed a cow and raided some fruit-stalls and devoured the stock; also it had met the municipal rubbish van and, when the driver jumped out and took to his heels, had turned the van over and inflicted violences upon it.

The Burmese sub-inspector and some Indian constables were waiting for me in the quarter where the elephant had been seen. It was a very poor quarter, a labyrinth of squalid bamboo huts, thatched with palm-leaf, winding all over a steep hillside. I remember that it was a cloudy, stuffy, morning at the beginning of the rains. We began questioning the people as to where the elephant had gone and, as usual, failed to get any definite information. That is invariably the case in the East; a story always sounds clear enough at a distance, but the nearer you get to the scene of events the vaguer it becomes. Some of the people said that the elephant had gone in one direction, some said that he had gone in another, some professed not even to have heard of any elephant. I had almost made up my mind that the whole story was a pack of lies, when we heard yells a little distance away. There was a loud, scandalized cry of "Go away, child! Go away this instant!" and an old woman with a switch in her hand came round the corner of a hut, violently shooing away a crowd of naked children. Some more women followed, clicking their tongues and exclaiming; evidently there was something that the children ought not to have seen. I rounded the hut and saw a man's dead body sprawling in the mud. He was an Indian, a black Dravidian coolie, almost naked, and he could not have been dead many minutes. The people said that the elephant had come suddenly upon him round the corner of the hut, caught him with its trunk, put its foot on his back and ground him into the earth. This was the rainy season and the ground was soft, and his face had scored a trench a foot deep and a couple of yards long. He was lying on his belly with arms crucified and head sharply twisted to one side. His face was coated with mud, the eyes wide open, the teeth bared and grinning with an expression of unendurable agony. (Never tell me, by the way, that the dead look peaceful. Most of the corpses I have seen looked devilish.) The friction of the great beast's foot had stripped the skin from his back as neatly as one skins a rabbit. As soon as I saw the dead man I sent an orderly to a friend's house nearby to borrow an elephant rifle. I had already sent back the pony, not wanting it to go mad with fright and throw me if it smelt the elephant.

5 The orderly came back in a few minutes with a rifle and five cartridges, and meanwhile some Burmans had arrived and told us that the elephant was in the paddy fields below, only a few hundred yards away. As I started forward practically the whole population of the quarter flocked out of the houses and followed me. They had seen the rifle and were all shouting excitedly that I was going to shoot the elephant. They had not shown much interest in the elephant when he was merely ravaging their homes, but it was different now that he was going to be shot. It was a bit of fun to them, as it would be to an English crowd; besides they wanted the meat. It made me vaguely uneasy. I had no intention of shooting the elephant—I had merely sent for the rifle to defend myself if necessary—and it is always unnerving to have a crowd following you. I marched down the hill, looking and feeling a fool, with the rifle over my shoulder and an evergrowing army of people jostling at my heels. At the bottom, when you got away from the huts, there was a metalled road and beyond that a miry waste of paddy fields a thousand yards across, not yet ploughed but soggy from the first rains and dotted with coarse grass. The elephant was standing eight yards from the road, his left side towards us. He took not the slightest notice of the crowd's approach. He was tearing up bunches of grass, beating them against his knees to clean them and stuffing them into his mouth.

I had halted on the road. As soon as I saw the elephant I knew with perfect certainty that I ought not to shoot him. It is a serious matter to shoot a working elephant—it is comparable to destroying a huge and costly piece of machinery—and obviously one ought not to do it if it can possibly be avoided. And at that distance, peacefully eating, the elephant looked no more dangerous than a cow. I thought then and I think now that his attack of "must" was already passing off; in which case he would merely wander harmlessly about until the mahout came back and caught him. Moreover, I did not in the least want to shoot him. I decided that I would watch him for a little while to make sure that he did not turn savage again, and then go home.

But at that moment I glanced round at the crowd that had followed me. It was an immense crowd, two thousand at the least and growing every minute. It blocked the road for a long distance on either side. I looked at the sea of yellow faces above the garish clothes—faces all happy and excited over this bit of fun, all certain that the elephant was going to be shot. They were watching me as they would watch a conjurer about to perform a trick. They did not like me, but with the magical rifle in my hands I was momentarily worth watching. And suddenly I realized that I should have to shoot the elephant after all. The people expected it of me and I had got to do it; I could feel their two thousand wills pressing me forward, irresistibly. And it was at this moment, as I stood there with the rifle in my hands, that I first grasped the hollowness, the futility of the white man's dominion in the East. Here was I, the white man with his gun, standing in front of the unarmed native crowd—seemingly the leading actor of the piece; but in reality I was only an absurd puppet pushed to and fro by the will of those yellow faces behind. I perceived in this moment that when the white man turns tyrant it is his own freedom that he destroys. He becomes a sort of hollow, posing dummy, the conventionalized figure of a sahib. For it is the condition of his rule that he shall spend his life in trying to impress the "natives," and so in every crisis he has got to do what the "natives" expect of him. He wears a mask, and his face grows to fit it. I had got to shoot the elephant. I had committed myself to doing it when I sent for the rifle. A sahib has got to act like a sahib; he has got to appear resolute, to know his own mind and do definite things. To come all that way, rifle in hand, with a thousand people marching at my heels, and then to trail feebly away, having done nothing—no, that was impossible. The crowd would laugh at me, And my whole life, every white man's life in the East, was one long struggle not to be laughed at.

But I did not want to shoot the elephant. I watched him beating his bunch of grass against his knees, with that preoccupied grandmotherly air that elephants have. It seemed to me that it would be murder to shoot him. At that age I was not squeamish about killing animals, but I had never shot an elephant and never wanted to. (Somehow it always seems worse to kill a *large* animal.) Besides, there was the beast's owner to be considered. Alive, the elephant was worth at least a hundred pounds; dead, he would only be worth the value of his tusks, five pounds, possibly. But I had got to act quickly. I turned to some experienced-looking Burmans who had been there when we arrived, and asked them how the elephant had been behaving. They all said the same thing, he took no notice of you if you left him alone, but he might charge if you went too close to him.

It was perfectly clear to me what I ought to do. I ought to walk up to within, say twenty-five yards of the elephant and test his behavior. If he charged, I could shoot; if he took no notice of me, it would be safe to leave him until the mahout came back. But also I knew that I was going to do no such thing. I was a poor shot with a rifle and the ground was soft mud into which one would sink at every step. If the elephant charged and I missed him, I should have about as much chance as a toad under a steam-roller. But even then I was not thinking particularly of my own skin, only of the watchful yellow faces behind. For at that moment, with the crowd watching me, I was not afraid in the ordinary sense, as I would have been if I had been alone. A white man mustn't be frightened in front of "natives"; and so, in general, he isn't frightened. The sole thought in my mind was that if anything went wrong those two thousand Burmans would see me pursued, caught, trampled on and reduced to a grinning corpse like that Indian up the hill. And if that happened it was quite probable that some of them would laugh. That would never do. There was only one alternative. I shoved the cartridges into the magazine and lay down on the road to get a better aim.

10 The crowd grew very still, and a deep, low, happy sigh, as of people who see the theatre curtain go up at last, breathed from innumerable throats. They were going to have their bit of fun after all. The rifle was a beautiful German thing with cross-hair sights. I did not then know that in shooting an elephant one would shoot to cut an imaginary bar running from ear-hole to ear-hole. I ought, therefore, as the elephant was sideways on, to have aimed straight at his ear-hole;

actually I aimed several inches in front of this, thinking the brain would be further forward.

When I pulled the trigger I did not hear the bang or feel the kick—one never does when a shot goes home—but I heard the devilish roar of glee that went up from the crowd. In that instant, in too short a time, one would have thought, even for the bullet to get there, a mysterious, terrible change had come over the elephant. He neither stirred nor fell, but every line of his body had altered. He looked suddenly stricken, shrunken, immensely old, as though the frightful impact of the bullet had paralysed him without knocking him down. At last, after what seemed a long time—it might have been five seconds, I dare say—he sagged flabbily to his knees. His mouth slobbered. An enormous senility seemed to have settled upon him. One could have imagined him thousands of years old. I fired again into the same spot. At the second shot he did not collapse but climbed with desperate slowness to his feet and stood weakly upright, with legs sagging and head drooping. I fired a third time. That was the shot that did for him. You could see the agony of it jolt his whole body and knock the last remnant of strength from his legs. But in failing he seemed for a moment to rise, for as his hind legs collapsed beneath him he seemed to tower upward like a huge rock toppling, his trunk reaching skywards like a tree. He trumpeted, for the first and only time. And then down he came, his belly towards me, with a crash that seemed to shake the ground even where I lay.

I got up. The Burmans were already racing past me across the mud. It was obvious that the elephant would never rise again, but he was not dead. He was breathing very rhythmically with long rattling gasps, his great mound of a side painfully rising and falling. His mouth was wide open—I could see far down into caverns of pale pink throat. I waited a long time for him to die, but his breathing did not weaken. Finally I fired my two remaining shots into the spot where I thought his heart must be. The thick blood welled out of him like red velvet, but still he did not die. His body did not even jerk when the shots hit him, the tortured breathing continued without a pause. He was dying, very slowly and in great agony, but in some world remote from me where not even a bullet could damage him further. I felt that I had got to put an end to that dreadful noise. It seemed dreadful to see the great beast lying there, powerless to move and yet powerless to die, and not even to be able to finish him. I sent back for my small rifle and poured shot after shot into his heart and down his throat. They seemed to make no impression. The tortured gasps continued as steadily as the ticking of a clock.

In the end I could not stand it any longer and went away. I heard later that it took him half an hour to die. Burmans were bringing dahs and baskets even before I left, and I was told they had stripped his body almost to the bones by the afternoon.

Afterwards, of course, there were endless discussions about the shooting of the elephant. The owner was furious, but he was only an Indian and could do nothing. Besides, legally I had done the right thing, for a mad elephant has to be killed, like a mad dog, if its owner fails to control it. Among the Europeans opinion was divided. The older men said I was right, the younger men said it was a damn shame to shoot an elephant for killing a coolie, because an elephant was worth more than any damn Coringhee coolie. And afterwards I was very glad that the coolie had been killed; it put me legally in the right and it gave me a sufficient pretext for shooting the elephant. I often wondered whether any of the others grasped that I had done it solely to avoid looking a fool.

## Questions on Meaning

1. Orwell confesses to many strong emotions about the Burmese people, such as his comment "I thought that the greatest joy in the world would be to drive a bayonet into a Buddhist priest's guts." Does he actually hate these people? Explain your answer with examples from the essay.
2. At the beginning of the third paragraph Orwell introduces the "tiny incident" that will for him reveal the "real motives for which despotic governments act." What are those motives, as revealed by the incident and Orwell's later comments?
3. Even before the incident with the elephant, Orwell tells us he had discovered that "imperialism was an evil thing." How many different kinds of "evil" are shown through the course of the essay?

## Questions on Rhetorical Strategy and Style

1. The primary rhetorical strategy used in this essay is narration—telling the story of shooting the elephant. In addition to the story itself, Orwell keeps up a sort of running commentary on the meaning of the story, helping us understand it as he analyzes the events of the story. Reread the essay and chart how Orwell moves back and forth between narration and analysis.
2. Orwell is particularly vivid in his descriptive language, often achieving a larger meaning through descriptive details and figurative language. Reread the section of the essay that describes the elephant's slow death as he seems "thousands of years old" (paragraph 11) What meanings are suggested by the language Orwell uses in this descriptive passage?

## Writing Assignments

1. Fear of embarrassment before others can be a powerful motivating force, as the young Orwell discovers in this incident. Search your memory for a time when you yourself took some action simply to avoid embarrassment. How did it feel at the time? Did you feel foolish afterwards? Would you do the same again now in the same circumstances? Try to be as honest in your self-evaluation as Orwell was in his.
2. Have you ever been among a large group of people very different from yourself, either in another country or in a different cultural

group in the United States? Did your concerns lead to fears or negative feelings about these others? Some social scientists have said that people naturally fear things or other people that are very different from themselves, that negative reactions are "normal" even if not healthy or fair to the others. Do you think there is such a natural impulse in people? What are the good and bad effects of this impulse? Present your thoughts in an essay exploring the topic.

3. We all have a "public self" and a "private self." Your public self may be the self you show to others in the academic world or on the job. It may be similar to your private self, what you really are like inside, or it may be very different. The two selves may be harmonious or in conflict, as they were for Orwell. Write an essay defining the difference between these two selves and exploring both the constructive and problematic aspects of this duality.

# RAPE: A BIGGER DANGER THAN FEMINISTS KNOW

## Camille Paglia

*Camille Paglia (1947– ) graduated from Harpur College (B.A., 1968) and Yale University (Ph.D., 1974). Paglia has taught at the University of the Arts in Philadelphia, Bennington College, Wesleyan University, and Yale. Best known for her book* Sexual Personnae: Art and Decadence From Nefertiti to Emily Dickinson *(1991), Paglia also wrote* Sex, Art, and American Culture: Essays *(1992) and* Vamps and Tramps: New Essays *(1994). In this essay, published in* Long Island Newsday *in 1988, Paglia characterizes the war of the sexes and offers women a dire warning.*

1 Rape is an outrage that cannot be tolerated in civilized society. 1
Yet feminism, which has waged a crusade for rape to be taken more seriously, has put young women in danger by hiding the truth about sex from them.

In dramatizing the pervasiveness of rape, feminists have told young women that before they have sex with a man, they must give consent as explicit as a legal contract's. In this way, young women have been convinced that they have been the victims of rape. On elite campuses in the Northeast and on the West Coast, they have held consciousness-raising sessions, petitioned administrations, demanded inquests. At Brown University, outraged, panicky "victims" have scrawled the names of alleged attackers on the walls of women's rest rooms. What marital rape was to the '70s, "date rape" is to the '90s.

The incidence and seriousness of rape do not require this kind of exaggeration. Real acquaintance rape is nothing new. It has been a horrible problem for women for all of recorded history. Once, father and brothers protected women from rape. Once, the penalty for rape

---

Reprinted by permission of the author.

was death. I come from a fierce Italian tradition where, not so long ago in the motherland, a rapist would end up knifed, castrated, and hung out to dry.

But the old clans and small rural communities have broken down. In our cities, on our campuses far from home, young women are vulnerable and defenseless. Feminism has not prepared them for this. Feminism keeps saying the sexes are the same. It keeps telling women they can do anything, go anywhere, say anything, wear anything. No, they can't. Women will always be in sexual danger.

5 One of my male students recently slept overnight with a friend in 5 a passageway of the Great Pyramid in Egypt. He described the moon and sand, the ancient silence and eerie echoes. I am a woman. I will never experience that. I am not stupid enough to believe I could ever be safe there. There is a world of solitary adventure I will never have. Women have always known these somber truths. But feminism, with its pie-in-the-sky fantasies about the perfect world, keeps young women from seeing life as it is.

We must remedy social injustice whenever we can. But there are some things we cannot change. There are sexual differences that are based in biology. Academic feminism is lost in a fog of social constructionism. It believes we are totally the product of our environment. This idea was invented by Rousseau. He was wrong. Emboldened by dumb French language theory, academic feminists repeat the same hollow slogans over and over to each other. Their view of sex is naive and prudish. Leaving sex to the feminists is like letting your dog vacation at the taxidermist's.

The sexes are at war. Men must struggle for identity against the overwhelming power of their mothers. Women have menstruation to tell them they are women. Men must do or risk something to be men. Men become masculine only when other men say they are. Having sex with a woman is one way a boy becomes a man.

College men are at their hormonal peak. They have just left their mothers and are questing for their male identity. In groups, they are dangerous. A woman going to a fraternity party is walking into Testosterone Flats, full of prickly cacti and blazing guns. If she goes, she should be armed with resolute alertness. She should arrive with girlfriends and leave with them. A girl who lets herself get dead drunk at a fraternity party is a fool. A girl who goes upstairs alone with a brother at a fraternity party is an idiot. Feminists call this "blaming the victim." I call it common sense.

For a decade, feminists have drilled their disciples to say, "Rape is a crime of violence but not of sex." This sugar-coated Shirley Temple nonsense has exposed young women to disaster. Misled by feminism, they do not expect rape from the nice boys from good homes who sit next to them in class.

Aggression and eroticism, in fact, are deeply intertwined. Hunt, pursuit and capture are biologically programmed into male sexuality. Generation after generation, men must be educated, refined, and ethically persuaded away from their tendency toward anarchy and brutishness. Society is not the enemy, as feminism ignorantly claims. Society is woman's protection against rape. Feminism, with its solemn Carry Nation repressiveness, does not see what is for men the eroticism or fun element in rape, especially the wild, infectious delirium of gang rape. Women who do not understand rape cannot defend themselves against it.

The date-rape controversy shows feminism hitting the wall of its own broken promises. The women of my '60s generation were the first respectable girls in history to swear like sailors, get drunk, stay out all night—in short, to act like men. We sought total sexual freedom and equality. But as time passed, we woke up to cold reality. The old double standard protected women. When anything goes, it's women who lose.

Today's young women don't know what they want. They see that feminism has not brought sexual happiness. The theatrics of public rage over date rape are their way of restoring the old sexual rules that were shattered by my generation. Yet nothing about the sexes has really changed. The comic film *Where the Boys Are* (1960), the ultimate expression of '50s man-chasing, still speaks directly to our time. It shows smart, lively women skillfully anticipating and fending off the dozens of strategies with which horny men try to get them into bed. The agonizing date-rape subplot and climax are brilliantly done. The victim, Yvette Mimieux, makes mistake after mistake, obvious to the other girls. She allows herself to be lured away from her girlfriends and into isolation with boys whose character and intentions she misreads. *Where the Boys Are* tells the truth. It shows courtship as a dangerous game in which the signals are not verbal but subliminal.

Neither militant feminism, which is obsessed with politically correct language, nor academic feminism, which believes that knowledge and experience are "constituted by" language, can understand preverbal or nonverbal communication. Feminism, focusing on sexual politics, cannot see that sex exists in and through the body. Sexual desire and arousal cannot be fully translated into verbal terms. This is why men and women misunderstand each other.

Trying to remake the future, feminism cut itself off from sexual history. It discarded and suppressed the sexual myths of literature, art and religion. Those myths show us the turbulence, the mysteries and passions of sex. In mythology we see men's sexual anxiety, their fear of woman's dominance. Much sexual violence is rooted in men's sense of psychological weakness toward women. It takes many men to deal with one woman. Woman's voracity is a persistent motif. Clara Bow, it was rumored, took on the USC football team on weekends. Marilyn Monroe, singing "Diamonds Are a Girl's Best Friend," rules a conga line of men in tuxes. Half-clad Cher, in the video for "If I Could Turn Back Time," deranges a battleship of screaming sailors and straddles a pink-lit cannon. Feminism, coveting social power, is blind to woman's cosmic sexual power.

15 To understand rape, you must study the past. There never was and never will be sexual harmony. Every woman must be prudent and cautious about where she goes and with whom. When she makes a mistake, she must accept the consequences and, through self-criticism, resolve never to make that mistake again. Running to mommy and daddy on the campus grievance committee is unworthy of strong women. Posting lists of guilty men in the toilet is cowardly, infantile stuff.

The Italian philosophy of life espouses high-energy confrontation. A male student makes a vulgar remark about your breasts? Don't slink off to whimper with the campus shrinking violets. Deal with it. On the spot. Say, "Shut up, you jerk! And crawl back to the barnyard where you belong!" In general, women who project this take-charge attitude toward life get harassed less often. I see too many dopey, immature, self-pitying women walking around like melting sticks of butter. It's the Yvette Mimieux syndrome: make me happy. And listen to me weep when I'm not.

The date-rape debate is already smothering in propaganda churned out by the expensive Northeastern colleges and universities, with their overconcentration of boring, uptight academic feminists and spoiled, affluent students. Beware of the deep manipulativeness of rich students who were neglected by their parents. They love to turn the campus into hysterical psychodramas of sexual transgression, followed by assertions of parental authority and concern. And don't look for sexual enlightenment from academe, which spews out mountains of books but never looks at life directly.

As a fan of football and rock music, I see in the simple, swaggering masculinity of the jock and in the noisy posturing of the heavy-metal guitarist certain fundamental, unchanging truths about sex. Masculinity is aggressive, unstable, combustible. It is also the most creative cultural force in history. Women must reorient themselves toward the elemental powers of sex, which can strengthen or destroy.

The only solution to date rape is female self-awareness and self-control. A woman's number-one line of defense against rape is herself. When a real rape occurs, she should report it to the police. Complaining to college committees because the courts "take too long" is ridiculous. College administrations are not a branch of the judiciary. They are not equipped or trained for legal inquiry. Colleges must alert incoming students to the problems and dangers of adulthood. Then colleges must stand back and get out of the sex game.

## Questions on Meaning

1. How does Paglia describe masculinity? Why does she believe it is "the most creative cultural force in history"?
2. Why does Paglia believe that women will always be "in sexual danger"? Why does she feel that that feminism has not prepared women for this natural vulnerability?
3. What advice does Paglia give college women for protecting themselves against unwanted sexual advances?

## Questions on Rhetorical Strategy and Style

1. Analyze how Paglia uses a cause and effect writing strategy to argue that the sexual revolution of her generation, during the 1960s, ultimately resulted in women losing. How does she relate the current outrage over "date rape" to the actions of feminists in the 1960s?
2. How does Paglia compare and contrast "militant feminism" with "academic feminism"? Why does she believe that neither of these approaches is effective? Why do their failures result in men and women misunderstanding each other?
3. Paglia often uses simple, declarative sentences in this essay. How did you respond to this staccato writing style? Rewrite her final paragraph into compound and complex sentences. How does your revision affect the tone and impact of the paragraph?

## Writing Assignments

1. Describe the awareness of "date rape" on your campus. If the campus has an established "date rape" policy, explain why you agree or disagree with it. Explain why, from your experience, you agree or disagree with Paglia's conclusion that "female self-awareness and self-control" is the only solution to "date rape." When should a woman "accept the consequences" for a mistake and when should she report it?
2. Research Rousseau's theories on the effect of environment. Write an essay on how these theories have been used by feminists and how you either agree or disagree with them. Use your experiences and your knowledge of the sexual characteristics of men and women to develop your argument.

3. What activities, dress, and actions do you feel are inherently risky for women? Write an essay in which you establish parameters—where women can go, what women can wear, how women can act—that maximize their safety. If you believe that women should have no limits, argue that point. What cautionary clues should women be alert to (such as catcalls and other undesirable attention)?

# THE ALLEGORY OF THE CAVE

## Plato

*Plato (c. 428–347 B.C.), one of the most influential philosophers in history, was born into a wealthy, aristocratic family, presumably in Athens. A pupil of Socrates (and teacher of Aristotle), Plato left Athens for nearly 20 years after his mentor's death in 399 B.C. Upon his return in 380 B.C., he established the Academy and taught there for the remainder of his life. Much of Plato's philosophy appears in his "dialogues"—conversations between Socrates and his students. Three of these "dialogues," the* Apology, *the* Crito, *and the* Phaedo, *immortalized Socrates' trial and final days. Other well-known works of Plato include the* Republic *and* Laws. *Plato's belief in the separate existence of the body and soul and the existence of an eternal order of Forms (the Theory of Forms) have influenced Western thought for more than 2,000 years. In "The Allegory of the Cave" (from the* Republic*), Plato argues the need to differentiate between the world of the senses and physical phenomena and the world of knowledge.*

*The den, the prisoners: the light at a distance;*

1 *Socrates:* And now, I said, let me show in a figure how far our nature is enlightened or unenlightened:—Behold! human beings living in an underground den, which has a mouth open towards the light and reaching all along the den; here they have been from their childhood, and have their legs and necks chained so that they cannot move, and can only see before them, being prevented by the chains from turning round their heads. Above and behind them a fire is blazing at a distance, and between the fire and the prisoners there is a raised way; and you will 1

see, if you look, a low wall built along the way, like the screen which marionette players have in front of them, over which they show the puppets.

*Glaucon:* I see.

And do you see, I said, men passing along the wall carrying all sorts of vessels, and statues and figures of animals made of wood and stone and various materials, which appear over the wall? Some of them are talking, others silent.

You have shown me a strange image, and they are strange prisoners.

Like ourselves, I replied; and they see only their own shadows, or the shadows of one another, which the fire throws on the opposite wall of cave?

*The low wall, and the moving figures of which the shadows are seen on the opposite wall of the den.*

True, he said; how could they see anything but the shadows if they were never allowed to move their heads?

And of the objects which are being carried in like manner they would only see the shadows?

Yes, he said.

And if they were able to converse with one another, would they not suppose that they were naming what was actually before them?

Very true.

And suppose further that the prison had an echo which came from the other side, would they not be sure to fancy when one of the passersby spoke that the voice which they heard came from the passing shadow?

*The prisoners would mistake the shadows for realities.*

No question, he replied.

To them, I said, the truth would be literally nothing but the shadows of the images.

That is certain.

And now look again, and see what will naturally follow if the prisoners are released and disabused of their error. At first, when any of them is liberated and compelled suddenly to stand up and turn his neck round and walk and look towards the light, he will suffer sharp pains; the glare will distress him, and he will be unable to see the realities of which in his former

*And when released, they would still persist in maintaining the superior truth of the shadows.*

state he had seen the shadows; and then conceive some one saying to him, that what he saw before was an illusion, but that now, when he is approaching nearer to being and his eye is turned towards more real existence, he has a clearer vision—what will be his reply? And you may further imagine that his instructor is pointing to the objects as they pass and requiring him to name them—will he not be perplexed? Will he not fancy that the shadows which he formerly saw are truer than the objects which are now shown to him?

Far truer.

And if he is compelled to look straight at the light, will he not have a pain in his eyes which will make him turn away to take refuge in the objects of vision which he can see, and which he will conceive to be in reality clearer than the things which are now being shown to him?

True, he said.

*When dragged upwards, they would be dazzled by excess of light.*

And suppose once more, that he is reluctantly dragged up a steep and rugged ascent, and held fast until he is forced into the presence of the sun himself, is he not likely to be pained and irritated? When he approaches the light his eyes will be dazzled, and he will not be able to see anything at all of what are now called realities.

Not all in a moment, he said.

He will require to grow accustomed to the sight of the upper world. And first he will see the shadows best, next the reflections of men and other objects in the water, and then the objects themselves; then he will gaze upon the light of the moon and the stars and the spangled heaven; and he will see the sky and the stars by night better than the sun or the light of the sun by day?

Certainly.

*At length they will see the sun and understand his nature.*

Last of all he will be able to see the sun, and not mere reflections of him in the water, but he will see him in his own proper place, and not in another; and he will contemplate him as he is.

Certainly.

He will then proceed to argue that this is he who gives the season and the years, and is the guardian of all that is in the visible world, and in a certain way the cause of all things which he and his fellows have been accustomed to behold?

Clearly, he said, he would first see the sun and then reason about him.

And when he remembered his old habitation, and the wisdom of the den and his fellow-prisoners, do you not suppose that he would felicitate himself on the change, and pity them?

*They would then pity their old companions of the den.*

Certainly, he would.

And if they were in the habit of conferring honours among themselves on those who were quickest to observe the passing shadows and to remark which of them went before, and which followed after, and which were together; and who were therefore best able to draw conclusions as to the future, do you think that he would care for such honors and glories, or envy the possessors of them? Would he not say with Homer, "Better to be the poor servant of a poor master," and to endure anything, rather than think as they do and live after their manner?

Yes, he said, I think that he would rather suffer anything than entertain those false notions and live in this miserable manner.

Imagine once more, I said, such as one coming suddenly out of the sun to be replaced in his old situation; would he not be certain to have his eyes full of darkness?

To be sure, he said.

And if there were a contest, and he had to compete in measuring the shadows with the prisoners who had never moved out of the den, while his sight was still weak, and before his eyes had become steady (and the time which would be needed to acquire this new habit of sight might be very considerable) would he not be ridiculous? Men would say of him that up

*But when they returned to the den they would see much worse than those who had never left it.*

he went and down he came without his eyes; and that it was better not even to think of ascending; and if any one tried to loose another and lead him up to the light, let them only catch the offender, and they would put him to death.

No question, he said.

35 This entire allegory, I said, you may not append, dear Glaucon, to the previous argument; the prison-house is the world of sight, the light of the fire is the sun, and you will not misapprehend me if you interpret the journey upwards to be the ascent of the soul into the intellectual world according to my poor belief, which, at your desire, I have expressed—whether rightly or wrongly God knows. But, whether true or false, my opinion is that in the world of knowledge the idea of good appears last of all, and is seen only with an effort; and when seen, is also inferred to be the universal author of all things beautiful and right, parent of light and of the lord of light in this visible world, and the immediate source of reason and truth in the intellectual; and that this is the power upon which he who would act rationally either in public or private life must have his eye fixed.

*The prison is the world of sight, the light of the fire is the sun.* 35

I agree, he said, as far as I am able to understand you.

## Questions on Meaning

1. What do the prisoners believe they are seeing as they watch the shadows on the wall? How do the echoes of the voices of the men who cast the shadows reinforce this belief?
2. What happens when a prisoner is released from the den and is "compelled to look straight at the light"? What will he see at first; what will he see as his eyes adjust? Why will he initially not accept that what he is seeing outside the cave is real? What does the prisoner see when he is returned to the cave? What does he then feel about reality? Why would the other prisoners distrust him and want to "put him to death"?

## Questions on Rhetorical Strategy and Style

1. What is the thesis of Plato's allegory? How would you summarize its application to life in general?
2. The dialogue presented here is built around a narration. Find where Plato also uses description and cause and effect within his story of the prisoners.
3. What do the den (the prison), the prisoners, the shadow, the sun, and the journey out of the cave and into sunlight symbolize in Plato's allegory? Why would Plato choose to use an allegory to present his ideas?

## Writing Assignments

1. Write an allegory to argue against the philosophy of a person or group with whom you disagree—such as white supremacists (race), monarchists (politics), or monopolists (business). Chose your symbolism to clarify the argument. As Plato learned from Socrates, ask rhetorical questions as you make each of your points to confirm that your reader follows—and does not disagree with—your arguments.
2. How might you apply Plato's teaching to your life? Write an essay about a time when your concept of reality was altered because of some knowledge you gained—it could be learning the truth about a friend or becoming aware of the facts about an event or situation. How did your "ascent into the intellectual world" change you? How did others respond to you once they realized that you no longer saw things as they did?

# WHY I HATE "FAMILY VALUES" (LET ME COUNT THE WAYS)

**Katha Pollitt**

*Katha Pollitt (1949- ), a poet and essayist, was born in Brooklyn, New York, and attended Radcliffe College (B. A., 1972). Pollitt, who has been an associate editor and columnist for* The Nation, *has been published in a number of other periodicals, including the* Atlantic Monthly, Mother Jones, The New York Times, *and* The New Yorker. *Her books include* Antarctic Traveler *(1982), a poetry compilation that received the National Book Circle Critics Award;* The Morning After: Sex, Fear, and Femininity on Campus; *and* Reasonable Creatures: Essays on Women and Feminism *(1994). She also has received a grant from the National Endowment for the Arts and a Guggenheim fellowship. In this 1992 essay from* The Nation, *Pollitt takes aim at the "family values" political platform.*

1 Unlike many of the commentators who have made Murphy 1
Brown the most famous unmarried mother since Ingrid Bergman ran off with Roberto Rossellini, I actually watched the notorious childbirth episode. After reading my sleepresistant 4-year-old her entire collection of Berenstain Bears books, television was all I was fit for. And that is how I know that I belong to the cultural elite: Not only can I spell "potato" correctly, and many other vegetables as well, I thought the show was a veritable riot of family values. First of all, Murph is smart, warm, playful, decent and rich: She'll be a great mom. Second, the dad is her ex-husband: The kid is as close to legitimate as the scriptwriters could manage, given that Murph is divorced. Third, her ex spurned her, not, as Dan Quayle implies, the

other way around. Fourth, she rejected abortion. On TV, women have abortions only in docudramas, usually after being raped, drugged with birth-defect-inducing chemicals or put into a coma. Finally, what does Murph sing to the newborn? "You make me feel like a natural woman"! Even on the most feminist sitcom in TV history (if you take points off *Kate and Allie* for never so much as mentioning the word "gay"), anatomy is destiny.

That a show as fluffy and genial as *Murphy Brown* has touched off a national debate about "family values" speaks volumes—and not just about the apparent inability of Dan Quayle to distinguish real life from a sitcom. (And since when are TV writers part of the cultural elite, anyway? I thought they were the crowd-pleasing lowbrows, and *intellectuals* were the cultural elite.) The *Murphy Brown* debate, it turns out, isn't really about Murphy Brown; it's about inner-city women, who will be encouraged to produce fatherless babies by Murph's example—the trickle-down theory of values. (Do welfare moms watch *Murphy Brown*? I thought it was supposed to be soap operas, as in "they just sit around all day watching the soaps." Marriage is a major obsession on the soaps—but never mind.) Everybody, it seems, understood this substitution immediately. After all, why get upset about Baby Boy Brown? Is there any doubt that he will be safe, loved, well schooled, taken for checkups, taught to respect the rights and feelings of others and treated to *The Berenstain Bears Visit the Dentist* as often as his little heart desires? Unlike millions of kids who live with both parents, he will never be physically or sexually abused, watch his father beat his mother (domestic assault is the leading cause of injury to women) or cower beneath the blankets while his parents scream at each other. And chances are excellent that he won't sexually assault a retarded girl with a miniature baseball bat, like those high school athletes in posh Glen Ridge, New Jersey; or shoot his lover's spouse, like Amy Fisher; or find himself on trial for rape, like William Kennedy Smith—children of intact and prosperous families every one of them. He'll probably go to Harvard and major in semiotics. Maybe that's the problem. Just think, if Murph were married, like Dan Quayle's mom, he could go to DePauw University and major in golf.

That there is something called "the family"—Papa Bear, Mama Bear, Brother Bear and Sister Bear—that is the best setting for raising children, and that it is in trouble because of a decline in "values," are bromides accepted by commentators of all political stripes. The right blames a left-wing cultural conspiracy: obscene rock lyrics, sex ed, abortion, prayerless schools, working mothers, promiscuity, homosexuality, decline of respect for authority and hard work, welfare and, of course, feminism. (On the *Chicago Tribune* Op-Ed page, Allan Carlson, president of the ultraconservative Rockford Institute, found a previously overlooked villain: federal housing subsidies. With all that square footage lying around, singles and unhappy spouses could afford to live on their own.) The left blames the ideology of postindustrial capitalism: consumerism, individualism, selfishness, alienation, lack of social supports for parents and children, atrophied communities, welfare and feminism. The center agonizes over teen sex, welfare moms, crime and divorce, unsure what the causes are beyond some sort of moral failure—probably related to feminism. Interesting how that word keeps coming up.

I used to wonder what family values are. As a matter of fact, I still do. If abortion, according to the right, undermines family values, then single motherhood (as the producers of *Murphy Brown* were quick to point out) must be in accord with them, no? Over on the left, if gender equality, love and sexual expressivity are desirable features of contemporary marriage, then isn't marriage bound to be unstable, given how hard those things are to achieve and maintain? Not really.

5 Just say no, says the right. Try counseling, says the left. Don't be 5
so lazy, says the center. Indeed, in its guilt-mongering cover story "Legacy of Divorce: How the Fear of Failure Haunts the Children of Broken Marriages," *Newsweek* was unable to come up with any explanation for the high American divorce rate except that people just didn't try hard enough to stay married.

When left, right and center agree, watch out. They probably don't know what they're talking about. And so it is with "the family" and "family values." In the first place, these terms lump together distinct social phenomena that in reality have virtually nothing to do with one another. The handful of fortysomething professionals like Murphy Brown who elect to have a child without a male partner have little in common with the millions of middle- and working-class divorced mothers who find themselves in desperate financial straits because their husbands fail to pay court-awarded child support. And neither category has much in common with inner-city girls like those a teacher friend of mine told me about the other day: a 13-year-old and a 12-year-old, impregnated by boyfriends twice their age and determined to bear and keep the babies—to spite abusive parents, to confirm their parents' low opinion of them, to have someone to love who loves them in return.

Beyond that, appeals to "the family" and its "values" frame the discussion as one about morals instead of consequences. In real life, for example, teen sex—the subject of endless sermons—has little relation with teen childbearing. That sounds counterfactual, but it's true. Western European teens have sex about as early and as often as American ones, but are much less likely to have babies. Partly it's because there are far fewer European girls whose lives are as marked by hopelessness and brutality as those of my friend's students. And partly it's because European youth have much better access to sexual information, birth control and abortion. Or consider divorce. In real life, parents divorce for all kinds of reasons, not because they lack moral fiber and are heedless of their children's needs. Indeed, many divorce because they do consider their kids, and the poisonous effects of growing up in a household marked by violence, craziness, open verbal warfare or simple lovelessness.

Perhaps this is the place to say that I come to the family-values debate with a personal bias. I am recently separated myself. I think my husband and I would fall under *Newsweek*'s "didn't try harder" rubric, although we thought about splitting up for years, discussed it for almost a whole additional year and consulted no fewer than four therapists, including a marital counselor who advised us that marriage was one of modern mankind's only means of self-transcendence (religion and psychoanalysis were the others, which should have warned me) and admonished us that we risked a future of shallow relationships if we shirked our spiritual mission, not to mention the damage we would "certainly" inflict on our daughter. I thought he was a jackass—shallow relationships? *moi*? But he got to me. Because our marriage wasn't some flaming disaster—with broken dishes and hitting and strange hotel charges showing up on the MasterCard bill. It was just unhappy, in ways that weren't going to change. Still, I think both of us would have been willing to trudge on to spare our child suffering. That's what couples do in women's magazines; that's what the Clintons say they did. But we saw it wouldn't work: As our daughter got older, she would see right through us, the way kids do. And, worse, no matter how hard I tried to put on a happy face, I would wordlessly communicate to her—whose favorite fairy tale is "Cinderella," and whose favorite game is Wedding, complete with bath-towel bridal veil—my resentment and depression and cynicism about relations between the sexes.

The family-values types would doubtless say that my husband and I made a selfish choice, which society should have impeded or even prevented. There's a growing sentiment in policy land to make divorce more difficult. In *When the Bough Breaks,* Sylvia Ann Hewlett argues that couples should be forced into therapy (funny how ready people are to believe that counseling, which even when voluntary takes years to modify garden-variety neuroses, can work wonders in months with resistant patients who hate each other). Christopher Lasch briefly supported a constitutional amendment forbidding divorce to couples with minor children, as if lack of a separation agreement would keep people living together (he's backed off that position, he told me recently). The Communitarians, who flood *The Nation*'s mailboxes with self-promoting worryfests, furrow their brows wondering "How can the family be saved without forcing women to stay at home or otherwise violating their rights?" (Good luck.) But I am still waiting for someone to explain why it would be better for my daughter to grow up in a joyless household than for her to live as she does now, with two reasonably cheerful parents living around the corner from each other, both committed to her support and cooperating, as they say on *Sesame Street,* in her care. We may not love each other, but we both love her. Maybe that's as much as parents can do for their children, and all that should be asked of them.

10 But, of course, civilized cooperation is exactly what many divorced parents find they cannot manage. The statistics on deadbeat and vanishing dads are shocking—less than half pay child support promptly and in full, and around half seldom or never see their kids within a few years of marital breakup. Surely, some of this male abdication can be explained by the very thinness of the traditional paternal role worshiped by the preachers of "values"; it's little more than bread-winning, discipline and fishing trips. How many diapers, after all, has Dan Quayle changed? A large percentage of American fathers

have never changed a single one. Maybe the reason so many fathers fade away after divorce is that they were never really there to begin with.

It is true that people's ideas about marriage are not what they were in the 1950s—although those who look back at the fifties nostalgically forget both that many of those marriages were miserable and that the fifties were an atypical decade in more than a century of social change. Married women have been moving steadily into the work force since 1890; beginning even earlier, families have been getting smaller; divorce has been rising; sexual activity has been initiated even earlier and marriage delayed; companionate marriage has been increasingly accepted as desirable by all social classes and both sexes. It may be that these trends have reached a tipping point, at which they come to define a new norm. Few men expect to marry virgins, and children are hardly "stigmatized" by divorce, as they might have been a mere fifteen or twenty years ago. But if people want different things from family life—if women, as Arlie Hochschild pointed out in *The Second Shift,* cite as a major reason for separation the failure of their husbands to share domestic labor; if both sexes are less willing to resign themselves to a marriage devoid of sexual pleasure, intimacy or shared goals; if single women decide they want to be mothers; if teenagers want to sleep together—why shouldn't society adapt? Society is, after all, just us. Nor are these developments unique to the United States. All over the industrialized world, divorce rates are high, single women are having babies by choice, homosexuals are coming out of the closet and infidelity, always much more common than anyone wanted to recognize, is on the rise. Indeed, in some ways America is behind the rest of the West: We still go to church, unlike the British, the French and, now that Franco is out of the way, the Spanish. More religious than Spain! Imagine.

I'm not saying that these changes are without cost—in poverty, loneliness, insecurity and stress. The reasons for this suffering, however, lie not in moral collapse but in our failure to acknowledge and adjust to changing social relations.

We still act as if mothers stayed home with children, wives didn't need to work, and men earned a "family wage." We'd rather preach about teenage "promiscuity" than teach young people—especially young women—how to negotiate sexual issues responsibly. If my friend's students had been prepared for puberty by schools and discussion groups and health centers, the way Dutch young people are, they might not have ended up pregnant, victims of what is, after all, statutory rape. And if women earned a dollar for every dollar earned by men, divorce and single parenthood would not mean poverty. Nobody worries about single fathers raising children, after all; indeed, paternal custody is the latest legal fad.

What is the point of trying to put the new wine of modern personal relations in the old bottles of the sexual double standard and indissoluble marriage? For that is what most of the current discourse on "family issues" amounts to. No matter how fallacious, the culture greets moralistic approaches to these subjects with instant agreement. Judith Wallerstein's travesty of social science, *Second Chances,* asserts that children are emotionally traumatized by divorce, and the fact that she had no control group is simply ignored by an ecstatic press. As it happens, a recent study in *Science* did use a control group. By following 17,000 children for four years, and comparing those whose parents split with those whose parents stayed in troubled marriages, the researchers found that the "divorce effect" disappeared entirely for boys and was very small for girls. Not surprisingly, this study attracted absolutely no attention.

15 Similarly, we are quick to blame poor unmarried mothers for all 15 manner of social problems—crime, unemployment, drops in reading scores, teen suicide. The solution? Cut off all welfare for additional children. Force teen mothers to live with their parents. Push women to marry in order to attach them to a male income. (So much for love—talk about marriage as legalized prostitution!)

New Jersey's new welfare reform law gives economic coercion a particularly bizarre twist. Welfare moms who marry can keep part of their dole, but only if the man is *not* the father of their children. The logic is that, married or not, Dad has a financial obligation to his kids, but Mr. Just Got Into Town does not. If the law's inventors are right that welfare policy can micromanage marital and reproductive choice, they have just guaranteed that no poor woman will marry her children's father. This is strengthening the family?

Charles Murray, of the American Enterprise Institute, thinks New Jersey does not go far enough. Get rid of welfare entirely, he argued in *The New York Times:* Mothers should marry or starve, and if they are foolish enough to prefer the latter, their kids should be put up for adoption or into orphanages. Mickey Kaus, who favors compulsory low-wage employment for the poor, likes orphanages too.

None of those punitive approaches will work. There is no evidence that increased poverty decreases family size, and welfare moms aren't likely to meet many men with family-sized incomes, or they'd probably be married already, though maybe not for long. The men who impregnated those seventh graders, for example, are much more likely to turn them out as prostitutes than to lead them to the altar. For one thing, those men may well be married themselves.

The fact is, the harm connected with the dissolution of "the family" is not a problem of values—at least not individual values—it's a problem of money. When the poor are abandoned to their fates, when there are no jobs, people don't get to display "work ethic," don't feel good about themselves and don't marry or stay married. The girls don't have anything to postpone motherhood for; the boys have no economic prospects that would make them reasonable marriage partners. This was as true in the slums of eighteenth-century London as it is today in the urban slums of Latin America and Africa, as well as the United States. Or take divorce: The real harm of divorce is that it makes lots of women, and their children, poor. One reason, which has got a fair amount of attention recently, is the scandalously low level of child support, plus the tendency of courts to award a disproportionate share of the marital assets to the man. The other reason is that women earn much less than men, thanks to gender discrimination and the failure of the workplace to adapt to the needs of working mothers. Instead of moaning about "family values" we should be thinking about how to provide the poor with decent jobs and social services, and about how to insure economic justice for working women. And let marriage take care of itself.

20 Family values and the cult of the nuclear family is, at bottom, just 20
another way to bash women, especially poor women. If only they would get married and stay married, society's ills would vanish. Inner-city crime would disappear because fathers would communicate manly values to their sons, which would cause jobs to spring up like mushrooms after rain. Welfare would fade away. Children would do well in school. (Irene Impellizeri, anti-condom vice president of the New York City Board of Education, recently gave a speech attributing inner-city children's poor grades and high dropout rates to the failure of their families to provide "moral models," the way immigrant

parents did in the good old days—a dangerous argument for her, in particular, to make; doesn't she know that Italian-American kids have dropout and failure rates only slightly lower than black and Latino teens?)

When pundits preach morality, I often find myself thinking of Samuel Johnson, literature's greatest enemy of cant and fatuity. What would the eighteenth-century moralist make of our current obsession with marriage? "Sir," he replied to Boswell, who held that marriage was a natural state, "it is so far from being natural for a man and woman to live in the state of marriage that we find all the motives which they have for remaining in that connection, and the restraints which civilized society imposes to prevent separation, are hardly sufficient to keep them together." Dr. Johnson knew what he was talking about: He and his wife lived apart. And what would he think of our confusion of moral preachments with practical solutions to social problems? Remember his response to Mrs. Thrale's long and flowery speech on the cost of children's clothes. "Nay, madam," he said, "when you are declaiming, declaim; and when you are calculating, calculate."

Which is it going to be? Declamation, which feeds no children, employs no jobless and reduces gender relations to an economic bargain? Or calculation, which accepts the fact that the Berenstain Bears, like Murphy Brown, are fiction. The people seem to be voting with their feet on "the family." It's time for our "values" to catch up.

## Questions on Meaning

1. Describe the "new norm" that Pollitt mentions. What has caused its formation? What does Pollitt feel society should do about the "new norm"?
2. According to Pollitt, what is the reason that many fathers "fade away" after divorce? How does she support that contention?
3. What is Pollitt's thesis? Restate it in your own words.

## Questions on Rhetorical Strategy and Style

1. Pollitt uses cause and effect throughout the essay to support her argument—such as why New Jersey welfare mothers are unlikely to marry the father of their children and why increased poverty *does not* decrease family size. Find three other examples of cause and effect.
2. Pollitt uses sometimes humorous, sometimes sardonic, parenthetical asides to air her views. What impact does this writing style have on the readability and comprehensibility of the essay? How would it affect Pollitt's argument if she had omitted these asides?
3. Find where Pollitt describes how the "left," the "right," and the "center" view the decline of family values? What point is she making by comparing and contrasting their perceptions?

## Writing Assignments

1. What do "family values" mean to you? Explain why you feel "family values" are or are not a valid issue in America. If you feel that "family values" are a valid issue, who should address them: politicians, churches, schools, and/or families? Describe how reading Pollitt's piece has affected your view of "family values."
2. Research specific trends on families in America today, such as the numbers of single-parent families, single home owners, same-sex living arrangements, and divorces. Write an essay on what you feel these data say about America.
3. Research employment and salary trends of women versus men. Write an essay describing your reactions to these data. What should be done to bring women's salaries in line with men's?

# FUTURE SHLOCK

## Neil Postman

*Neil Postman (1931– ) was born in Brooklyn, New York. He was educated at the State University of New York and Columbia, and he has taught communications arts and sciences at New York University. A well-known spokesman for educational reform, Postman has written for a number of periodicals, including the* Atlantic *and* The Nation. *Postman's books include* Teaching as a Conserving Activity *(1980),* The Disappearance of Childhood *(1982),* Amusing Ourselves to Death: Public Discourse in the Age of Show Business *(1985), and* Conscientious Objections: Stirring Up Trouble About Language, Technology, and Education *(1988). Also, he coauthored* Linguistics: A Revolution in Teaching *(1966),* Teaching as a Subversive Activity *(1969), and* The Soft Revolution *(1971). Postman edited* Et Cetera, *the journal of general semantics, for a decade. In this essay, Postman attacks the trivialization of American culture and the loss of intelligent discourse by the show business mindset of mass media.*

1 Human intelligence is among the most fragile things in nature. 1
It doesn't take much to distract it, suppress it, or even annihilate it. In this century, we have had some lethal examples of how easily and quickly intelligence can be defeated by any one of its several nemeses: ignorance, superstition, moral fervor, cruelty, cowardice, neglect. In the late 1920s, for example, Germany was, by any measure, the most literate, cultured nation in the world. Its legendary seats of learning attracted scholars from every corner. Its philosophers, social critics, and scientists were of the first rank; its humane traditions

From *Conscientious Objections* by Neil Postman. Published by Alfred A. Knopf, Inc.

an inspiration to less favored nations. But by the mid-1930s—that is, in less than ten years—this cathedral of human reason had been transformed into a cesspool of barbaric irrationality. Many of the most intelligent products of German culture were forced to flee—for example, Einstein, Freud, Karl Jaspers, Thomas Mann, and Stefan Zweig. Even worse, those who remained were either forced to submit their minds to the sovereignty of primitive superstition, or—worse still—willingly did so: Konrad Lorenz, Werner Heisenberg, Martin Heidegger, Gerhardt Hauptmann. On May 10, 1933, a huge bonfire was kindled in Berlin and the books of Marcel Proust, André Gide, Emile Zola, Jack London, Upton Sinclair, and a hundred others were committed to the flames, amid shouts of idiot delight. By 1936, Joseph Paul Goebbels, Germany's Minister of Propaganda, was issuing a proclamation which began with the following words: "Because this year has not brought an improvement in art criticism, I forbid once and for all the continuance of art criticism in its past form, effective as of today." By 1936, there was no one left in Germany who had the brains or courage to object.

Exactly why the Germans banished intelligence is a vast and largely unanswered question. I have never been persuaded that the desperate economic depression that afflicted Germany in the 1920s adequately explains what happened. To quote Aristotle: Men do not become tyrants in order to keep warm. Neither do they become stupid—at least not *that* stupid. But the matter need not trouble us here. I offer the German case only as the most striking example of the fragility of human intelligence. My focus here is the United States in our own time, and I wish to worry you about the rapid erosion of our own intelligence. If you are confident that such a thing cannot happen, your confidence is misplaced, I believe, but it is understandable.

After all, the United States is one of the few countries in the world founded by intellectuals—men of wide learning, of extraordinary rhetorical powers, of deep faith in reason. And although we have had our moods of anti-intellectualism, few people have been more generous in support of intelligence and learning than Americans. It was the United States that initiated the experiment in mass education that is, even today, the envy of the world. It was America's churches that laid the foundation of our admirable system of higher education; it was the Land-Grant Act of 1862 that made possible our great state universities; and it is to America that scholars and writers have fled when freedom of the intellect became impossible in their own nations. This is why the great historian of American civilization Henry Steele Commager called America "the Empire of Reason." But Commager was referring to the United States of the eighteenth and nineteenth centuries. What term he would use for America today, I cannot say. Yet he has observed, as others have, a change, a precipitous decline in our valuation of intelligence, in our uses of language, in the disciplines of logic and reason, in our capacity to attend to complexity. Perhaps he would agree with me that the Empire of Reason is, in fact, gone, and that the most apt term for America today is the Empire of Shlock.

In any case, this is what I wish to call to your notice: the frightening displacement of serious, intelligent public discourse in American culture by the imagery and triviality of what may be called show business. I do not see the decline of intelligent discourse in America leading to the barbarisms that flourished in Germany, of course. No scholars, I believe, will ever need to flee America. There will be no bonfires to burn books. And I cannot imagine any proclamations forbidding once and for all art criticism, or any other kind of criticism. But this is not a cause for complacency, let alone celebration. A culture does not have to force scholars to flee to render them impotent. A culture does not have to burn books to assure that they will not be read. And a culture does not need a Minister of Propaganda issuing proclamations to silence criticism. There are other ways to achieve stupidity, and it appears that, as in so many other things, there is a distinctly American way.

5 To explain what I am getting at, I find it helpful to refer to two 5
films, which taken together embody the main lines of my argument. The first film is of recent vintage and is called *The Gods Must Be Crazy.* It is about a tribal people who live in the Kalahari Desert plains of southern Africa, and what happens to their culture when it is invaded by an empty Coca-Cola bottle tossed from the window of a small plane passing overhead. The bottle lands in the middle of the village and is construed by these gentle people to be a gift from the gods, for they not only have never seen a bottle before but have never seen glass either. The people are almost immediately charmed by the gift, and not only because of its novelty. The bottle, it turns out, has multiple uses, chief among them the intriguing music it makes when one blows into it.

But gradually a change takes place in the tribe. The bottle becomes an irresistible preoccupation. Looking at it, holding it, thinking of things to do with it displace other activities once thought essential. But more than this, the Coke bottle is the only thing these people have ever seen of which there is only one of its kind. And so those who do not have it try to get it from the one who does. And the one who does refuses to give it up. Jealousy, greed, and even violence enter the scene, and come very close to destroying the harmony that has characterized their culture for a thousand years. The people begin to love their bottle more than they love themselves, and are saved only when the leader of the tribe, convinced that the gods must be crazy, returns the bottle to the gods by throwing it off the top of a mountain.

The film is great fun and it is also wise, mainly because it is about a subject as relevant to people in Chicago or Los Angeles or New York as it is to those of the Kalahari Desert. It raises two questions of extreme importance to our situation: How does a culture change when new technologies are introduced to it? And is it always desirable for a culture to accommodate itself to the demands of new technologies? The leader of the Kalahari tribe is forced to confront these questions in a way that Americans have refused to do. And because his vision is not obstructed by a belief in what Americans call "technological progress," he is able with minimal discomfort to decide that the songs of the Coke bottle are not so alluring that they are worth admitting envy, egotism, and greed to a serene culture.

The second film relevant to my argument was made in 1967. It is Mel Brooks's first film, *The Producers. The Producers* is a rather raucous comedy that has at its center a painful joke: An unscrupulous theatrical producer has figured out that it is relatively easy to turn a buck by producing a play that fails. All one has to do is induce dozens of backers to invest in the play by promising them exorbitant percentages of its profits. When the play fails, there being no profits to disperse, the producer walks away with thousands of dollars that can never be claimed. Of course, the central problem he must solve is to make sure that his play is a disastrous failure. And so he hits upon an excellent idea: he will take the most tragic and grotesque story of our century—the rise of Adolf Hitler—and make it into a musical.

Because the producer is only a crook and not a fool, he assumes that the stupidity of making a musical on this theme will be immediately grasped by audiences and that they will leave the theater in dumbfounded rage. So he calls his play *Springtime for Hitler,* which is also the name of its most important song. The song begins with the words:

> *Springtime for Hitler and Germany;*
> *Winter for Poland and France.*

The melody is catchy, and when the song is sung it is accompanied by a happy chorus line. (One must understand, of course, that *Springtime for Hitler* is no spoof of Hitler, as was, for example, Charlie Chaplin's *The Great Dictator.* The play is instead a kind of denial of Hitler in song and dance; as if to say, it was all in fun.)

The ending of the movie is predictable. The audience loves the play and leaves the theater humming *Springtime for Hitler.* The musical becomes a great hit. The producer ends up in jail, his joke having turned back on him. But Brooks's point is that the joke is on us. Although the film was made years before a movie actor became President of the United States, Brooks was making a kind of prophecy about that—namely, that the producers of American culture will increasingly turn our history, politics, religion, commerce, and education into forms of entertainment, and that we will become as a result a trivial people, incapable of coping with complexity, ambiguity, uncertainty, perhaps even reality. We will become, in a phrase, a people amused into stupidity.

For those readers who are not inclined to take Mel Brooks as seriously as I do, let me remind you that the prophecy I attribute here to Brooks was, in fact, made many years before by a more formidable social critic than he. I refer to Aldous Huxley, who wrote *Brave New World* at the time that the modern monuments to intellectual stupidity were taking shape: Nazism in Germany, fascism in Italy, communism in Russia. But Huxley was not concerned in his book with such naked and crude forms of intellectual suicide. He saw beyond them, and mostly, I must add, he saw America. To be more specific, he foresaw that the greatest threat to the intelligence and humane creativity of our culture would not come from Big Brother and Ministries of Propaganda, or gulags and concentration camps. He prophesied, if I may put it this way, that there is tyranny lurking in a Coca-Cola bottle; that we could be ruined not by what we fear and hate but by what we welcome and love, by what we construe to be a gift from the gods.

And in case anyone missed his point in 1932, Huxley wrote *Brave New World Revisited* twenty years later. By then, George Orwell's *1984* had been published, and it was inevitable that Huxley would compare Orwell's book with his own. The difference, he said, is that in Orwell's book people are controlled by inflicting pain. In *Brave New World,* they are controlled by inflicting pleasure.

The Coke bottle that has fallen in our midst is a corporation of dazzling technologies whose forms turn all serious public business into a kind of *Springtime for Hitler* musical. Television is the principal instrument of this disaster, in part because it is the medium Americans most dearly love, and in part because it has become the command center of our culture. Americans turn to television not only for their light entertainment but for their news, their weather, their politics, their religion, their history—all of which may be said to be their serious entertainment. The light entertainment is not the problem. The least dangerous things on television are its junk. What I am talking about is television's preemption of our culture's most serious business. It would be merely banal to say that television presents us with entertaining subject matter. It is quite another thing to say that on television all subject matter is presented as entertaining. And that is how television brings ruin to any intelligent understanding of public affairs.

15 Political campaigns, for example, are now conducted largely in the 15
form of television commercials. Candidates forgo precision, complexity, substance—in some cases, language itself—for the arts of show business: music, imagery, celebrities, theatrics. Indeed, political figures have become so good at this, and so accustomed to it, that they do television commercials even when they are not campaigning, as, for example, Geraldine Ferraro for Diet Pepsi and former vice-presidential candidate William Miller and the late Senator Sam Ervin for American Express. Even worse, political figures appear on variety shows, soap operas, and sitcoms. George McGovern, Ralph Nader, Ed Koch, and Jesse Jackson have all hosted "Saturday Night Live." Henry Kissinger and former President Gerald Ford have done cameo roles on "Dynasty." Tip O'Neill and Governor Michael Dukakis have appeared on "Cheers." Richard Nixon did a short stint on "Laugh-In." The late Senator from Illinois, Everett Dirksen, was on "What's My Line?" a prophetic question if ever there was one. What *is* the line of these people? Or, more precisely, *where* is the line that one ought to be able to draw between politics and entertainment? I would suggest that television has annihilated it.

It is significant, I think, that although our current President, a former Hollywood movie actor, rarely speaks accurately and never precisely, he is known as the Great Communicator; his telegenic charm appears to be his major asset, and that seems to be quite good enough in an entertainment-oriented politics. But lest you think his election to two terms is a mere aberration, I must remind you that, as I write [1988], Charlton Heston is being mentioned as a possible candidate for the Republican nomination in 1988. Should this happen, what alternative would the Democrats have but to nominate Gregory Peck? Two idols of the silver screen going one on one. Could even the fertile imagination of Mel Brooks have foreseen this? Heston giving us intimations of Moses as he accepts the nomination; Peck re-creating the courage of his biblical David as he accepts the challenge of running against a modern Goliath. Heston going on the stump as Michelangelo; Peck countering with Douglas MacArthur. Heston accusing Peck of insanity because of *The Boys From Brazil.* Peck replying with the charge that Heston blew the world up in *Return to Planet of the Apes. Springtime for Hitler* could be closer than you think.

But politics is only one arena in which serious language has been displaced by the arts of show business. We have all seen how religion is packaged on television, as a kind of Las Vegas stage show, devoid of ritual, sacrality, and tradition. Today's electronic preachers are in no way like America's evangelicals of the past. Men like Jonathan Edwards, Charles Finney, and George Whitefield were preachers of theological depth, authentic learning, and great expository power. Electronic preachers such as Jimmy Swaggart, Jim Bakker, and Jerry Falwell are merely performers who exploit television's visual power and their own charisma for the greater glory of themselves.

We have also seen "Sesame Street" and other educational shows in which the demands of entertainment take precedence over the rigors of learning. And we well know how American businessmen, working under the assumption that potential customers require amusement rather than facts, use music, dance, comedy, cartoons, and celebrities to sell their products.

Even our daily news, which for most Americans means television news, is packaged as a kind of show, featuring handsome news readers, exciting music, and dynamic film footage. Most especially, film footage. When there is no film footage, there is no story. Stranger still, commercials may appear anywhere in a news story—before, after, or in the middle. This reduces all events to trivialities, sources of public entertainment and little more. After all, how serious can a bombing in Lebanon be if it is shown to us prefaced by a happy United Airlines commercial and summarized by a Calvin Klein jeans commercial? Indeed, television newscasters have added to our grammar a new part of speech—what may be called the "Now . . . this" conjunction, a conjunction that does not connect two things, but disconnects them. When newscasters say, "Now . . . this," they mean to indicate that what you have just heard or seen has no relevance to what you are about to hear or see. There is no murder so brutal, no political blunder so costly, no bombing so devastating that it cannot be erased from our minds by a newscaster saying, "Now . . . this." He means that you have thought long enough on the matter (let us say, for forty seconds) and you must now give your attention to a commercial. Such a situation is not "the news." It is merely a daily version of *Springtime for Hitler,* and in my opinion accounts for the fact that Americans are among the most ill-informed people in the world. To be sure, we know *of* many things; but we know *about* very little.

To provide some verification of this, I conducted a survey a few years back on the subject of the Iranian hostage crisis. I chose this subject because it was alluded to on television *every day for more than a year.* I did not ask my subjects for their opinions about the hostage situation. I am not interested in opinion polls; I am interested in knowledge polls. The questions I asked were simple and did not require deep knowledge. For example, Where is Iran? What language do the Iranians speak? Where did the Shah come from? What religion do the Iranians practice, and what are its basic tenets? What does "Ayatollah" mean? I found that almost everybody knew practically nothing about Iran. And those who did know something said they had learned it from *Newsweek* or *Time* or the *New York Times.* Television, in other words, is not the great information machine. It is the great disinformation machine. A most nerve-wracking confirmation of this came some time ago during an interview with the producer and the writer of the TV mini-series *Peter the Great.* Defending the historical inaccuracies in the drama—which included a fabricated meeting between Peter and Sir Isaac Newton—the producer said that no one would watch a dry, historically faithful biography. The writer added that it is better for audiences to learn something that is untrue, if it is entertaining, than not to learn anything at all. And just to put some icing on the cake, the actor who played Peter, Maximilian Schell, remarked that he does not believe in historical truth and therefore sees no reason to pursue it.

I do not mean to say that the trivialization of American public discourse is all accomplished on television. Rather, television is the paradigm for all our attempts at public communication. It conditions our minds to apprehend the world through fragmented pictures and forces other media to orient themselves in that direction. You know the standard question we put to people who have difficulty understanding even simple language: we ask them impatiently, "Do I have to draw a picture for you?" Well, it appears that, like it or not, our culture will draw pictures for us, will explain the world to us in pictures. As a medium for conducting public business, language has receded in importance; it has been moved to the periphery of culture and has been replaced at the center by the entertaining visual image.

Please understand that I am making no criticism of the visual arts in general. That criticism is made by God, not by me. You will remember that in His Second Commandment, God explicitly states that "Thou shalt not make unto thee any graven image, nor any likeness of anything that is in Heaven above, or that is in the earth beneath, or the waters beneath the earth." I have always felt that God was taking a rather extreme position on this, as is His way. As for myself, I am arguing from the standpoint of a symbolic relativist. Forms of communication are neither good nor bad in themselves. They become good or bad depending on their relationship to other symbols and on the functions they are made to serve within a social order. When a culture becomes overloaded with pictures; when logic and rhetoric lose their binding authority; when historical truth becomes irrelevant; when the spoken or written word is distrusted or makes demands on our attention that we are incapable of giving; when our politics, history, education, religion, public information, and commerce are expressed largely in visual imagery rather than words, then a culture is in serious jeopardy.

Neither do I make a complaint against entertainment. As an old song has it, life is not a highway strewn with flowers. The sight of a few blossoms here and there may make our journey a trifle more endurable. But in America, the least amusing people are our professional entertainers. In our present situation, our preachers, entrepreneurs, politicians, teachers, and journalists are committed to entertaining us through media that do not lend themselves to serious, complex discourse. But these producers of our culture are not to be blamed. They, like the rest of us, believe in the supremacy of technological progress. It has never occurred to us that the gods might be crazy. And even if it did, there is no mountaintop from which we can return what is dangerous to us.

We would do well to keep in mind that there are two ways in which the spirit of a culture may be degraded. In the first—the Orwellian—culture becomes a prison. This was the way of the Nazis, and it appears to be the way of the Russians. In the second—the Huxleyan—culture becomes a burlesque. This appears to be the way of the Americans. What Huxley teaches is that in the Age of Advanced Technology, spiritual devastation is more likely to come from an enemy with a smiling countenance than from one whose face exudes suspicion and hate. In the Huxleyan prophecy, Big Brother does not watch us, by his choice; we watch him, by ours. When a culture becomes distracted by trivia; when political and social life are redefined as a perpetual round of entertainments; when public conversation becomes a form of baby talk; when a people become, in short, an audience and their public business a vaudeville act, then—Huxley argued—a nation finds itself at risk and culture-death is a clear possibility. I agree.

## Questions on Meaning

1. Why does Postman believe that human intelligence is so fragile? What can damage or destroy it? What example does he provide to show the quick destruction of an intelligent society?
2. Explain why the two films Postman describes—*The Gods Must Be Crazy* and *The Producers*— "embody" his argument. What did the tribal leader in the first film do that Postman states Americans have refused to do? What was the "prophecy" of the second film that will, in Postman's words, turn Americans into "a people amused into stupidity"?
3. Why does Postman single out television as the root of the problem?

## Questions on Rhetorical Strategy and Style

1. What is the primary rhetorical strategy of this essay? Show where Postman supports it with example, narration, and cause and effect.
2. How does Postman compare and contrast Huxley's *Brave New World* and Orwell's *1984*? What is the major difference between Huxley's future society and the society described by Orwell? During the 20th century, what has been the fate of well-known Orwellian societies, such as Nazi Germany and communist Russia? Why does Postman characterize American society as becoming Huxleyan?
3. How does Postman compare and contrast the cultures of pre-World War II Germany with the United States? Why does he state that scholars will not have to flee America and books will not need to be burned for the American culture to become "stupid"?

## Writing Assignments

1. Postman criticizes the presentation and format of television news—show business—as trivializing what should be serious, blurring the lines between what is important (a bombing in Lebanon) to what isn't (Calvin Klein jeans). Study the evening news for a few nights. Determine how much time is spent on serious news, human interest, and advertising. Note the transitions from the serious to the trivial. Write down your reactions to the studio newsreaders and the reporters in the field—how do their

mannerisms and delivery affect the meaning of the news? Do you agree with Postman's criticisms?

2. Much to the amazement and dismay of many thinking people—such as Postman—former President Ronald Reagan was often called "The Great Communicator." Read something about Reagan's legendary communications skills. How did Reagan, who often bungled facts and could discuss few topics without cue cards, earn such a reputation? What other important elected position did Reagan hold?
3. Write an essay about the trend today to make history alive and real through theme parks, documentaries, and other forms of dramatization. Where must we draw the line between entertainment and distortion? Is it possible for most consumers to be sufficiently discerning to know what to believe and what to question? Is there value in giving half-accurate information versus no information at all?

# THE C WORD IN THE HALLWAYS

## Anna Quindlen

*Anna Quindlen (1953– ) grew up in Philadelphia and graduated from Barnard College. She first worked as a journalist for the* New York Post *and the* New York Times, *where she became a personal opinion columnist. Her writing for the* Times *"Hers" column covers many topics such as motherhood, family relations, and marriage, and her own column is titled, "Life in the Thirties." The best of her columns have been collected in* Living Out Loud *(1988) and* Thinking Out Loud *(1993). She won the Pulitzer Prize for Commentary in 1992. Her work in fiction includes the novels* Object Lessons *(1992),* One True Thing *(1994), and* Black and Blue *(1998). In the following essay, Quindlen questions society's refusal to acknowledge and treat serious mental health problems in adolescents—problems that she claims contribute to the dramatic rise in teen suicide and homicide.*

1 The saddest phrase I've read in a long time is this one: psychological autopsy. That's what the doctors call it when a kid kills himself and they go back over the plowed ground of his short life, and discover all the hidden markers that led to the rope, the blade, the gun.

There's a plague on all our houses, and since it doesn't announce itself with lumps or spots or protest marches, it has gone unremarked in the quiet suburbs and busy cities where it has been laying waste. The number of suicides and homicides committed by teenagers, most often young men, has exploded in the last three decades, until it has

"The C Word in the Hallways," by Anna Quindlen, reprinted from *Newsweek*, November 29, 1999, pp. 112.

become commonplace to have black-bordered photographs in yearbooks and murder suspects with acne problems. And everyone searches for reasons, and scapegoats, and solutions, most often punitive. Yet one solution continues to elude us, and that is ending the ignorance about mental health, and moving it from the margins of care and into the mainstream where it belongs. As surely as any vaccine, this would save lives.

So many have already been lost. This month Kip Kinkel was sentenced to life in prison in Oregon for the murders of his parents and a shooting rampage at his high school that killed two students. A psychiatrist who specializes in the care of adolescents testified that Kinkel, now 17, had been hearing voices since he was 12. Sam Manzie is also 17. He is serving a 70-year sentence for luring an 11-year-old boy named Eddie Werner into his New Jersey home and strangling him with the cord of an alarm clock because his Sega Genesis was out of reach. Manzie had his first psychological evaluation in the first grade.

Excuses, excuses. That's what so many think of the underlying pathology in such unimaginable crimes. In the 1956 movie "The Bad Seed," little Patty McCormack played what was then called a homicidal maniac, and the film censors demanded a ludicrous mock curtain call in which the child actress was taken over the knee of her screen father and spanked. There are still some representatives of the "good spanking" school out there, although today the spanking may wind up being life in prison. And there's still plenty of that useless adult "what in the world does a 16-year-old have to be depressed about" mind-set to keep depressed 16-year-olds from getting help.

5 It's true that both the Kinkel and the Manzie boys had already been introduced to the mental-health system before their crimes. Concerned by her son's fascination with weapons, Faith Kinkel took him for nine sessions with a psychologist in the year before the shootings. Because of his rages and his continuing relationship with a pedophile, Sam's parents had tried to have him admitted to a residential facility just days before their son invited Eddie in.

But they were threading their way through a mental-health system that is marginalized by shame, ignorance, custom, the courts, even by business practice. Kip Kinkel's father made no secret of his disapproval of therapy. During its course he bought his son the Glock that Kip would later use on his killing spree, which speaks sad volumes about our peculiar standards of masculinity. Sam's father, on the other hand, spent days trying to figure out how much of the cost of a home for troubled kids his insurance would cover. In the meantime, a psychiatrist who examined his son for less time than it takes to eat a Happy Meal concluded that he was no danger to himself or others, and a judge lectured Sam from the bench: "you know the difference between what's right and wrong, don't you?"

The federal Center for Mental Health Services estimates that at least 6 million children in this country have some serious emotional disturbance, and for some of them, right and wrong takes second seat to the voices in their heads. Fifty years ago their parents might have surrendered them to life in an institution, or a doctor flying blind with an ice pick might have performed a lobotomy, leaving them to loll away their days. Now lots of them wind up in jail. Warm fuzzies aside, consider this from a utilitarian point of view: psychological intervention is cheaper than incarceration.

The most optimistic estimate is that two thirds of these emotionally disturbed children are not getting any treatment. Imagine how we would respond if two thirds of America's babies were not being immunized. Many health-insurance plans do not provide coverage for necessary treatment, or financially penalize those who need a psychiatrist instead of an oncologist. Teachers are not trained to recognize mental illness, and some dismiss it, "Bad Seed" fashion, as bad behavior. Parents are afraid, and ashamed, creating a home environment, and a national atmosphere, too, that tells teenagers their demons are a disgrace.

And then there are the teenagers themselves, slouching toward adulthood in a world that loves conformity. Add to the horror of creeping depression or delusions that of peer derision, the sound of the C word in the hallways: crazy, man, he's crazy, haven't you seen him, didn't you hear? Boys, especially, still suspect that talk therapy, or even heartfelt talk, is somehow sissified, weak. Sometimes even their own fathers think so, at least until they have to identify the body.

10 Another sad little phrase is "If only," and there are always plenty 10
of them littering the valleys of tragedy. If only there had been long-term intervention and medication, Kip Kinkel might be out of jail, off the taxpayer's tab and perhaps leading a productive life. If only Sam Manzie had been treated aggressively earlier, new psychotropic drugs might have slowed or stilled his downward slide. And if only those things had happened, Faith Kinkel, William Kinkel, Mikael Nicko-

lauson, Ben Walker and Eddie Werner might all be alive today. Mental-health care is health care, too, and mental illness is an illness, not a character flaw. Insurance providers should act like it. Hospitals and schools should act like it. Above all, we parents should act like it. Then maybe the kids will believe it.

## Questions on Meaning

1. According to Quindlen, what is one of the hidden causes behind the increasing number of teenage suicides and homicides? What other possible causes have been presented in news accounts of such violence?
2. At one point Quindlen refers to "our peculiar standards of masculinity." To what is she referring? What other examples of such standards appear in the essay?
3. How does Quindlen characterize teenagers' responses to people like Kip Kinkel and Sam Manzie? Based on your own experience, how accurate is her characterization? Explain your response.

## Questions on Rhetorical Strategy and Style

1. In order to persuade her readers, Quindlen balances reason and emotion. Cite one example of each of these appeals, and explain how each contributes to the effectiveness of her argument.
2. An example is effective only to the extent that it represents the primary issues addressed in the essay. How do the examples of Kip Kinkel and Sam Manzie represent specific issues raised by Quindlen?
3. Quindlen ends her essay with four short sentences, the first three of which end with the words "should act like it" and the last with "will believe it." What purpose does this repetition of phrases and rhythms serve? How effective is this technique in concluding the argument?

## Writing Assignments

1. To what extent do you agree or disagree with Quindlen? Write an essay in which you offer evidence supporting your position on the causes of teenage violence. Refer to additional cases from recent years, for example, one or more of the school shootings covered extensively in the media.
2. Rent and watch the 1956 film *The Bad Seed*, paying particular attention to the psychological analysis of the child's behavior in the film as opposed to the implicit "common-sense" analysis in the

curtain call. Write a review of the film, highlighting the discrepancies between the two analyses and commenting on what these discrepancies say about society.

3. Quindlen makes two literary references in this essay, first to Shakespeare's *Romeo and Juliet* ("a plague on all our houses") and second to William Butler Yeats's "The Second Coming" ("slouching toward adulthood"). Using either the prince's speech in the play or the Yeats poem, write an essay explaining the relevance of the literary work to Quindlen's argument.

# THE FEAR OF LOSING A CULTURE

**Richard Rodriguez**

*Richard Rodriguez (1944– ) was born in San Francisco. A child of Mexican immigrants, Rodriguez spoke Spanish until he went to a Catholic school at age 6. As a youth, he delivered newspapers and worked as a gardener. Rodriguez received a B.A. from Stanford University, an M.A. from Columbia University, and a Ph.D. in English Renaissance literature from the University of California at Berkeley; he later attended the Warburg Institute in London on a Fulbright fellowship. A noted prose stylist, Rodriguez has worked as a teacher, journalist, and educational consultant, in addition to writing, lecturing, and appearing frequently on the Public Broadcast System (PBS) program, "The MacNeil-Lehrer News Hour." Rodriguez's books include* Hunger of Memory: The Education of Richard Rodriguez *(1982), a collection of autobiographical essays;* Mexico's Children *(1990); and* Days of Obligation: An Argument With My Mexican Father *(1992), which was nominated for a National Book Award. In addition, he has been published in* The American Scholar, Change, College English, Harper's, Mother Jones, Reader's Digest, *and* Time. *A controversial writer, Rodriguez often speaks out against affirmative action and bilingual education. In this essay, Rodriguez discusses the importance of the Hispanic culture to America, and how assimilation of the cultures will redefine the nation.*

1 What is culture? 1

The immigrant shrugs. Latin American immigrants come to the United States with only the things they need in mind—not abstractions like culture. Money. They need dollars. They need food. Maybe they need to get out of the way of bullets.

Most of us who concern ourselves with Hispanic-American culture, as painters, musicians, writers—or as sons and daughters—are the children of immigrants. We have grown up on this side of the border, in the land of Elvis Presley and Thomas Edison; our lives are prescribed by the mall, by the DMV and the Chinese restaurant. Our imagination yet vascillates between an Edenic Latin America (the blue door)—which nevertheless betrayed our parents—and the repellent plate glass of a real American city—which has been good to us.

Hispanic-American culture is where the past meets the future. Hispanic-American culture is not an Hispanic milestone only, not simply a celebration at the crossroads. America transforms into pleasure what America cannot avoid. Is it any coincidence that at a time when Americans are troubled by the encroachment of the Mexican desert, Americans discover a chic in cactus, in the decorator colors of the Southwest? In sand?

5 Hispanic-American culture of the sort that is now showing (the teen movie, the rock songs) may exist in an hourglass; may in fact be irrelevant to the epic. The U.S. Border Patrol works through the night to arrest the flow of illegal immigrants over the border, even as Americans wait in line to get into "La Bamba." Even as Americans vote to declare, once and for all, that English shall be the official language of the United States, Madonna starts recording in Spanish.

But then so is Bill Cosby's show irrelevant to the 10 o'clock news, where families huddle together in fear on porches, pointing at the body of the slain boy bagged in tarpoline. Which is not to say that Bill Cosby or Michael Jackson are irrelevant to the future or without neo-Platonic influence. Like players within the play, they prefigure, they resolve. They make black and white audiences aware of a bond that may not yet exist.

Before a national TV audience, Rita Moreno tells Geraldo Rivera that her dream as an actress is to play a character rather like herself: "I speak English perfectly well . . . I'm not dying from poverty . . . I want to play *that* kind of Hispanic woman, which is to say, an American citizen." This is an actress talking, these are show-biz pieties. But Moreno expresses as well the general Hispanic-American predicament. Hispanics want to belong to America without betraying the past.

Hispanics fear losing ground in any negotiation with the American city. We come from an expansive, an intimate culture that has been judged second-rate by the United States of America. For reasons of pride, therefore, as much as of affection, we are reluctant to give up our past. Hispanics often express a fear of "losing" culture. Our fame in the United States has been our resistance to assimilation.

The symbol of Hispanic culture has been the tongue of flame—Spanish. But the remarkable legacy Hispanics carry from Latin America is not language—an inflatable skin—but breath itself, capacity of soul, an inclination to live. The genius of Latin America is the habit of synthesis.

10 We assimilate. Just over the border there is the example of Mex- 10
ico, the country from which the majority of U.S. Hispanics come. Mexico is mestizo—Indian and Spanish. Within a single family, Mexicans are light-skinned and dark. It is impossible for the Mexican to say, in the scheme of things, where the Indian begins and the Spaniard surrenders.

In culture as in blood, Latin America was formed by a rape that became a marriage. Due to the absorbing generosity of the Indian, European culture took on new soil. What Latin America knows is that people create one another as they marry. In the music of Latin America you will hear the litany of bloodlines—the African drum, the German accordian, the cry from the minaret.

The United States stands as the opposing New World experiment. In North America the Indian and the European stood apace. Whereas Latin America was formed by a medieval Catholic dream of one world—of meltdown conversion—the United States was built up from Protestant individualism. The American melting pot washes away only embarrassment; it is the necessary initiation into public life. The American faith is that our national strength derives from separateness, from "diversity." The glamour of the United States is a carnival promise: You can lose weight, get rich as Rockefeller, tough up your roots, get a divorce.

Immigrants still come for the promise. But the United States wavers in its faith. As long as there was space enough, sky enough, as long as economic success validated individualism, loneliness was not too high a price to pay. (The cabin on the prairie or the Sony Walkman.)

As we near the end of the American century, two alternative cultures beckon the American imagination—both highly communal cultures—the Asian and the Latin American. The United States is a literal culture. Americans devour what we might otherwise fear to become. Sushi will make us corporate warriors. Combination Plate #3, smothered in mestizo gravy, will burn a hole in our hearts.

15 Latin America offers passion. Latin America has a life—I mean 15 *life*—big clouds, unambiguous themes, death, birth, faith, that the United States, for all its quality of life, seems without now. Latin America offers communal riches: an undistressed leisure, a kitchen table, even a full sorrow. Such is the solitude of America, such is the urgency of American need, Americans reach right past a fledgling, homegrown Hispanic-American culture for the real thing—the darker bottle of Mexican beer; the denser novel of a Latin American master.

For a long time, Hispanics in the United States withheld from the United States our Latin American gift. We denied the value of assimilation. But as our presence is judged less foreign in America, we will produce a more generous art, less timid, less parochial. Carlos Santana, Luis Valdez, Linda Ronstadt—Hispanic Americans do not have a "pure" Latin American art to offer. Expect bastard themes, expect ironies, comic conclusions. For we live on this side of the border, where Kraft manufactures bricks of "Mexican style" Velveeta, and where Jack in the Box serves "Fajita Pita."

*The flame-red Chevy floats a song down the Pan American Highway: From a rolled-down window, the grizzled voice of Willie Nelson rises in disembodied harmony with the voice of Julio Iglesias. Gabby Hayes and Cisco are thus resolved.*

Expect marriage. We will change America even as we will be changed. We will disappear with you into a new miscegenation.

Along the border, real conflicts remain. But the ancient tear separating Europe from itself—the Catholic Mediterranean from the Protestant north—may yet heal itself in the New World. For generations, Latin America has been the place—the bed—of a confluence of so many races and cultures that Protestant North America shuddered to imagine it.

20 Imagine it. 20

## Questions on Meaning

1. What symbols of America and of Latin America does Rodriguez provide? Describe them in terms of tangible or intangible, material or immaterial characteristics. What is Rodriguez's message in his choice of symbols?
2. Rodriguez notes that those who concern themselves with Hispanic-American culture tend to be "painters, musicians, writers" or "sons and daughters." What are the cultural concerns of these different groups?
3. According to Rodriguez, what is Hispanics' fame in the United States? Why? How does Rodriguez feel about that fame?

## Questions on Rhetorical Strategy and Style

1. Rodriguez offers a number of examples of pop culture (Hispanic-theme movies like "La Bamba") and reality (the U.S. Border Patrol trying to prevent Mexicans from coming over the border). Find other examples of how the essay compares and contrasts pop culture and reality in America today.
2. Rodriguez often uses the third-person "American" (as though he were an observer) in the same sentence with the first-person "we." What is the effect of this style? Locate two or three examples of this writing style and substitute "American" for "we" and then "we" for "American." What happens to the rhythm and meaning of these passages when you swap words?

## Writing Assignments

1. Rodriguez sees assimilation not as a Hispanic loss, but as an American gain. Choose an element of cultural assimilation—music, food, language, family, sexuality, art, literature—and write an essay describing the Hispanic influences you are now aware of. Compare the gains and losses you see with the cultural blending taking place. What are the forces pushing and resisting the assimilation?
2. Rodriguez notes that "Hispanics want to belong to America without betraying the past." Try to identify a time when you or someone you know has betrayed their past. You might have dropped an old family custom, stopped speaking your parent's native tongue, or tossed out those artifacts of your grandparents. Why

did you decide to take that action? How did you feel about it months or years later? What would you do if you had to make that decision again?

3. Rodriguez states that "America transforms into pleasure what America cannot avoid" and "Americans devour what we might otherwise fear." Identify cultural changes that you have experienced or see coming that you either would like to avoid or are apprehensive of. Talk to friends and relatives and compare your reactions to theirs. Write an essay in which you describe the various cultural forces involved, and then explain your perceptions and feelings.

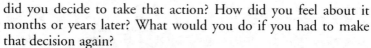

# THE REWARDS OF LIVING A SOLITARY LIFE


## May Sarton


*May Sarton (1912–1995) was born in Wondelgem, Belgium, and grew up in Cambridge, Massachusetts. Sarton trained at the Civic Repertory Theatre in New York City and taught at a number of schools. A poet, short story writer, and novelist, she published many poetry collections, more than twenty novels, and a memoir. Sarton's better-known books include* Faithful Are the Wounds *(1955),* Plant Dreaming Deep *(1968),* Kinds of Love *(1970),* Magnificent Spinster *(1985), and* Endgame: A Journal of the Seventy-Ninth Year *(1992). In this essay, Sarton argues that true solitude allows an individual to come to a full appreciation of his or her life experiences.*

1 The other day an acquaintance of mine, a gregarious and charming man, told me he had found himself unexpectedly alone in New York for an hour or two between appointments. He went to the Whitney and spent the "empty" time looking at things in solitary bliss. For him it proved to be a shock nearly as great as falling in love to discover that he could enjoy himself so much alone. 1

What had he been afraid of, I asked myself? That, suddenly alone, he would discover that he bored himself, or that there was, quite simply, no self there to meet? But having taken the plunge, he is now on the brink of adventure; he is about to be launched into his own inner space, space as immense, unexplored, and sometimes frightening as outer space to the astronaut. His every perception will come to him with a new freshness and, for a time, seem startingly original. For anyone who can see things for himself with a naked eye becomes, for a moment or two, something of a genius. With another human being present vision becomes double vision, inevitably. We are busy wondering, what does my companion see or think of this, and what do I think of it? The original impact gets lost, or diffused.

"Music I heard with you was more than music." Exactly. And therefore music *itself* can only be heard alone. Solitude is the salt of personhood. It brings out the authentic flavor of every experience.

"Alone one is never lonely: the spirit adventures, walking/In a quiet garden, in a cool house, abiding single there."

5 Loneliness is most acutely felt with other people, for with others, 5
even with a lover sometimes, we suffer from our differences of taste, temperament, mood. Human intercourse often demands that we soften the edge of perception, or withdraw at the very instant of personal truth for fear of hurting, or of being inappropriately present, which is to say naked, in a social situation. Alone we can afford to be wholly whatever we are, and to feel whatever we feel absolutely. That is a great luxury!

For me the most interesting thing about a solitary life, and mine has been that for the last twenty years, is that it becomes increasingly rewarding. When I can wake up and watch the sun rise over the ocean, as I do most days, and know that I have an entire day ahead, uninterrupted, in which to write a few pages, take a walk with my dog, lie down in the afternoon for a long think (why does one think better in a horizontal position?), read and listen to music, I am flooded with happiness.

I am lonely only when I am overtired, when I have worked too long without a break, when for the time being I feel empty and need filling up. And I am lonely sometimes when I come back home after a lecture trip, when I have seen a lot of people and talked a lot, and am full to the brim with experience that needs to be sorted out.

Then for a little while the house feels huge and empty, and I wonder where my self is hiding. It has to be recaptured slowly by watering the plants, perhaps, and looking again at each one as though it were a person, by feeding the two cats, by cooking a meal.

It takes a while, as I watch the surf blowing up in fountains at the end of the field, but the moment comes when the world falls away, and the self emerges again from the deep unconscious, bringing back all I have recently experienced to be explored and slowly understood, when I can converse again with my hidden powers, and so grow, and so be renewed, till death do us part.

## Questions on Meaning

1. What did Sarton's acquaintance discover from his couple of hours of "empty" time? Why was he so surprised? Why was Sarton *not* surprised?
2. Explain why Sarton contends that "alone one is never lonely" and "loneliness is most acutely felt with other people." Under what circumstances does she admit to being "lonely"?
3. What is the importance of "self" to one who chooses solitude, such as Sarton? Why did she wonder if her friend, alone in New York City, might discover he had "no self to meet"?

## Questions on Rhetorical Strategy and Style

1. How does Sarton compare and contrast the perceptions of a person who is alone to those of a person sharing an experience with another? What does she mean by the comment that "present vision becomes double vision"?
2. How does Sarton define "solitude"? What impact does she believe solitude has on experiences? Explain why you agree or disagree with her that solitude can be "a great luxury."
3. What examples does Sarton provide to show why her solitary life has been rewarding? Explain why these examples would or would not convince you to live alone.

## Writing Assignments

1. Describe an experience you have had when you enjoyed an extended period of time to yourself—such as weekend when a roommate was gone, or a solo camping trip. Did you choose not to seek the company of others? How do you think you would react if you had the opportunity to live truly alone, such as on an uninhabited island?
2. In many ways, it is *difficult* to be out of contact with other people today because of cellular telephones, the Internet, beepers, fax machines, answering machines, and other means of communications. Write an essay about the impact of omnipresent electronic communications on one's personal development. How does the ability to communicate with other people at all times from nearly everywhere in the world affect one's self-reliance? Explain why you do or do not like to be out of touch with your friends and family at different times. If you do like to disconnect, explain how you achieve it.

# THE KNIFE

## Richard Selzer

*Richard Selzer (1928– ) was born in Troy, New York and earned his M.D. from Albany Medical College. As a surgeon he has maintained a practice in New Haven, Connecticut, and has been a professor of surgery at Yale University School of Medicine. He has written a number of books about medicine and related subjects, beginning with* Mortal Lessons: Notes on the Art of Surgery *(1974). His essays on the issues doctors and surgeons face have been published in* Esquire *and a number of other books, including* Confessions of a Knife *(1979) and* Letters to a Young Doctor *(1982). Selzer is best known for looking at the human side of medicine, including the unpleasant realities we often do not want to think about. The essay "The Knife" was published in* Mortal Lessons. *It offers an interesting perspective on the work of surgeons.*

1 One holds the knife as one holds the bow of a cello or a tulip— 1
by the stem. Not palmed nor gripped nor grasped, but lightly, with the tips of the fingers. The knife is not for pressing. It is for drawing across the field of skin. Like a slender fish, it waits, at the ready, then, go! It darts, followed by a fine wake of red. The flesh parts, falling away to yellow globules of fat. Even now, after so many times I still marvel at its power—cold, gleaming, silent. More, I am still struck with a kind of dread that it is I in whose hand the blade travels, that my hand is its vehicle, that yet again this terrible steel-bellied thing and I have conspired for a most unnatural purpose, the laying open of the body of a human being.

A stillness settles in my heart and is carried to my hand. It is the quietude of resolve layered over fear. And it is this resolve that lowers us, my knife and me, deeper and deeper into the person beneath. It is an entry into the body that is nothing like a caress; still, it is among the gentlest of acts. Then stroke and stroke again, and we are joined by other instruments, hemostats and forceps, until the wound blooms with strange flowers whose looped handles fall to the sides in steely array.

There is sound, the tight click of clamps fixing teeth into severed blood vessels, the snuffle and gargle of the suction machine clearing the field of blood for the next stroke, the litany of monosyllables with which one prays his way down and in: *clamp, sponge, suture, tie, cut.* And there is color. The green of the cloth, the white of the sponges, the red and yellow of the body. Beneath the fat lies the fascia, the tough fibrous sheet encasing the muscles. It must be sliced and the red beef of the muscles separated. Now there are refractors to hold apart the wound. Hands move together, part, weave. We are fully engaged, like children absorbed in a game or the craftsmen of some place like Damascus.

Deeper still. The peritoneum, pink and gleaming and membranous, bulges into the wound. It is grasped with forceps, and opened. For the first time we can see into the cavity of the abdomen. Such a primitive place. One expects to find drawings of buffalo on the walls. The sense of trespassing is keener now, heightened by the world's light illuminating the organs, their secret colors revealed—maroon and salmon and yellow. The vista is sweetly vulnerable at this moment, a kind of welcoming. An arc of the liver shines high and on the right, like a dark sun. It laps over the pink sweep of the stomach, from whose lower border the gauzy omentum is draped, and through which veil one sees, sinuous, slow as just-fed snakes, the indolent coils of the intestine.

5 You turn aside to wash your gloves. It is a ritual cleansing. One enters this temple doubly washed. Here is man as microcosm, representing in all his parts the earth, perhaps the universe.

I must confess that the priestliness of my profession has even been impressed on me. In the beginning there are vows, taken with all solemnity. Then there is the endless harsh novitiate of training, much fatigue, much sacrifice. At last one emerges as celebrant, standing close to the truth lying curtained in the Ark of the body. Not surplice and cassock but mask and gown are your regalia. You hold no chalice, but a knife. There is no wine, no wafer. There are only the facts of blood and flesh.

And if the surgeon is like a poet, then the scars you have made on countless bodies are like verses into the fashioning of which you have poured your soul. I think that if years later I were to see the trace from an old incision of mine, I should know it at once, as one recognizes his pet expressions.

But mostly you are a traveler in a dangerous country, advancing into the moist and jungly cleft your hands have made. Eyes and ears are shuttered from the land you left behind; mind empties itself of all other thought. You are the root of groping fingers. It is a fine hour for the fingers, their sense of touch so enhanced. The blind must know this feeling. Oh, there is risk everywhere. One goes lightly. The spleen. No! No! Do not touch the spleen that lurks below the left leaf of the diaphragm, a manta ray in a coral cave, its bloody tongue protruding. One poke and it might rupture, exploding with sudden hemorrhage. The filmy omentum must not be torn, the intestine scraped or denuded. The hand finds the liver, palms it, fingers running along its sharp lower edge, admiring. Here are the twin mounds of the kidneys, the apron of the omentum hanging in front of the intestinal coils. One lifts it aside and the fingers dip among the loops, searching, mapping territory, establishing boundaries. Deeper still, and the womb is touched, then held like a small muscular bottle—the womb and its earlike appendages, the ovaries. How they do nestle in the cup of a man's hand, their power all dormant. They are frailty itself.

There is a hush in the room. Speech stops. The hands of the others, assistants and nurses, are still. Only the voice of the patient's respiration remains. It is the rhythm of a quiet sea, the sound of waiting. Then you speak, slowly, the terse entries of a Himalayan climber reporting back.

"The stomach is okay. Greater curvature clean. No sign of ulcer. Pylorus, duodenum fine. Now comes the gallbladder. No stones. Right kidney, left, all right. Liver . . . uh-oh."

Your speech lowers to a whisper, falters, stops for a long, long moment, then picks up again at the end of a sigh that comes through your mask like a last exhalation.

"Three big hard ones in the left lobe, one on the right. Metastatic deposits. Bad, bad. Where's the primary? Got to be coming from somewhere."

The arm shifts direction and the fingers drop lower and lower into the pelvis—the body impaled now upon the arm of the surgeon to the hilt of the elbow.

"Here it is."

The voice goes flat, all business now.

"Tumor in the sigmoid colon, wrapped all around it, pretty tight. We'll take out a sleeve of the bowel. No colostomy. Not that, anyway. But, God, there's a lot of it down there. Here, you take a feel."

You step back from the table, and lean into a sterile basin of water, resting on stiff arms, while the others locate the cancer. . . .

What is it, then, this thing, the knife, whose shape is virtually the same as it was three thousand years ago, but now with its head grown detachable? Before steel, it was bronze. Before bronze, stone then back into unremembered time. Did man invent it or did the knife precede him here, hidden under ages of vegetation and hoofprints, lying in wait to be discovered, picked up, used?

The scalpel is in two parts, the handle and the blade. Joined, it is six inches from tip to tip. At one end of the handle is a narrow notched prong upon which the blade is slid, then snapped into place. Without the blade, the handle has a blind, decapitated look. It is helpless as a trussed maniac. But slide on the blade, click it home, and the knife springs instantly to life. It is headed now, edgy, leaping to mount the fingers for the gallop to its feast.

Now is the moment from which you have turned aside, from which you have averted your gaze, yet toward which you have been hastened. Now the scalpel sings along the flesh again, its brute run unimpeded by germs or other frictions. It is a slick slide home, a barracuda spurt, a rip of embedded talon. One listens, and almost hears the whine—nasal, high, delivered through that gleaming metallic snout. The flesh splits with its own kind of moan. It is like the penetration of rape.

The breasts of women are cut off, arms and legs sliced to the bone to make ready for the saw, eyes freed from sockets, intestines lopped. The hand of the surgeon rebels. Tension boils through his pores, like sweat. The flesh of the patient retaliates with hemorrhage, and the blood chases the knife wherever it is withdrawn.

Within the belly a tumor squats, toadish, fungoid. A gray mother and her brood. The only thing it does not do is croak. It too is hacked from its bed as the carnivore knife lips the blood, turning in it in a kind of ecstasy of plenty, a gluttony after a long fast. It is just for this that the knife was created, tempered, heated, its violence beaten into paper-thin force. At last a little thread is passed into the wound and tied. The monstrous booming fury is stilled by a tiny thread. The tempest is silenced. The operation is over. On the table, the knife lies spent, on its side, the bloody meal smear-dried upon its flanks. The knife rests. And waits.

## Questions on Meaning

1. Since the goal of surgery is to help cure the body and enhance life, you might think the tone of an essay like this should be more positive and affirming. Yet it does not feel that way. Describe the essay's tone and explain why you think Selzer wrote it this way.
2. Explain what Selzer means with this metaphor for the interior of the abdomen: "Such a primitive place. One expects to find drawings of buffalo on the walls."
3. Why is there such a change in the operating room when the surgeon's hand reaches deep into the abdomen seeking the disease?

## Questions on Rhetorical Strategy and Style

1. Selzer uses a series of analogies to describe the surgeon: priest, poet, "traveler in a dangerous country." Explain how each helps clarify what he is saying about surgeons.
2. What do you make of the two-part structure of the essay, moving from a focus on the surgeon to a focus on the knife?
3. Is Selzer's style too flamboyant? Reread paragraphs 20 and 21. Does his figurative language and powerful imagery here enhance or detract from the reading? How?

## Writing Assignments

1. The essay reveals the enormous power of the surgeon and the utter dependence of the patient on his or her skill. Think of other professions that have similar power over people's welfare, in which the practitioner must be trusted completely. We trust the employees of the water company to ensure our water is free of bacteria, for example, and we trust our architects and contractors to build buildings that will not fall down upon us. You should be able to think of many such jobs and roles. Does your awareness of your implicit trust in such people make you feel more vulnerable? Write a brief essay exploring the concept that society depends on people in many such positions who hold power—for better or worse.
2. Selzer personifies the knife as a surgeon. As an exercise in writing style, write a brief narrative in which you decribe the process of something happening through the perspective of an inanimate object in the process. For example, your car driving to campus,

your fork feeding you, your bathroom plumbing giving you a shower. Be creative and have some fun as you write, as you personify the object and use its point of view.

# BEAUTY

## Susan Sontag

*Susan Sontag (1933-) was born in New York City and reared in Arizona and California. She attended the University of California at Berkeley, the University of Chicago (from which she graduated at age 18), received a graduate degree from Harvard University, and served as an instructor and writer-in-residence at several colleges. Accomplished as both a fiction and nonfiction writer, Sontag is best known for her social commentary, often focusing on trends in literature, art, and film. Her books include* Against Interpretation and Other Essays *(1966),* Death Kit *(1967),* Trip to Hanoi *(1968),* The Style of Radical Will *(1969),* On Photography *(1976),* Illness as a Metaphor *(1978),* AIDS and Its Metaphors *(1989),* The Volcano Lover *(1992), and* Alice in Bed *(1993). She also has written and directed four movies:* Duet for Cannibals *(1969),* Brother Carl *(1971),* Promised Lands *(1974), and* Unguided Tour *(1975). In this 1975 essay, Sontag argues that our society traps women into an endless preoccupation with outward appearance by associating beauty with femininity.*

1 For the Greeks, beauty was a virtue: a kind of excellence. Persons 1
then were assumed to be what we now have to call—lamely, enviously—whole persons. If it did occur to the Greeks to distinguish between a person's "inside" and "outside," they still expected that inner beauty would be matched by beauty of the other kind. The well-born young Athenians who gathered around Socrates found it quite paradoxical that their hero was so intelligent, so brave, so honorable, so seductive—and so ugly. One of Socrates' main pedagogical acts was to be ugly—and teach those innocent, no doubt splendid-looking disciples of his how full of paradoxes life really was.

---

Originally titled "A Woman's Beauty: Put Down or Power Source" by Susan Sontag. Published by Wylie, Aitken & Stone, Inc. 

They may have resisted Socrates' lesson. We do not. Several thousand years later, we are more wary of the enchantments of beauty. We not only split off—with the greatest facility—the "inside" (character, intellect) from the "outside" (looks); but we are actually surprised when someone who is beautiful is also intelligent, talented, good.

It was principally the influence of Christianity that deprived beauty of the central place it had in classical ideals of human excellence. By limiting excellence (*virtus* in Latin) to *moral* virtue only, Christianity set beauty adrift—as an alienated, arbitrary, superficial enchantment. And beauty has continued to lose prestige. For close to two centuries it has become a convention to attribute beauty to only one of the two sexes: the sex which, however Fair, is always Second. Associating beauty with women has put beauty even further on the defensive, morally.

A beautiful woman, we say in English. But a handsome man. "Handsome" is the masculine equivalent of—and refusal of—a compliment which has accumulated certain demeaning overtones, by being reserved for women only. That one can call a man "beautiful" in French and in Italian suggests that Catholic countries—unlike those countries shaped by the Protestant version of Christianity—still retain some vestiges of the pagan admiration for beauty. But the difference, if one exists, is of degree only. In every modern country that is Christian or post-Christian, women *are* the beautiful sex—to the detriment of the notion of beauty as well as of women.

5 To be called beautiful is thought to name something essential to women's character and concerns. (In contrast to men—whose essence is to be strong, or effective, or competent.) It does not take someone in the throes of advanced feminist awareness to perceive that the way women are taught to be involved with beauty encourages narcissism, reinforces dependence and immaturity. Everybody (women and men) knows that. For it is "everybody," a whole society, that has identified being feminine with caring about how one *looks.* (In contrast to being masculine—which is identified with caring about what one *is* and *does* and only secondarily, if at all, about how one looks.) Given these stereotypes, it is no wonder that beauty enjoys, at best, a rather mixed reputation.

It is not, of course, the desire to be beautiful that is wrong but the obligation to be—or to try. What is accepted by most women as a flattering idealization of their sex is a way of making women feel inferior to what they actually are—or normally grow to be. For the ideal of beauty is administered as a form of self-oppression. Women are taught to see their bodies in *parts,* and to evaluate each part separately.

Breasts, feet, hips, waistline, neck, eyes, nose, complexion, hair, and so on—each in turn is submitted to an anxious, fretful, often despairing scrutiny. Even if some pass muster, some will always be found wanting. Nothing less than perfection will do.

In men, good looks is a whole, something taken in at a glance. It does not need to be confirmed by giving measurements of different regions of the body, nobody encourages a man to dissect his appearance, feature by feature. As for perfection, that is considered trivial—almost unmanly. Indeed, in the ideally good-looking man a small imperfection or blemish is considered positively desirable. According to one movie critic (a woman) who is a declared Robert Redford fan, it is having that cluster of skin-colored moles on one cheek that saves Redford from being merely a "pretty face." Think of the depreciation of women—as well as of beauty—that is implied in that judgment.

"The privileges of beauty are immense," said Cocteau. To be sure, beauty is a form of power. And deservedly so. What is lamentable is that it is the only form of power that most women are encouraged to seek. This power is always conceived in relation to men; it is not the power to do but the power to attract. It is a power that negates itself. For this power is not one that can be chosen freely—at least, not by women—or renounced without social censure.

To preen, for a woman, can never be just a pleasure. It is also a duty. It is her work. If a woman does real work—and even if she has clambered up to a leading position in politics, law, medicine, business, or whatever—she is always under pressure to confess that she still works at being attractive. But in so far as she is keeping up as one of the Fair Sex, she brings under suspicion her very capacity to be objective, professional, authoritative, thoughtful. Damned if they do—women are. And damned if they don't.

10 One could hardly ask for more important evidence of the dangers of considering persons as split between what is "inside" and what is "outside" than that interminable half-comic half-tragic tale, the oppression of women. How easy it is to start off by defining women as caretakers of their surfaces, and then to disparage them (or find them adorable) for being "superficial." It is a crude trap, and it has worked for too long. But to get out of the trap requires that women get some critical distance from that excellence and privilege which is beauty, enough distance to see how much beauty itself has been abridged in order to prop up the mythology of the "feminine." There should be a way of saving beauty *from* women—and *for* them.

## Questions on Meaning

1. Why does Sontag say that beauty carries "demeaning overtones"? Was this always so throughout history?
2. Sontag points out that beauty is a form of power. Why does she feel that this power can work against women? How can beauty be detrimental to a woman in the workplace?
3. What does Sontag say that Socrates tried to teach his students about beauty, ugliness, and life's paradoxes? If Socrates' beauty was not physical, where did it lie?

## Questions on Rhetorical Strategy and Style

1. In explaining why beauty is a form of self-oppression for women, Sontag compares and contrasts how women and men are seen and see themselves. What major differences does she expose in terms of the quest for perfection?
2. Find where Sontag uses cause and effect to describe the impact of Christianity on perceptions of beauty. How does she compare the *virtue* of beauty of the ancient Greeks with the Christian view?

## Writing Assignments

1. How does Sontag relate the perceptions of beauty to women's character? How does this compare with perceptions associated with the term *masculine*?
2. What role does physical beauty play in your life? How much time and money do you spend on your appearance—clothes, makeup, hair styling, etc.? How does your interest in your appearance compare with your friends' interest in their appearance? What is your motivation (or lack thereof) for your attention (inattention) to your appearance?
3. When Sontag wrote this essay in 1975, feminists such as Sontag were alerting Americans to the stigmas and stereotypes in society that harmed women. How is the concept of "femininity" attached to perceptions of "beauty" today? Have things changed? How do advertising and the media affect women's ability to be seen as a "whole" person in the classical Greek sense of the word?
4. Choose a person you admire greatly—a parent, teacher, neighbor, friend, politician, or friend—and write an essay describing the elements that make him or her a "whole" person. Why are you

attracted to this person? Do you aspire to be like him or her? What characteristics of this person reflect his or her "inner beauty"?

# THE JACKET

## Gary Soto

*Gary Soto (1952– ) was born in Fresno, California. In addition to teaching at the University of California at Berkeley, Soto has written poetry, memoirs, essays, and children's fiction. His books, which often reflect his Mexican-American roots, include the poetry collections* The Elements of San Joaquin *(1977) and* Black Hair *(1985) and the memoirs* Living Up the Street *(1985),* Small Faces *(1986),* Lesser Evils *(1988), and* A Summer Life *(1990). Soto describes the sometimes overwhelming significance of clothing to adolescents in this essay from* Small Faces.

1 My clothes have failed me. I remember the green coat that I 1
wore in fifth and sixth grade when you either danced like a champ or pressed yourself against a greasy wall, bitter as a penny toward the happy couples.

When I needed a new jacket and my mother asked what kind I wanted, I described something like bikers wear: black leather and silver studs, with enough belts to hold down a small town. We were in the kitchen, steam on the windows from her cooking. She listened so long while stirring dinner that I thought she understood for sure the kind I wanted. The next day when I got home from school, I discovered draped on my bedpost a jacket the color of day-old guacamole. I threw my books on the bed and approached the jacket slowly, as if it were a stranger whose hand I had to shake. I touched the vinyl sleeve, the collar, and peeked at the mustard-colored lining.

From the kitchen mother yelled that my jacket was in the closet. I closed the door to her voice and pulled at the rack of clothes in the closet, hoping the jacket on the bedpost wasn't for me but my mean brother. No luck. I gave up. From my bed, I stared at the jacket. I wanted to cry because it was so ugly and so big that I knew I'd have to wear it a long time. I was a small kid, thin as a young tree, and it would be years before I'd have a new one. I stared at the jacket, like an enemy, thinking bad things before I took off my old jacket, whose sleeves climbed halfway to my elbow.

I put the big jacket on. I zipped it up and down several times and rolled the cuffs up so they didn't cover my hands. I put my hands in the pockets and flapped the jacket like a bird's wings. I stood in front of the mirror, full face, then profile, and then looked over my shoulder as if someone had called me. I sat on the bed, stood against the bed, and combed my hair to see what I would look like doing something natural. I looked ugly. I threw it on my brother's bed and looked at it for a long time before I slipped it on and went out to the backyard, smiling a "thank you" to my mom as I passed her in the kitchen. With my hands in my pockets I kicked a ball against the fence, and then climbed it to sit looking into the alley. I hurled orange peels at the mouth of an open garbage can, and when the peels were gone I watched the white puffs of my breath thin to nothing.

5 I jumped down, hands in my pockets, and in the backyard, on my 5
knees, I teased my dog, Brownie, by swooping my arms while making bird calls. He jumped at me and missed. He jumped again and again, until a tooth sunk deep, ripping an L-shaped tear on my left sleeve. I pushed Brownie away to study the tear as I would a cut on my arm. There was no blood, only a few loose pieces of fuzz. Damn dog, I thought, and pushed him away hard when he tried to bite again. I got up from my knees and went to my bedroom to sit with my jacket on my lap, with the lights out.

That was the first afternoon with my new jacket. The next day I wore it to sixth grade and got a D on a math quiz. During the morning recess Frankie T., the playground terrorist, pushed me to the ground and told me to stay there until recess was over. My best friend, Steve Negrete, ate an apple while looking at me, and the girls turned away to whisper on the monkey bars. The teachers were no help: they looked my way and talked about how foolish I looked in my new jacket. I saw their heads bob with laughter, their hands half covering their mouths.

Even though it was cold, I took off the jacket during lunch and played kickball in a thin shirt, my arms feeling like braille from goose bumps. But when I returned to class I slipped the jacket on and shivered until I was warm. I sat on my hands, heating them up, while my teeth chattered like a cup of crooked dice. Finally warm, I slid out of the jacket but put it back on a few minutes later when the fire bell rang. We paraded out into the yard where we, the sixth graders, walked past all the other grades to stand against the back fence. Everybody saw me. Although they didn't say out loud, "Man, that's ugly," I heard the buzz-buzz of gossip and even laughter that I knew was meant for me.

And so I went, in my guacamole-colored jacket. So embarrassed, so hurt, I couldn't even do my homework. I received C's on quizzes and forgot the state capitals and the rivers of South America, our friendly neighbor. Even the girls who had been friendly blew away like loose flowers to follow the boys in neat jackets.

I wore that thing for three years until the sleeves grew short and my forearms stuck out like the necks of turtles. All during that time no love came to me—no little dark girl in a Sunday dress she wore on Monday. At lunchtime I stayed with the ugly boys who leaned against the chainlink fence and looked around with propellers of grass spinning in our mouths. We saw girls walk by alone, saw couples, hand in hand, their heads like bookends pressing air together. We saw them and spun our propellers so fast our faces were blurs.

10 I blame that jacket for those bad years. I blame my mother for her bad taste and her cheap ways. It was a sad time for the heart. With a friend I spent my sixth-grade year in a tree in the alley, waiting for something good to happen to me in that jacket, which had become the ugly brother who tagged along wherever I went. And it was about that time that I began to grow. My chest puffed up with muscle and, strangely, a few more ribs. Even my hands, those fleshy hammers, showed bravely through the cuffs, the fingers already hardening for the coming fights. But that L-shaped rip on the left sleeve got bigger; bits of stuffing coughed out from its wound after a hard day of play. I finally Scotch-taped it closed, but in rain or cold weather the tape peeled off like a scab and more stuffing fell out until that sleeve shriveled into a palsied arm. That winter the elbows began to crack and whole chunks of green began to fall off. I showed the cracks to my mother, who always seemed to be at the stove with steamed-up glasses, and she said that there were children in Mexico who would love that jacket. I told her that this was America and yelled that Debbie, my sister, didn't have a jacket like mine. I ran outside, ready to cry, and climbed the tree by the alley to think bad thoughts and watch my breath puff white and disappear.

But whole pieces still casually flew off my jacket when I played hard, read quietly, or took vicious spelling tests at school. When it became so spotted that my brother began to call me "camouflage," I flung it over the fence into the alley. Later, however, I swiped the jacket off the ground and went inside to drape it across my lap and mope.

I was called to dinner: steam silvered my mother's glasses as she said grace; my brother and sister with their heads bowed made ugly faces at their glasses of powdered milk. I gagged too, but eagerly ate big rips of buttered tortilla that held scooped-up beans. Finished, I went outside with my jacket across my arm. It was a cold sky. The faces of clouds were piled up, hurting. I climbed the fence, jumping down with a grunt. I started up the alley and soon slipped into my jacket, that green ugly brother who breathed over my shoulder that day and ever since.

## Questions on Meaning

1. What is Soto able to predict about his life with his new jacket when he notices how large it is?
2. Why does Soto smile a "thank you" to his mother as he goes outside wearing his new jacket? What does this comment tell you about his lifestyle, his mother's intentions, and Soto's acceptance of them?
3. What are the various terms Soto uses to describe his jacket? What meaning is conveyed by them?

## Questions on Rhetorical Strategy and Style

1. How does Soto compare and contrast the jacket he desired with the jacket he received? What do these descriptions say about his self image—or the image he wanted to project?
2. Find where Soto uses a rhtetorical strategy of cause and effect to blame misfortune on his jacket. Explain why you feel he did or did not actually believe these examples of cause and effect.
3. Reread Soto's narrative and mark each of his similes and metaphors. Which of these writing tools are most effective in this essay?

## Writing Assignments

1. Describe an article of clothing that you have had that you disliked intensely. How did you acquire it? Why was it so onerous to you? How did it make you feel? Why did you have to wear it? What finally happened to rid you of it?
2. Write an essay on the role you feel clothes play in creating the whole person. As you write the essay, compare and contrast the attributes of people you know who are terribly clothes-conscious and those who appear to care less about what they wear. What role does a person's personality and self-assuredness play in how clothes look on him or her? How can really ugly clothes (like Soto's jacket) be cool or trendy because of their distastefulness?

# THE IMPORTANCE OF WORK

## Gloria Steinem

*Gloria Steinem (1934– ) was born in Toledo, Ohio, and after graduating from Smith College went on to further studies at the University of Delhi and the University of Calcutta. She began a career in political journalism with her column for* New York *magazine in the late 1960s. In 1971 she cofounded* Ms. *magazine and became its editor, a position she held until 1987. Steinem has been a key figure in the feminist movement and has worked with the National Women's Political Caucus and the Women's Action Alliance. She published her first collection of essays and columns,* Outrageous Acts and Everyday Rebellions, *in 1983, in which the following essay was published, followed by* Revolution from Within *(1992) and* Moving Beyond Words *(1994). "The Importance of Work" explores not only women's right to work but the larger meaningfulness of work for women.*

1 Toward the end of the 1970s, the *Wall Street Journal* devoted an 1
eight-part front-page series to "the working woman"—that is, the influx of women into the paid-labor force—as the greatest change in American life since the Industrial Revolution.

Many women readers greeted both the news and the definition with cynicism. After all, women have always worked. If all the productive work of human maintenance that women do in the home were valued at its replacement cost, the gross national product of the United States would go up by 26 percent. It's just that we are now more likely than ever before to leave our poorly rewarded, low-security, high-risk job of homemaking (though we're still trying to explain that it's a perfectly good one and that the problem is male society's refusal both to do it and to give it an economic value) for more secure, independent and better-paid jobs outside the home.

Obviously, the real work revolution won't come until all productive work is rewarded—including child rearing and other jobs done in the home—and men are integrated into so-called women's work as well as vice versa. But the radical change being touted by the *Journal* and other media is one part of that long integration process: the unprecedented flood of women into salaried jobs, that is, into the labor force as it has been male-defined and previously occupied by men. We are already more than 41 percent of it—the highest proportion in history. Given the fact that women also make up a whopping 69 percent of the "discouraged labor force" (that is, people who need jobs but don't get counted in the unemployment statistics because they've given up looking), plus an official female unemployment rate that is substantially higher than men's, it's clear that we could expand to become fully half of the national work force by 1990.

Faced with this determination of women to find a little independence and to be paid and honored for our work, experts have rushed to ask: "Why?" It's a question rarely directed at male workers. Their basic motivations of survival and personal satisfaction are taken for granted. Indeed, men are regarded as "odd" and therefore subjects for sociological study and journalistic reports only when they *don't* have work, even if they are rich and don't need jobs or are poor and can't find them. Nonetheless, pollsters and sociologists have gone to great expense to prove that women work outside the home because of dire financial need, or if we persist despite the presence of a wage-earning male, out of some desire to buy "little extras" for our families, or even out of good old-fashioned penis envy.

5 Job interviewers and even our own families may still ask salaried 5
women the big "Why?" If we have small children at home or are in some job regarded as "men's work," the incidence of such questions increases. Condescending or accusatory versions of "What's a nice girl like you doing in a place like this?" have not disappeared from the workplace.

How do we answer these assumptions that we are "working" out of some pressing or peculiar need? Do we feel okay about arguing that it's as natural for us to have salaried jobs as for our husbands whether or not we have young children at home? Can we enjoy strong career ambitions without worrying about being thought "unfeminine"? When we confront men's growing resentment of women competing in the work force (often in the form of such guilt-producing accusations as "You're taking men's jobs away" or "You're damaging your children"), do we simply state that a decent job is a basic human right for everybody?

I'm afraid the answer is often no. As individuals and as a movement, we tend to retreat into some version of a tactically questionable defense: "Womenworkbecausewehaveto." The phrase has become one word, one key on the typewriter—an economic form of the socially "feminine" stance of passivity and self-sacrifice. Under attack, we still tend to present ourselves as creatures of economic necessity and familial devotion. "Womenworkbecausewehaveto" has become the easiest thing to say.

Like most truisms, this one is easy to prove with statistics. Economic need *is* the most consistent work motive—for women as well as men. In 1976, for instance, 43 percent of all women in the paid-labor force were single, widowed, separated, or divorced, and working to support themselves and their dependents. An additional 21 percent were married to men who had earned less than ten thousand dollars in the previous year, the minimum then required to support a family of four. In fact, if you take men's pensions, stocks, real estate, and various forms of accumulated wealth into account, a good statistical case can be made that there are more women who "have" to work (that is, who have neither the accumulated wealth, nor husbands whose work or wealth can support them for the rest of their lives) than there are men with the same need. If we were going to ask one group "Do you really need this job?" we should ask men.

But the first weakness of the whole "have to work" defense is its deceptiveness. Anyone who has ever experienced dehumanized life on welfare or any other confidence-shaking dependency knows that a paid job may be preferable to the dole, even when the handout is coming from a family member. Yet the will and self-confidence to work on one's own can diminish as dependency and fear increase. That may explain why—contrary to the "have to" rationale—wives of men who earn less than three thousand dollars a year are actually *less* likely to be employed than wives whose husbands make ten thousand dollars a year or more.

10 Furthermore, the greatest proportion of employed wives is found 10 among families with a total household income of twenty-five to fifty thousand dollars a year. This is the statistical underpinning used by some sociologists to prove that women's work is mainly important for boosting families into the middle or upper middle class. Thus, women's incomes are largely used for buying "luxuries" and "little extras": a neat double-whammy that renders us secondary within our families, and makes our jobs expendable in hard times. We may even go along with this interpretation (at least, up to the point of getting fired so a male can have our job). It preserves a husbandly ego-need to be seen as the primary breadwinner, and still allows us a safe "feminine" excuse for working.

But there are often rewards that we're not confessing. As noted in *The Two-Career Couple,* by Francine and Douglas Hall: "Women who hold jobs by choice, even blue-collar routine jobs, are more satisfied with their lives than are the full-time housewives."

In addition to personal satisfaction, there is also society's need for all its members' talents. Suppose that jobs were given out on only a "have to work" basis to both women and men—one job per household. It would be unthinkable to lose the unique abilities of, for instance, Eleanor Holmes Norton, the distinguished chair of the Equal Employment Opportunity Commission. But would we then be forced to question the important work of her husband, Edward Norton, who is also a distinguished lawyer? Since men earn more than twice as much as women on the average, the wife in most households would be more likely to give up her job. Does that mean the nation could do as well without millions of its nurses, teachers, and secretaries? Or that the rare man who earns less than his wife should give up his job?

It was this kind of waste of human talents on a society-wide scale that traumatized millions of unemployed or underemployed Americans during the Depression. Then, a one-job-per-household rule seemed somewhat justified, yet the concept was used to displace women workers only, create intolerable dependencies, and waste female talent that the country needed. That Depression experience, plus the energy and example of women who were finally allowed to work during the manpower shortage created by World War II, led Congress to reinterpret the meaning of the country's full-employment goal in its Economic Act of 1946. Full employment was officially defined as "the employment of those who want to work, without regard to whether their employment is, by some definition, necessary. This goal applies equally to men and women." Since bad economic times are again creating a resentment of employed women—as well as creating more need for women to be employed—we need such a goal more than ever. Women are again being caught in a tragic double bind: We are required to be strong and then punished for our strength.

Clearly, anything less than government and popular commitment to this 1946 definition of full employment will leave the less powerful groups, whoever they may be, in danger. Almost as important as the financial penalty paid by the powerless is the suffering that comes from being shut out of paid and recognized work. Without it, we lose much of our self-respect and our ability to prove that we are alive by making some difference in the world. That's just as true for the suburban woman as it is for the unemployed steel worker.

But it won't be easy to give up the passive defense of "weworkbecausewehaveto."

When a woman who is struggling to support her children and grandchildren on welfare sees her neighbor working as a waitress, even though that neighbor's husband has a job, she may feel resentful; and the waitress (of course, not the waitress's husband) may feel guilty. Yet unless we establish the obligation to provide a job for everyone who is willing and able to work, that welfare woman may herself be penalized by policies that give out only one public-service job per household. She and her daughter will have to make a painful and divisive decision about which of them gets that precious job, and the whole household will have to survive on only one salary.

A job as a human right is a principle that applies to men as well as women. But women have more cause to fight for it. The phenomenon of the "working woman" has been held responsible for everything from an increase in male impotence (which turned out, incidentally, to be attributable to medication for high blood pressure) to the rising cost of steak (which was due to high energy costs and beef import restrictions, not women's refusal to prepare the cheaper, slower-cooking cuts). Unless we see a job as part of every citizen's right to autonomy and personal fulfillment, we will continue to be vulnerable to someone else's idea of what "need" is, and whose "need" counts the most.

In many ways, women who do not have to work for simple survival, but who choose to do so nonetheless, are on the frontier of asserting this right for all women. Those with well-to-do husbands are dangerously easy for us to resent and put down. It's easier still to resent women from families of inherited wealth, even though men generally control and benefit from that wealth. (There is no Rockefeller Sisters Fund, no J. P. Morgan & Daughters, and sons-in-law may be the ones who really sleep their way to power.) But to prevent a woman whose husband or father is wealthy from earning her own living, and from gaining the self-confidence that comes with that ability, is to keep her needful of that unearned power and less willing to disperse it. Moreover, it is to lose forever her unique talents.

Perhaps modern feminists have been guilty of a kind of reverse snobbism that keeps us from reaching out to the wives and daughters of wealthy men; yet it was exactly such women who refused the restrictions of class and financed the first wave of feminist revolution.

For most of us, however, "womenworkbecausewehaveto" is just true enough to be seductive as a personal defense.

If we use it without also staking out the larger human right to a job, however, we will never achieve that right. And we will always be subject to the false argument that independence for women is a luxury affordable only in good economic times. Alternatives to layoffs will not be explored, acceptable unemployment will always be used to frighten those with jobs into accepting low wages, and we will never remedy the real cost, both to families and to the country, of dependent women and a massive loss of talent.

Worst of all, we may never learn to find productive, honored work as a natural part of ourselves and as one of life's basic pleasures.

## Questions on Meaning

1. What's wrong with the explanation "Women work because we have to"? Why does Steinem say this explanation—even when true—is counterproductive for women?
2. Is there naturally a "right" to a job? Does the essay explicitly argue for this right, or simply assume that it exists?
3. Is Steinem arguing for some specific actions to be taken, such as some legislation or new policies for the workplace? If so, what specifically does she want as solutions for the present problem? If not, what exactly is she arguing for?

## Questions on Rhetorical Strategy and Style

1. What kinds of evidence does Steinem bring into the essay to strengthen her argument? Identify several examples of these in the essay.
2. Steinem uses the rhetorical strategy of comparison and contrast to explore similarities and differences in men and women working. Go through the essay and mark each such comparison. How does this strategy develop the key ideas of the essay?
3. Is Steinem writing only to women? When she uses the pronoun "we" apparently to refer to both women in general and the reader, does that help solidify her argument or alienate her male readers? Examine the "we" throughout the essay and comment on the effects of specific examples.

## Writing Assignments

1. Have society and the working world changed since 1983 when this was first printed? Do you still see the same resentment toward women working that Steinem describes? If so, how is it manifested today, when an even higher percentage of women are working and are working higher level jobs? If not, what has changed since that time to account for present differences?
2. Consider your own experience with work, regardless of whether you are a man or a woman. Have all the jobs you have held given you a sense of fulfillment? Imagine for a moment that you just won the lottery and never needed to work again. Would you? Why or why not? Is this kind of not working any different from not working because your spouse makes plenty of money? Explore

the difference in an essay in which you formulate your own thesis about the value of work.

3. Steinem cites one study that shows women who work by choice are more satisfied with their lives than full-time housewives, but she does not go on to argue or explain this in any detail. Think about the concept of satisfaction. Why are women who do not work less satisfied with their lives, since presumably they have more time to engage in a variety of fulfilling activities? What is it about work that provides an important sense of satisfaction for both men and women? Write an essay that presents your thoughts on this phenomenon.

# NOTES ON PUNCTUATION

## Lewis Thomas

*Lewis Thomas (1913–1994), a physician, scientist, educator, and literary figure of some repute, was born in Flushing, New York. Educated at Princeton (B.S.), Harvard Medical School (M.D.), and Yale (M.A.), Lewis established a career in medical research, education, and administration. He was dean of the School of Medicine at New York University and Yale University and director of the Sloan-Kettering Cancer Center in New York City. Throughout his career in medicine, Thomas published extensively. Although much of his writing appeared in specialized scientific journals, his love of language and his ability to communicate complex topics to uninformed readers enabled him to gain an appreciative lay audience. Thomas's recognition as a skilled and enjoyable essayist began in the mid-1970s, when a series of columns written for the venerable* New England Journal of Medicine *and collected in the book* Lives of a Cell, *won the National Book Award for Arts and Letters. Thomas assembled four additional collections of his essays, including* The Medusa and the Snail *(1979), from which this essay was taken. In this essay, Thomas's love of learning and good humor and optimism are evident, as they are in his scientific writing.*

1 There are no precise rules about punctuation (Fowler lays out some general advice (as best he can under the complex circumstances of English prose (he points out, for example, that we possess only four stops (the comma, the semicolon, the colon and the period (the question mark and exclamation point are not, strictly 1

speaking, stops; they are indicators of tone (oddly enough, the Greeks employed the semicolon for their question mark (it produces a strange sensation to read a Greek sentence which is a straightforward question: Why weepest thou; (instead of Why weepest thou? (and, of course, there are parentheses (which are surely a kind of punctuation making this whole matter much more complicated by having to count up the left-handed parentheses in order to be sure of closing with the right number (but if the parentheses were left out, with nothing to work with but the stops, we would have considerably more flexibility in the deploying of layers of meaning than if we tried to separate all the clauses by physical barriers (and in the latter case, while we might have more precision and exactitude for our meaning, we would lose the essential flavor of language, which is its wonderful ambiguity)))))))))))).

The commas are the most useful and usable of all the stops. It is highly important to put them in place as you go along. If you try to come back after doing a paragraph and stick them in the various spots that tempt you you will discover that they tend to swarm like minnows into all sorts of crevices whose existence you hadn't realized and before you know it the whole long sentence becomes immobilized and lashed up squirming in commas. Better to use them sparingly, and with affection, precisely when the need for each one arises, nicely, by itself.

I have grown fond of semicolons in recent years. The semicolon tells you that there is still some question about the preceding full sentence; something needs to be added; it reminds you sometimes of the Greek usage. It is almost always a greater pleasure to come across a semicolon than a period. The period tells you that that is that; if you didn't get all the meaning you wanted or expected, anyway you got all the writer intended to parcel out and now you have to move along. But with a semicolon there you get a pleasant little feeling of expectancy; there is more to come; read on; it will get clearer.

Colons are a lot less attractive, for several reasons: firstly, they give you the feeling of being rather ordered around, or at least having your nose pointed in a direction you might not be inclined to take if left to yourself, and, secondly, you suspect you're in for one of those sentences that will be labeling the points to be made: firstly, secondly and so forth, with the implication that you haven't sense enough to keep track of a sequence of notions without having them numbered. Also, many writers use this system loosely and incompletely, starting out with number one and number two as though counting off on their fingers but then going on and on without the succession of labels you've been led to expect, leaving you floundering about searching for the ninethly or seventeenthly that ought to be there but isn't.

Exclamation points are the most irritating of all. Look! they say, look at what I just said! How amazing is my thought! It is like being forced to watch someone else's small child jumping up and down crazily in the center of the living room shouting to attract attention. If a sentence really has something of importance to say, something quite remarkable, it doesn't need a mark to point it out. And if it is really, after all, a banal sentence needing more zing, the exclamation point simply emphasizes its banality!

Quotation marks should be used honestly and sparingly, when there is a genuine quotation at hand, and it is necessary to be very rigorous about the words enclosed by the marks. If something is to be quoted, the *exact* words must be used. If part of it must be left out because of space limitations, it is good manners to insert three dots to indicate the omission, but it is unethical to do this if it means connecting two thoughts which the original author did not intend to have tied together. Above all, quotation marks should not be used for ideas that you'd like to disown, things in the air so to speak. Nor should they be put in place around clichés; if you want to use a cliché you must take full responsibility for it yourself and not try to fob it off on anon., or on society. The most objectionable misuse of quotation marks, but one which illustrates the dangers of misuse in ordinary prose, is seen in advertising, especially in advertisements for small restaurants, for example "just around the corner," or "a good place to eat." No single, identifiable, citable person ever really said, for the record, "just around the corner," much less "a good place to eat," least likely of all for restaurants of the type that use this type of prose.

The dash is a handy device, informal and essentially playful, telling you that you're about to take off on a different tack but still in some way connected with the present course—only you have to remember that the dash is there, and either put a second dash at the end of the notion to let the reader know that he's back on course, or else end the sentence, as here, with a period.

The greatest danger in punctuation is for poetry. Here it is necessary to be as economical and parsimonious with commas and periods as with the words themselves, and any marks that seem to carry their own subtle meanings, like dashes and little rows of periods, even semicolons and question marks, should be left out altogether rather than inserted to clog up the thing with ambiguity. A single exclamation point in a poem, no matter what else the poem has to say, is enough to destroy the whole work.

The things I like best in T. S. Eliot's poetry, especially in the *Four Quartets,* are the semicolons. You cannot hear them, but they are there, laying out the connections between the images and the ideas. Sometimes you get a glimpse of a semicolon coming, a few lines farther on, and it is like climbing a steep path through woods and seeing a wooden bench just at a bend in the road ahead, a place where you can expect to sit for a moment, catching your breath.

Commas can't do this sort of thing; they can only tell you how the different parts of a complicated thought are to be fitted together, but you can't sit, not even take a breath, just because of a comma,

## Questions on Meaning

1. On the surface, Thomas's opening sentence contradicts what we have been taught about punctuation. Do you agree? List some rules of punctuation that you have learned. What is your feeling about the rigidity of these rules after reading this essay?
2. Thomas states that commas must be "put . . . in place as you go along." How does he illustrate this point?

## Questions on Rhetorical Strategy and Style

1. Thomas uses offhand humor to make serious comments about punctuation. "And if it is, really, after all," he writes, "a banal sentence needing more zing, the exclamation point simply emphasizes its banality!" Underline similar comments on other punctuation marks.
2. Reflecting his scientific training, Thomas uses the writing strategy of classification and division through the essay. Outline his presentation as he moves from his overview in the first paragraph through his detailed discussions in subsequent paragraphs. Do you feel his presentation is orderly? How else might he have outlined the essay?
3. Thomas provides examples of good and bad punctuation usage throughout the essay, often humorously. Do you agree with his points about these examples? Choose three examples of his punctuation usage that you question and explain why you disagree with Thomas. Show how you would have punctuated the sentence(s), passage(s), or paragraph(s).
4. Thomas's lighthearted tone and "playful" adjectives can be disarming. Do you think he would have made his points about punctuation more effectively if he had been less casual? Rewrite paragraph 7 as a serious commentary on the dash, and then compare it to Thomas's paragraph. What do you feel about his style now?

## Writing Assignments

1. Evaluate the punctuation in something you have written. Did you think much about punctuation when you were writing? Should punctuation marks play a visible role in writing, or should they sit quietly in the background? Are they an embellishment or a

tool? Locate instances where you used punctuation ineffectively and places where punctuation enhanced your writing. Describe the major weaknesses and strengths in your use of punctuation.

2. Punctuation is applied differently in different writing styles. Select two very different types of writing—such as in a magazine ad and in an academic journal—and compare/contrast the use of punctuation. How has the use of punctuation contributed to the effectiveness of the written material?

# THE PLACE WHERE I WAS BORN

## Alice Walker

*Alice Walker (1944– ) was born in Georgia to sharecropper parents. She attended Spelman College and Sarah Lawrence College and was active in the civil rights movement of the 1960s. Publishing her first novel,* The Third Life of Grange Copeland, *at the age of 26, she has been a prolific writer since. In all, she has published five novels, two short story collections, two collections of essays, and several books of poems. Her novel* The Color Purple *(1982) is perhaps her best known, having won the American Book Award, the Pulitzer Prize, and the Candace Award of the National Coalition of 100 Black Women. The novel was also made into a prize-winning film by director Steven Spielberg. Walker's topics run the gamut of human experience and include some harsh realities such as incest and racial violence as well as relationships within families and society. In the following essay, first published in the June, 1991* Essence, *Walker compares her present home to her childhood home and reveals something larger about the meaning of place.*

1 I am a displaced person. I sit here on a swing on the deck of my 1
house in northern California admiring how the fog has turned the valley below into a lake. For hours nothing will be visible below me except this large expanse of vapor; then slowly, as the sun rises and gains in intensity, the fog will start to curl up and begin its slow rolling drift toward the ocean. People here call it the dragon; and, indeed, a dragon is what it looks like, puffing and coiling, winged, flaring and in places thin and discreet, as it races before the sun, back to its ocean

---

From *Her Blue Body,* in Essence, June 1991, pp. 58–59. 

coast den. Mornings I sit here in awe and great peace. The mountains across the valley come and go in the mist; the redwoods and firs, oaks and giant bays appear as clumpish spires, enigmatic shapes of green, like the stone forests one sees in Chinese paintings of Guilin.

It is incredibly beautiful where I live. Not fancy at all, or exclusive. But from where I sit on my deck I can look down on the backs of hawks, and the wide, satiny wings of turkey vultures glistening in the sun become my present connection to ancient Egyptian Africa. The pond is so still below me that the trees reflected in it seem, from this distance, to be painted in its depths.

All this—the beauty, the quiet, the cleanliness, the peace—is what I love. I realize how lucky I am to have found it here. And yet, there are days when my view of the mountains and redwoods makes me nostalgic for small rounded hills easily walked over, and for the look of big-leaf poplar and the scent of pine.

I am nostalgic for the land of my birth, the land I left forever when I was 13—moving first to the town of Eatonton, Georgia, and then, at 17, to the city of Atlanta.

5 I cried one day as I talked to a friend about a tree I loved as a child. 5
A tree that had sheltered my father on his long cold walk to school each morning: It was midway between his house and the school and because there was a large cavity in its trunk, a fire could be made inside it. During my childhood, in a tiny, overcrowded house in a tiny dell below it, I looked up at it frequently and felt reassured by its age, its generosity despite its years of brutalization (the fires, I knew, had to hurt), and its tall, old-growth pine nobility. When it was struck by lightning and killed, and then was cut down and made into firewood, I grieved as if it had been a person. Secretly. Because who among the members of my family would not have laughed at my grief?

I have felt entirely fortunate to have had this companion, and even today remember it with gratitude. But why the tears? my friend wanted to know. And it suddenly dawned on me that perhaps it *was* sad that it was a tree and not a member of my family to whom I was so emotionally close.

As a child I assumed I would always have the middle Georgia landscape to live in, as Br'er Rabbit, a native also, and relative, had his brier patch. It was not to be. The pain of racist oppression, and its consequence, economic impoverishment, drove me to the four corners of the earth in search of justice and peace, and work that affirmed my whole being. I have come to rest here, weary from travel, on a deck—not a southern front porch—overlooking another world.

I am content; and yet, I wonder what my life would have been like if I had been able to stay home.

I remember early morning fogs in Georgia, not so dramatic as California ones, but magical too because out of the southern fog of memory tramps my dark father, smiling and large, glowing with rootedness, and talking of hound dogs, biscuits and coons. And my equally rooted mother bustles around the corner of our house preparing to start a wash, the fire under the black wash pot extending a circle of warmth in which I, a grave-eyed child, stand. There is my sister Ruth, beautiful to me and dressed elegantly for high school In gray felt skirt and rhinestone brooch, hurrying up the road to catch the yellow school bus which glows like a large glowworm in the early morning fog.

## Questions on Meaning

1. Why does Walker say she left Georgia? Why does she use one brief paragraph to explain her reasons for leaving?
2. Walker describes both her parents as "rooted" in Georgia. Is Walker herself rooted in some respect? Speculate about differences between her and her parents that led to her leaving and their apparent staying.
3. What do you make of the story of the large tree in the middle of the essay? How does this description fit in with the rest of the essay? Walker comments that she was emotionally closer to the tree than to members of her family—why do you think that was so?

## Questions on Rhetorical Strategy and Style

1. Walker begins the essay with a description of the fog near her northern California home and closes it with a description of the fog near her childhood home in Georgia. What is the effect of this image on your reading experience? Reread these fog passages and analyze the mood and meaning that emerge from them.
2. Walker uses the rhetorical device of comparison and contrast in describing her present home and her childhood home. In addition to the fog, what aspects of each home are compared? What meaning emerges from this comparison? What is the effect of an incomplete comparison, such as when Walker comments that Georgia held the "pain of racist oppression" but does not explicitly state what she has experienced in California; what are you meant to conclude?

## Writing Assignments

1. Remember a place that was special to you in your childhood. How clearly and specifically can you describe it now? Write a paragraph or two of physical description, avoiding the temptation to explain what it means to you but allowing the images to reveal this meaning through the description itself. How well do you feel you can capture the spirit of the place? Why is it that even apparently simple physical descriptions require such careful attention to writing?
2. An implied theme in Walker's essay is that place affects people's behavior. Consider your own experience. Choose two different

places you have lived, perhaps your current college setting and the place where you grew up, and think about differences in people in those two places. Write an essay in which you analyze these differences while comparing and contrasting those different groups of people.

# ONCE MORE TO THE LAKE

## E.B. White

*E.B. White (1899–1985) was born in Mt. Vernon, New York, and attended Cornell University. He was a career writer of newspaper pieces and essays for the magazines* The New Yorker *and* Harper's. *His three children's books have become classics:* Stuart Little, Charlotte's Web, *and* The Trumpet of the Swan. *As an accomplished stylist, he revised the grammar book by Strunk that he had himself used as a student—which is now known universally as Strunk and White's* Elements of Style. *The essay "Once More to the Lake" was originally published in White's* One Man's Meat *in 1941. It examines what seems to be White's idyllic childhood of summers at a lake in Maine, revisited decades later by an older White who at first seems nostalgic. The essay gives us much more, however, than wistful memories of a happy time in a beautiful place.*

1 One summer, along about 1904, my father rented a camp on 1 a lake in Maine and took us all there for the month of August. We all got ringworm from some kittens and had to rub Pond's Extract on our arms and legs night and morning, and my father rolled over in a canoe with all his clothes on; but outside of that the vacation was a success and from then on none of us ever thought there was any place in the world like that lake in Maine. We returned summer after summer—always on August 1st for one month. I have since become a salt-water man, but sometimes in summer there are days when the restlessness of the tides and the fearful cold of the sea water and the incessant wind which blows across the afternoon and into the evening make me wish for the placidity of a lake in the woods. A few weeks ago this feeling got so strong I bought myself a couple of

bass hooks and a spinner and returned to the lake where we used to go, for a week's fishing and to revisit old haunts.

I took along my son, who had never had any fresh water up his nose and who had seen lily pads only from train windows. On the journey over to the lake I began to wonder what it would be like. I wondered how time would have marred this unique, this holy spot—the coves and streams, the hills that the sun set behind, the camps and the paths behind the camps. I was sure the tarred road would have found it out and I wondered in what other ways it would be desolated. It is strange how much you can remember about places like that once you allow your mind to return into the grooves which lead back. You remember one thing, and that suddenly reminds you of another thing. I guess I remembered clearest of all the early mornings, when the lake was cool and motionless, remembered how the bedroom smelled of the lumber it was made of and of the wet woods whose scent entered through the screen. The partitions in the camp were thin and did not extend clear to the top of the rooms, and as I was always the first up I would dress softly so as not to wake the others, and sneak out into the sweet outdoors and start out in the canoe, keeping close along the shore in the long shadows of the pines. I remembered being very careful never to rub my paddle against the gunwale for fear of disturbing the stillness of the cathedral.

The lake had never been what you would call a wild lake. There were cottages sprinkled around the shores, and it was in farming country although the shores of the lake were quite heavily wooded. Some of the cottages were owned by nearby farmers, and you would live at the shore and eat your meals at the farmhouse. That's what our family did. But although it wasn't wild, it was a fairly large and undisturbed lake and there were places in it which, to a child at least, seemed infinitely remote and primeval.

I was right about the tar: it led to within half a mile of the shore. But when I got back there, with my boy, and we settled into a camp near a farmhouse and into the kind of summertime I had known, I could tell that it was going to be pretty much the same as it had been before I knew it, lying in bed the first morning, smelling the bedroom, and hearing the boy sneak quietly out and go off along the shore in a boat. I began to sustain the illusion that he was I, and therefore, by simple transposition, that I was my father. This sensation persisted, kept cropping up all the time we were there. It was not an entirely new feeling, but in this setting it grew much stronger. I seemed to be living a dual existence. I would be in the middle of some simple act, I would be picking up a bait box or laying down a table fork, or I would be saying something, and suddenly it would be not I but my father who was saying the words or making the gesture. It gave me a creepy sensation.

5 We went fishing the first morning. I felt the same damp moss covering the worms in the bait can, and saw the dragonfly alight on the tip of my rod as it hovered a few inches from the surface of the water. It was the arrival of this fly that convinced me beyond any doubt that everything was as it always had been, that the years were a mirage and there had been no years. The small waves were the same, chucking the rowboat under the chin as we fished at anchor, and the boat was the same boat, the same color green and the ribs broken in the same places, and under the floor-boards the same freshwater leavings and débris—the dead helgramite, the wisps of moss, the rusty discarded fishhook, the dried blood from yesterday's catch. We stared silently at the tips of our rods, at the dragonflies that came and went. I lowered the tip of mine into the water, tentatively, pensively dislodging the fly, which darted two feet away, poised, darted two feet back, and came to rest again a little farther up the rod. There had been no years between the ducking of this dragonfly and the other one—the one that was part of memory. I looked at the boy, who was silently watching his fly, and it was my hands that held his rod, my eyes watching. I felt dizzy and didn't know which rod I was at the end of.

We caught two bass, hauling them in briskly as though they were mackerel, pulling them over the side of the boat in a businesslike manner without any landing net, and stunning them with a blow on the back of the head. When we got back for a swim before lunch, the lake was exactly where we had left it, the same number of inches from the dock, and there was only the merest suggestion of a breeze. This seemed an utterly enchanted sea, this lake you could leave to its own devices for a few hours and come back to, and find that it had not stirred, this constant and trustworthy body of water. In the shallows, the dark, water-soaked sticks and twigs, smooth and old, were undulating in clusters on the bottom against the clean ribbed sand, and the track of the mussel was plain. A school of minnows swam by, each minnow with its small individual shadow, doubling the attendance, so clear and sharp in the sunlight. Some of the other campers were in swimming, along the shore, one of them with a cake of soap, and the water felt thin and clear and unsubstantial. Over the years there had been this person with the cake of soap, this cultist, and here he was. There had been no years.

Up to the farmhouse to dinner through the teeming, dusty field, the road under our sneakers was only a two-track road. The middle track was missing, the one with the marks of the hooves and the splotches of dried, flaky manure. There had always been three tracks to choose from in choosing which track to walk in; now the choice was narrowed down to two. For a moment I missed terribly the middle alternative. But the way led past the tennis court, and something about the way it lay there in the sun reassured me; the tape had loosened along the backline, the alleys were green with plantains and other weeds, and the net (installed in June and removed in September) sagged in the dry noon, and the whole place steamed with midday heat and hunger and emptiness. There was a choice of pie for dessert, and one was blueberry and one was apple, and the waitresses were the same country girls, there having been no passage of time, only the illusion of it as in a dropped curtain—the waitresses were still fifteen; their hair had been washed, that was the only difference—they had been to the movies and seen the pretty girls with the clean hair.

Summertime, oh summertime, pattern of life indelible, the fadeproof lake, the woods unshatterable, the pasture with the sweetfern and the juniper forever and ever, summer without end; this was the background, and the life along the shore was the design, the cottages with their innocent and tranquil design, their tiny docks with the flagpole and the American flag floating against the white clouds in the blue sky, the little paths over the roots of the trees leading from camp to camp and the paths leading back to the outhouses and the can of lime for sprinkling, and at the souvenir counters at the store the miniature birch-bark canoes and the post cards that showed things looking a little better than they looked. This was the American family at play, escaping the city heat, wondering whether the newcomers in the camp at the head of the cove were "common" or "nice," wondering whether it was true that the people who drove up for Sunday dinner at the farmhouse were turned away because there wasn't enough chicken.

It seemed to me, as I kept remembering all this, that those times and those summers had been infinitely precious and worth saving.

There had been jollity and peace and goodness. The arriving (at the beginning of August) had been so big a business in itself, at the railway station the farm wagon drawn up, the first smell of the pine-laden air, the first glimpse of the smiling farmer, and the great importance of the trunks and your father's enormous authority in such matters, and the feel of the wagon under you for the long ten-mile haul, and at the top of the last long hill catching the first view of the lake after eleven months of not seeing this cherished body of water. The shouts and cries of the other campers when they saw you, and the trunks to be unpacked, to give up their rich burden. (Arriving was less exciting nowadays, when you sneaked up in your car and parked it under a tree near the camp and took out the bags and in five minutes it was all over, no fuss, no loud wonderful fuss about trunks.)

10 Peace and goodness and jollity. The only thing that was wrong now, really, was the sound of the place, an unfamiliar nervous sound of the outboard motors. This was the note that jarred, the one thing that would sometimes break the illusion and set the years moving. In those other summertimes all motors were inboard; and when they were at a little distance, the noise they made was a sedative, an ingredient of summer sleep. They were one-cylinder and two-cylinder engines, and some were make-and-break and some were jump-spark, but they all made a sleepy sound across the lake. The one-lungers throbbed and fluttered, and the twin-cylinder ones purred and purred, and that was a quiet sound too. But now the campers all had outboards. In the daytime, in the hot mornings, these motors made a petulant, irritable sound; at night, in the still evening when the afterglow lit the water, they whined about one's ears like mosquitoes. My boy loved our rented outboard, and his great desire was to achieve singlehanded mastery over it, and authority, and he soon learned the trick of choking it a little (but not too much), and the adjustment of the needle valve. Watching him I would remember the things you could do with the old one-cylinder engine with the heavy flywheel, how you could have it eating out of your hand if you got really close to it spiritually. Motor boats in those days didn't have clutches, and you would make a landing by shutting off the motor at the proper time and coasting in with a dead rudder. But there was a way of reversing them, if you learned the trick, by cutting the switch and putting it on again exactly on the final dying revolution of the flywheel, so that it would kick back against compression and begin reversing. Approaching a

dock in a strong following breeze, it was difficult to slow up sufficiently by the ordinary coasting method, and if a boy felt he had complete mastery over his motor, he was tempted to keep it running beyond its time and then reverse it a few feet from the dock. It took a cool nerve, because if you threw the switch a twentieth of a second too soon you would catch the flywheel when it still had speed enough to go up past center, and the boat would leap ahead, charging bull-fashion at the dock.

We had a good week at the camp. The bass were biting well and the sun shone endlessly, day after day. We would be tired at night and lie down in the accumulated heat of the little bedrooms after the long hot day and the breeze would stir almost imperceptibly outside and the smell of the swamp drift in through the rusty screens. Sleep would come easily and in the morning the red squirrel would be on the roof, tapping out his gay routine. I kept remembering everything, lying in bed in the mornings—the small steamboat that had a long rounded stern like the lip of a Ubangi, and how quietly she ran on the moonlight sails, when the older boys played their mandolins and the girls sang and we ate doughnuts dipped in sugar, and how sweet the music was on the water in the shining night, and what it had felt like to think about girls then. After breakfast we would go up to the store and the things were in the same place—the minnows in a bottle, the plugs and spinners disarranged and pawed over by the youngsters from the boys' camp, the fig newtons and the Beeman's gum. Outside, the road was tarred and cars stood in front of the store. Inside, all was just as it had always been, except there was more Coca-Cola and not so much Moxie and root beer and birch beer and sarsaparilla. We would walk out with a bottle of pop apiece and sometimes the pop would backfire up our noses and hurt. We explored the streams, quietly, where the turtles slid off the sunny logs and dug their way into the soft bottom; and we lay on the town wharf and fed worms to the tame bass. Everywhere we went I had trouble making out which was I, the one walking at my side, the one walking in my pants.

One afternoon while we were there at that lake a thunderstorm came up. It was like the revival of an old melodrama that I had seen long ago with childish awe. The second-act climax of the drama of the electrical disturbance over a lake in America had not changed in any important respect. This was the big scene, still the big scene. The whole thing was so familiar, the first feeling of oppression and heat and a general air around camp of not wanting to go very far away. In midafternoon (it was all the same) a curious darkening of the sky, and a lull in everything that had made life tick; and then the way the boats suddenly swung the other way at their moorings with the coming of a breeze out of the new quarter, and the premonitory rumble. Then the kettle drum, then the snare, then the bass drum and cymbals, then crackling light against the dark, and the gods grinning and licking their chops in the hills. Afterward the calm, the rain steadily rustling in the calm lake, the return of light and hope and spirits, and the campers running out in joy and relief to go swimming in the rain, their bright cries perpetuating the deathless joke about how they were getting simply drenched, and the children screaming with delight at the new sensation of bathing in the rain, and the joke about getting drenched linking the generations in a strong indestructible chain. And the comedian who waded in carrying an umbrella.

When the others went swimming my son said he was going in too. He pulled his dripping trunks from the line where they had hung all through the shower, and wrung them out. Languidly, and with no thought of going in, I watched him, his hard little body, skinny and bare, saw him wince slightly as he pulled up around his vitals the small, soggy, icy garment. As he buckled the swollen belt suddenly my groin felt the chill of death.

## Questions on Meaning

1. What was your first impression when you reached the abrupt shift in tone in the essay's conclusion, the "chill of death"? Had you sensed anything like that coming? What effect does that dramatic ending have on the rather upbeat essay preceding it?
2. Although the narrator emphasizes throughout the essay that there has been no change—"There had been no years"—he does still describe things that have changed, such as the missing third track in the road and the sound of the outboard engines. Are such changes merely incidental details or signs of some larger, more significant change? Explain your answer.
3. White refers to his own father in the opening and again in reference to past arrivals carrying trunks from the railway, but White never actually says whether his father has died or is still alive. Does he need to say it, or can we safely assume the reality based on things White does not say? How does his increasing identification with his father throughout the essay help us understand his sudden thought of death at the end?

## Questions on Rhetorical Strategy and Style

1. One of White's great strengths as a writer is his imagery: the clear concrete moments of experience we experience with our senses. Choose one passage in the essay, such as the experience of fishing with his son, and reread it carefully, noting how he vividly builds the scene through descriptions of even tiny details. How does this use of imagery contribute to the whole reading experience and ultimately also to the ending theme?
2. Note that until the end of the essay White does not describe his own son's name, age, or appearance, even though the son is clearly a significant part of the experience. (Only in the last sentence do we learn anything about him—and then, only that he is skinny and little.) Could this omission of detail be an essential part of the essay's successful unfolding? Explain your answer.
3. In this essay White's primary rhetorical strategy is narration, or story telling. Indeed, in many ways this reads more like a short story than an essay. Think about typical differences between fiction and essays and about how the two genres might almost overlap. Ultimately, would you argue this is an essay rather than a piece of fiction? Why, or why not? Does it matter whether the "I" telling the story is White himself or a fictional character speaking?

## Writing Assignments

1. The essay is in part about memory. Take a few minutes to remember a place from your own childhood, somewhere you have not been in more than ten years. Draw a map of the place, as White did when he wrote *Charlotte's Web.* Close your eyes and try to visualize details, including sounds and smells. Can you make it feel real? How do you think it would feel if you were to return to it now?
2. Another theme present in the essay is the power of imagination, as White at different moments imagines himself as both his father and his son. As he comments, the experience can be dizzying. Try to put yourself in the mind of one of your own parents or guardians, thinking of you yourself from the point of view of the other. Is this difficult to do? Imagine being the other watching you interacting with a friend. Write a few paragraphs on what this experience feels like.
3. White also uses the rhetorical strategy of description to let us see how he feels about the lake setting. Think of a physical place in your own life that has meant much to you. Using description, write an essay exploring the meaning of that place.

# HATE RADIO

## Patricia J. Williams

*Patricia Williams (1951– ) was born in Boston, Massachusetts and educated amongst the privileged students of Wellesley and Harvard Law School. She has written articles for newspapers such as the* Boston Globe, *the* Christian Science Monitor, *and the* Washington Post*; as well as for magazines such as* Ms., The Nation, *and the* New Yorker. *She has written two books on race issues:* The Alchemy of Race and Rights *(1991) and* The Rooster's Egg: On the Persistence of Prejudice *(1995). She has taught at Golden Gate University, the City University of New York, the University of Wisconsin, and presently teaches at Columbia University. In this essay first published in* Ms. *in 1994, Williams describes an unattractive aspect of the post-modern environment, the rise of radio programming that uses extremist views involving racism and sexism as "entertainment."*

1 Three years ago I stood at my sink, washing the dishes and listening to the radio. I was tuned to rock and roll so I could avoid thinking about the big news from the day before—George Bush had just nominated Clarence Thomas to replace Thurgood Marshall on the Supreme Court. I was squeezing a dot of lemon Joy into each of the wineglasses when I realized that two smoothly radio-cultured voices, a man's and a woman's, had replaced the music. 1

"I think it's a stroke of genius on the president's part," said the female voice.

"Yeah," said the male voice. "Then those blacks, those African Americans, those Negroes—hey 'Negro' is good enough for Thurgood Marshall—whatever, they can't make up their minds [what] they want to be called. I'm gonna call them Blafricans. Black Africans. Yeah, I like it. Blafricans. Then they can get all upset because now the president appointed a Blafrican."

'Yeah, well, that's the way those liberals think. It's just crazy."

"And then after they turn down his nomination the president can say he tried to please 'em, and then he can appoint someone with some intelligence."

Back then, this conversation seemed so horrendously unusual, so singularly hateful, that I picked up a pencil and wrote it down. I was certain that a firestorm of protest was going to engulf the station and purge those foul radio mouths with the good clean soap of social outrage.

I am so naive. When I finally turned on the radio and rolled my dial to where everyone else had been tuned while I was busy watching Cosby reruns, it took me a while to understand that there's a firestorm all right, but not of protest. In the two and a half years since Thomas has assumed his post on the Supreme Court, the underlying assumptions of the conversation I heard as uniquely outrageous have become commonplace, popularly expressed, and louder in volume. I hear the style of that snide polemicism everywhere, among acquaintances, on the street, on television in toned-down versions. It is a crude demagoguery that makes me heartsick. I feel more and more surrounded by that point of view, the assumptions of being without intelligence, the coded epithets, the "Blafrican"-like stand-ins for "nigger," the mocking angry glee, the endless tirades filled with nonspecific, nonempirically based slurs against "these people" or "those minorities" or "feminazis" or "liberals" or "scumbags" or "pansies" or "jerks" or "sleazeballs" or "loonies" or "animals" or "foreigners."

At the same time I am not so naive as to suppose that this is something new. In clearheaded moments I realize I am not listening to the radio anymore, I am listening to a large segment of white America think aloud in ever louder resurgent thoughts that have generations of historical precedent. It's as though the radio has split open like an egg, Morton Downey, Jr.'s clones and Joe McCarthy's ghost spilling out, broken yolks, a great collective of sometimes clever, sometimes small, but uniformly threatened brains—they have all come gushing out. Just as they were about to pass into oblivion, Jack Benny and his humble black sidekick Rochester get resurrected in the ungainly bodies of Howard Stern and his faithful black henchwoman, Robin Quivers. The culture of Amos and Andy has been revived and reassembled in

Bob Grant's radio minstrelry and radio newcomer Daryl Gates's sanctimonious imprecations on behalf of decent white people. And in striking imitation of Jesse Helms's nearly forgotten days as a radio host, the far Right has found its undisputed king in the personage of Rush Limbaugh—a polished demagogue with a weekly radio audience of at least twenty million, a television show that vies for ratings with the likes of Jay Leno, a newsletter with a circulation of 380,000, and two best-selling books whose combined sales are closing in on six million copies.

From Churchill to Hitler to the old Soviet Union, it's clear that radio and television have the power to change the course of history, to proselytize, and to coalesce not merely the good and the noble, but the very worst in human nature as well. Likewise, when Orson Welles made his famous radio broadcast "witnessing" the landing of a spaceship full of hostile Martians, the United States ought to have learned a lesson about the power of radio to appeal to mass instincts and incite mass hysteria. Radio remains a peculiarly powerful medium even today, its visual emptiness in a world of six trillion flashing images allowing one of the few remaining playgrounds for the aural subconscious. Perhaps its power is attributable to our need for an oral tradition after all, some conveying of stories, feelings, myths of ancestors, epics of alienation, and the need to rejoin ancestral roots, even ignorant bigoted roots. Perhaps the visual quiescence of radio is related to the popularity of E-mail or electronic networking. Only the voice is made manifest, unmasking worlds that cannot—or dare not?—be seen. Just yet. Nostalgia crystallizing into a dangerous future. The preconscious voice erupting into the expressed, the prime time.

10 What comes out of the modern radio mouth could be the *Iliad,* 10
the *Rubáiyát,* the griot's song of our times. If indeed radio is a vessel for the American "Song of Songs," then what does it mean that a manic, adolescent Howard Stern is so popular among radio listeners, that Rush Limbaugh's wittily smooth sadism has gone the way of prime-time television, and that both vie for the number one slot on all the best-selling book lists? What to make of the stories being told by our modern radio evangelists and their tragic unloved chorus of callers? Is it really just a collapsing economy that spawns this drama of grown people sitting around scaring themselves to death with fantasies of black feminist Mexican able-bodied gay soldiers earning $100,000

a year on welfare who are so criminally depraved that Hillary Clinton or the Antichrist-of-the-moment had no choice but to invite them onto the government payroll so they can run the country? The panicky exaggeration reminds me of a child's fear. . . . *And then, and then, a huge lion jumped out of the shadows and was about to gobble me up, and I can't ever sleep again for a whole week.*

As I spin the dial on my radio, I can't help thinking that this stuff must be related to that most poignant of fiber-optic phenomena, phone sex. Aural Sex, Radio Racism and a touch of S & M. High-priest hosts with the power and run-amok ego to discipline listeners, to smack with the verbal back of the hand, to smash the button that shuts you up once and for all. "Idiot!" shouts New York City radio demagogue Bob Grant and then the sound of droning telephone emptiness, the voice of dissent dumped out some trapdoor in aural space.

As I listened to a range of such programs what struck me as the most unifying theme was not merely the specific intolerance on such hot topics as race and gender, but a much more general contempt for the world, a verbal stoning of anything different. It is like some unusually violent game of "Simon Says," this mockery and shouting down of callers, this roar of incantations, the insistence on agreement.

But, ah, if you *will* but only agree, what sweet and safe reward, what soft enfolding by a stern and angry radio god. And as an added bonus, the invisible shield of an AM community, a family of fans who are Exactly Like You, to whom you can express, in anonymity, all the filthy stuff you imagine "them" doing to you. The comfort and relief of being able to ejaculate, to those who understand, about the dark imagined excess overtaking, robbing, needing to be held down and taught a good lesson, needing to put it in its place before the ravenous demon enervates all that is true and good and pure in this life.

The audience for this genre of radio flagellation is mostly young, white, and male. Two thirds of Rush Limbaugh's audience is male. According to *Time* magazine, 75 percent of Howard Stern's listeners are white men. Most of the callers have spent their lives walling themselves off from any real experience with blacks, feminists, lesbians, or gays. In this regard, it is probably true, as former Secretary of Education William Bennett says, that Rush Limbaugh "tells his audience that what you believe inside, you can talk about in the marketplace." Unfortunately, what's "inside" is then mistaken for what's outside, treated as empirical and political reality. The *National Review* extols

Limbaugh's conservative leadership as no less than that of Ronald Reagan, and the Republican party provides Limbaugh with books to discuss, stories, angles, and public support. "People were afraid of censure by gay activists, feminists, environmentalists—now they are not because Rush takes them on," says Bennett.

U.S. history has been marked by cycles in which brands of this or that hatred come into fashion and go out, are unleashed and then restrained. If racism, homophobia, jingoism, and woman-hating have been features of national life in pretty much all of modern history, it rather begs the question to spend a lot of time wondering if right-wing radio is a symptom or a cause. For at least 400 years, prevailing attitudes in the West have considered African Americans less intelligent. Recent statistics show that 53 percent of people in the United States agree that blacks and Latinos are less intelligent than whites, and a majority believe that blacks are lazy, violent, welfare-dependent, and unpatriotic.

I think that what has made life more or less tolerable for "out" groups have been those moments in history when those "inside" feelings were relatively restrained. In fact, if I could believe that right-wing radio were only about idiosyncratic, singular, rough-hewn individuals thinking those inside thoughts, I'd be much more inclined to agree with Columbia University media expert Everette Dennis, who says that Stern's and Limbaugh's popularity represents the "triumph of the individual" or with *Time* magazine's bottom line that "the fact that either is seriously considered a threat . . . is more worrisome than Stern or Limbaugh will ever be." If what I were hearing had even a tad more to do with real oppressions, with real white *and* black levels of joblessness and homelessness, or with the real problems of real white men, then I wouldn't have bothered to slog my way through hours of Howard Stern's miserable obsessions.

Yet at the heart of my anxiety is the worry that Stern, Limbaugh, Grant, et al. represent the very antithesis of individualism's triumph. As the *National Review* said of Limbaugh's ascent, "It was a feat not only of the loudest voice but also of a keen political brain to round up, as Rush did, the media herd and drive them into the conservative corral." When asked about his political aspirations, Bob Grant gloated to the *Washington Post,* "I think I would make rather a good dictator."

The polemics of right-wing radio are putting nothing less than hate onto the airwaves, into the marketplace, electing it to office, teaching it in schools, and exalting it as freedom. What worries me is the increasing-to-constant commerce of retribution, control, and lashing out, fed not by fact but fantasy. What worries me is the reemergence, more powerfully than at any time since the institution of Jim Crow, of a socio-centered self that excludes "the likes of," well, me for example, from the civic circle, and that would rob me of my worth and claim and identity as a citizen. As the *Economist* rightly observes, "Mr. Limbaugh takes a mass market—white, mainly male, middle-class, ordinary America—and talks to it as an endangered minority."

I worry about this identity whose external reference is a set of beliefs, ethics, and practices that excludes, restricts, and acts in the world on me, or mine, as the perceived if not real enemy. I am acutely aware of losing *my* mythic individualism to the surface shapes of my mythic group fearsomeness as black, as female, as left wing. "I" merge not fluidly but irretrievably into a category of "them." I become a suspect self, a moving target of loathsome properties, not merely different but dangerous. And that worries me a lot.

What happens in my life with all this translated license, this permission to be uncivil? What happens to the social space that was supposedly at the sweet mountaintop of the civil rights movement's trail? Can I get a seat on the bus without having to be reminded that I *should* be standing? Did the civil rights movement guarantee us nothing more than to use public accommodations while surrounded by raving lunatic bigots? "They didn't beat this idiot [Rodney King] enough," says Howard Stern.

Not long ago I had the misfortune to hail a taxicab in which the driver was listening to Howard Stern undress some woman. After some blocks, I had to get out. I was, frankly, afraid to ask the driver to turn it off—not because I was afraid of "censoring" him, which seems to be the only thing people will talk about anymore, but because the driver was stripping me too, as he leered through the rearview mirror. "Something the matter?" he demanded, as I asked him to pull over and let me out well short of my destination. (I'll spare you the full story of what happened from there—trying to get another cab, as the cabbies stopped for all the white businessmen who so much as scratched their heads near the curb; a nice young white man, seeing my plight, giving me his cab, having to thank him, he hero, me saved-but-humiliated, cabdriver pissed and surly. I fight my way to my destination, finally arriving in bad mood, militant black woman, cranky feminazi.)

When Yeltsin blared rock music at his opponents holed up in the parliament building in Moscow, in imitation of the U.S. Marines trying to torture Manuel Noriega in Panama, all I could think of was that it must be like being trapped in a crowded subway car when all the portable stereos are tuned to Bob Grant or Howard Stem. With Howard Stern's voice a tinny, screeching backdrop, with all the faces growing dreamily mean as though some soporifically evil hallucinogen were gushing into their bloodstreams, I'd start begging to surrender.

Surrender to what? Surrender to the laissez-faire resegregation that is the metaphoric significance of the hundreds of "Rush rooms" that have cropped up in restaurants around the country; rooms broadcasting Limbaugh's words, rooms for your listening pleasure, rooms where bigots can capture the purity of a Rush-only lunch counter, rooms where all those unpleasant others just "choose" not to eat? Surrender to the naughty luxury of a room in which a Ku Klux Klan meeting could take place in orderly, First Amendment fashion? Everyone's "free" to come in (and a few of you outsiders do), but mostly the undesirable nonconformists are gently repulsed away. It's a high-tech world of enhanced choice. Whites choose mostly to sit in the Rush room. Feminists, blacks, lesbians, and gays "choose" to sit elsewhere. No need to buy black votes, you just pay them not to vote; no need to insist on white-only schools, you just sell the desirability of black-only schools. Just sit back and watch it work, like those invisible shock shields that keep dogs cowering in their own backyards.

How real is the driving perception behind all the Sturm und Drang of this genre of radio-harangue—the perception that white men are an oppressed minority, with no power and no opportunity in the land that they made great? While it is true that power and opportunity are shrinking for all but the very wealthy in this country (and would that Limbaugh would take that issue on), the fact remains that white men are still this country's most privileged citizens and market actors. To give just a small example, according to the *Wall Street Journal,* blacks were the only racial group to suffer a net job loss during the 1990–91 economic downturn at the companies reporting to the Equal Employment Opportunity Commission. Whites, Latinos, and Asians, meanwhile, gained thousands of jobs. While whites gained 71,144 jobs at these companies, Latinos gained 60,040, Asians gained 55,104, and blacks lost 59,479. If every black were hired in the United States tomorrow, the numbers would not be sufficient to account for white men's expanding balloon of fear that they have been specifically dispossessed by African Americans.

Given deep patterns of social segregation and general ignorance of history, particularly racial history, media remain the principal source of most Americans' knowledge of each other. Media can provoke violence or induce passivity. In San Francisco, for example, a radio show on KMEL called "Street Soldiers" has taken this power as a responsibility with great consequence: "Unquestionably," writes Ken Auletta in *The New Yorker*, "the show has helped avert violence. When a Samoan teenager was slain, apparently by Filipino gang members, in a drive-by shooting, the phones lit up with calls from Samoans wanting to tell [the hosts] they would not rest until they had exacted revenge. Threats filled the air for a couple of weeks. Then the dead Samoan's father called in, and, in a poignant exchange, the father said he couldn't tolerate the thought of more young men senselessly slaughtered. There would be no retaliation, he vowed. And there was none." In contrast, we must wonder at the phenomenon of the very powerful leadership of the Republican party, from Ronald Reagan to Robert Dole to William Bennett, giving advice, counsel, and friendship to Rush Limbaugh's passionate divisiveness.

The outright denial of the material crisis at every level of U.S. society, most urgently in black inner-city neighborhoods but facing us all, is a kind of political circus, dissembling as it feeds the frustrations of the moment. We as a nation can no longer afford to deal with such crises by *imagining* an excess of bodies, of babies, of job-stealers, of welfare mothers, of overreaching immigrants, of too-powerful (Jewish, in whispers) liberal Hollywood, of lesbians and gays, of gang members ("gangsters" remain white, and no matter what the atrocity, less vilified than "gang members," who are black), of Arab terrorists, and uppity women. The reality of our social poverty far exceeds these scapegoats. This right-wing backlash resembles, in form if not substance, phenomena like anti-Semitism in Poland: there aren't but a handful of Jews left in that whole country, but the giant balloon of heated anti-Semitism flourishes apace, Jews blamed for the world's evils.

The overwhelming response to right-wing excesses in the United States has been to seek an odd sort of comfort in the fact that the First Amendment is working so well that you can't suppress this sort of thing. Look what's happened in Eastern Europe. Granted. So let's not talk about censorship or the First Amendment for the next ten minutes. But in Western Europe, where fascism is rising at an appalling rate, suppression is hardly the problem. In Eastern and Western Europe as well as the United States, we must begin to think just a little bit about the fiercely coalescing power of media to spark mistrust, to fan it into forest fires of fear and revenge. We must begin to think about the levels of national and social complacence in the face of such resolute ignorance. We must ask ourselves what the expected result is, not of censorship or suppression, but of so much encouragement, so much support, so much investment in the fashionability of hate. What future is it that we are designing with the devotion of such tremendous resources to the disgraceful propaganda of bigotry?

## Questions on Meaning

1. Explain what specifically offended Williams in the radio conversation she reports.
2. What does Williams suggest is the appeal of "hate" radio to its primary audience—young, white males? What are the negative social effects of this kind of radio program?
3. Is Williams suggesting that hate radio should be censored? What actions does she seem to endorse to combat its messages?

## Questions on Rhetorical Strategy and Style

1. The radio programs Williams objects to are politically conservative in their orientation. Does Williams seem like a political liberal who is attacking the programs for partisan reasons? Do her political leanings affect the persuasiveness of her message?
2. Did any of Williams's opinions annoy you? Did any cause you to react with enthusiastic agreement? Explain.
3. Re-examine the third paragraph from the end of the article, the one beginning "Given deep patterns of social segregation and general ignorance. . . ." Evaluate the paragraph's effectiveness in conveying Willliams's central point.

## Writing Assignments

1. Tune in to Rush Limbaugh, Howard Stern, Dr. Laura or some other conservative commentators. Listen and take notes (or tape-record) the program and analyze its attitudes. Who does the program host attack? Who is defended? What examples of language might offend certain parties? Write an essay that evaluates Williams's idea that there is a connection between political conservatism and hatred.
2. Look up the first amendment to the Constitution. Then research recent freedom of speech cases such as the People vs. Larry Flynt and the debates on prayer in the schools. In an essay, discuss the definition of the right to freedom of speech including appropriate restraints on that right.

# THE LIBRARY CARD

## Richard Wright

*Richard Wright (1908–1960) was born on a plantation in Natchez, Mississippi. When he was young, his family was frequently displaced as his mother moved about looking for work. Eventually his family dissolved and Wright spent time in a number of orphanages and foster homes. At age 15, Wright took off on his own, supporting himself with odd jobs. In 1943 he moved to Chicago and later joined the Federal Writer's Project. A member of the "radical left," Wright published in such publications as the* Daily Worker, Left Front, *and* New Masses, *in addition to more mainstream publications, such as* Harper's. *His first novel,* Uncle Tom's Children: Four Novellas *(1938) won him the critical acclaim that led to a Guggenheim Fellowship. His novel* Native Son *(1940) became a classic in American literature. Other books by Wright include* Eight Men *(1940),* Black Boy *(1945),* The Outsider *(1953),* Black Power *(1954), and* The Long Dream *(1958). In 1946, Wright emigrated to France. In this essay, an excerpt from* Black Boy, *Wright reveals how his introduction to books both expanded his intellectual horizons and revealed the limits imposed on him by the American South of the 1920s.*

1 One morning I arrived early at work and went into the bank lobby where the Negro porter was mopping. I stood at a counter and picked up the Memphis *Commercial Appeal* and began my free reading of the press. I came finally to the editorial page and saw an article dealing with one H. L. Mencken. I knew by hearsay that he was the editor of the *American Mercury,* but aside from that I 1

knew nothing about him. The article was a furious denunciation of Mencken, concluding with one hot, short sentence: Mencken is a fool.

I wondered what on earth this Mencken had done to call down upon him the scorn of the South. The only people I had ever heard denounced in the South were Negroes, and this man was not a Negro. Then what ideas did Mencken hold that made a newspaper like the *Commercial Appeal* castigate him publicly? Undoubtedly he must be advocating ideas that the South did not like. Were there, then, people other than Negroes who criticized the South? I knew that during the Civil War the South had hated northern whites, but I had not encountered such hate during my life. Knowing no more of Mencken than I did at that moment, I felt a vague sympathy for him. Had not the South, which had assigned me the role of a non-man, cast at him its hardest words?

Now, how could I find out about this Mencken? There was a huge library near the riverfront, but I knew that Negroes were not allowed to patronize its shelves any more than they were the parks and playgrounds of the city. I had gone into the library several times to get books for the white men on the job. Which of them would now help me to get books? And how could I read them without causing concern to the white men with whom I worked? I had so far been successful in hiding my thoughts and feelings from them, but I knew that I would create hostility if I went about this business of reading in a clumsy way.

I weighed the personalities of the men on the job. There was Don, a Jew; but I distrusted him. His position was not much better than mine and I knew that he was uneasy and insecure; he had always treated me in an offhand, bantering way that barely concealed his contempt. I was afraid to ask him to help me to get books; his frantic desire to demonstrate a racial solidarity with the whites against Negroes might make him betray me.

Then how about the boss? No, he was a Baptist and I had the suspicion that he would not be quite able to comprehend why a black boy would want to read Mencken. There were other white men on the job whose attitudes showed clearly that they were Kluxers or sympathizers, and they were out of the question.

There remained only one man whose attitude did not fit into an anti-Negro category, for I had heard the white men refer to him as a "Pope lover." He was an Irish Catholic and was hated by the white Southerners. I knew that he read books, because I had got him volumes from the library several times. Since he, too, was an object of hatred, I felt that he might refuse me but would hardly betray me. I hesitated, weighing and balancing the imponderable realities.

One morning I paused before the Catholic fellow's desk.

"I want to ask you a favor," I whispered to him.

"What is it?"

"I want to read. I can't get books from the library. I wonder if you'd let me use your card?"

He looked at me suspiciously.

"My card is full most of the time," he said.

"I see," I said and waited, posing my question silently.

"You're not trying to get me into trouble, are you, boy?" he asked, staring at me.

"Oh, no, sir."

"What book do you want?"

"A book by H. L. Mencken."

"Which one?"

"I don't know. Has he written more than one?"

"He has written several."

"I didn't know that."

"What makes you want to read Mencken?"

"Oh, I just saw his name in the newspaper," I said.

"It's good of you to want to read," he said. "But you ought to read the right things."

I said nothing. Would he want to supervise my reading?

"Let me think," he said. "I'll figure out something."

I turned from him and he called me back. He stared at me quizzically.

"Richard, don't mention this to the other white men," he said.

"I understand," I said. "I won't say a word."

A few days later he called me to him.

"I've got a card in my wife's name," he said. "Here's mine."

"Thank you, sir."

"Do you think you can manage it?"

"I'll manage fine," I said.

"If they suspect you, you'll get in trouble," he said.

"I'll write the same kind of notes to the library that you wrote when you sent me for books," I told him. "I'll sign your name."

He laughed.

"Go ahead. Let me see what you get," he said.

That afternoon I addressed myself to forging a note. Now, what were the names of books written by H. L. Mencken? I did not know any of them. I finally wrote what I thought would be a foolproof note: *Dear Madam: Will you please let this nigger boy*—I used the word "nigger" to make the librarian feel that I could not possibly be the author of the note—*have some books by H. L. Mencken?* I forged the white man's name.

I entered the library as I had always done when on errands for whites, but I felt that I would somehow slip up and betray myself. I doffed my hat, stood a respectful distance from the desk, looked as unbookish as possible, and waited for the white patrons to be taken care of. When the desk was clear of people, I still waited. The white librarian looked at me.

"What do you want, boy?"

As though I did not possess the power of speech, I stepped forward and simply handed her the forged note, not parting my lips.

"What books by Mencken does he want?" she asked.

"I don't know, ma'am," I said, avoiding her eyes.

"Who gave you this card?"

"Mr. Falk," I said.

"Where is he?"

"He's at work, at the M—Optical Company," I said. "I've been in here for him before."

"I remember," the woman said. "But he never wrote notes like this."

Oh, God, she's suspicious. Perhaps she would not let me have the books? If she had turned her back at that moment, I would have ducked out the door and never gone back. Then I thought of a bold idea.

"You can call him up, ma'am," I said, my heart pounding.

"You're not using these books, are you?" she asked pointedly.

"Oh, no, ma'am. I can't read."

"I don't know what he wants by Mencken," she said under her breath.

I knew now that I had won; she was thinking of other things and the race question had gone out of her mind. She went to the shelves. Once or twice she looked over her shoulder at me, as though she was still doubtful. Finally she came forward with two books in her hand.

"I'm sending him two books," she said. "But tell Mr. Falk to come in next time, or send me the names of the books he wants. I don't know what he wants to read."

I said nothing. She stamped the card and handed me the books. Not daring to glance at them, I went out of the library, fearing that the woman would call me back for further questioning. A block away from the library I opened one of the books and read a title: *A Book of Prefaces.* I was nearing my nineteenth birthday and I did not know how to pronounce the word "preface." I thumbed the pages and saw strange words and strange names. I shook my head, disappointed. I looked at the other book; it was called *Prejudices.* I knew what that word meant; I had heard it all my life. And right off I was on guard against Mencken's books. Why would a man want to call a book *Prejudices*? The word was so stained with all my memories of racial hate that I could not conceive of anybody using it for a title. Perhaps I had made a mistake about Mencken? A man who had prejudices must be wrong.

When I showed the books to Mr. Falk, he looked at me and frowned.

"That librarian might telephone you," I warned him.

"That's all right," he said. "But when you're through reading those books, I want you to tell me what you get out of them."

That night in my rented room, while letting the hot water run over my can of pork and beans in the sink, I opened *A Book of Prefaces* and began to read. I was jarred and shocked by the style, the clear, clean, sweeping sentences. Why did he write like that? And how did one write like that? I pictured the man as a raging demon, slashing with his pen, consumed with hate, denouncing everything American, extolling everything European or German, laughing at the weaknesses of people, mocking God, authority. What was this? I stood up, trying to realize what reality lay behind the meaning of the words. . . . Yes, this man was fighting, fighting with words. He was using words as a weapon, using them as one would use a club. Could words be weapons? Well, yes, for here they were. Then, maybe, perhaps, I could use them as a weapon? No. It frightened me. I read on and what amazed me was not what he said, but how on earth anybody had the courage to say it.

Occasionally I glanced up to reassure myself that I was alone in the room. Who were these men about whom Mencken was talking so passionately? Who was Anatole France? Joseph Conrad? Sinclair Lewis, Sherwood Anderson, Dostoevski, George Moore, Gustave Flaubert, Maupassant, Tolstoy, Frank Harris, Mark Twain, Thomas Hardy, Arnold Bennett, Stephen Crane, Zola, Norris, Gorky, Bergson,

Ibsen, Balzac, Bernard Shaw, Dumas, Poe, Thomas Mann, O. Henry, Dreiser, H. G. Wells, Gogol, T. S. Eliot, Gide, Baudelaire, Edgar Lee Masters, Stendhal, Turgenev, Huneker, Nietzsche, and scores of others? Were these men real? Did they exist or had they existed? And how did one pronounce their names?

I ran across many words whose meanings I did not know, and I either looked them up in a dictionary or, before I had a chance to do that, encountered the word in a context that made its meaning clear. But what strange world was this? I concluded the book with the conviction that I had somehow overlooked something terribly important in life. I had once tried to write, had once reveled in feeling, had let my crude imagination roam, but the impulse to dream had been slowly beaten out of me by experience. Now it surged up again and I hungered for books, new ways of looking and seeing. It was not a matter of believing or disbelieving what I read, but of feeling something new, of being affected by something that made the look of the world different.

As dawn broke I ate my pork and beans, feeling dopey, sleepy. I went to work, but the mood of the book would not die; it lingered, coloring everything I saw, heard, did. I now felt that I knew what the white men were feeling. Merely because I had read a book that had spoken of how they lived and thought, I identified myself with that book. I felt vaguely guilty. Would I, filled with bookish notions, act in a manner that would make the whites dislike me?

65 I forged more notes and my trips to the library became frequent. 65
Reading grew into a passion. My first serious novel was Sinclair Lewis's *Main Street.* It made me see my boss, Mr. Gerald, and identify him as an American type. I would smile when I saw him lugging his golf bags into the office. I had always felt a vast distance separating me from the boss, and now I felt closer to him, though still distant. I felt now that I knew him, that I could feel the very limits of his narrow life. And this had happened because I had read a novel about a mythical man called George F. Babbitt.

The plots and stories in the novels did not interest me so much as the point of view revealed. I gave myself over to each novel without reserve, without trying to criticize it; it was enough for me to see and feel something different. And for me, everything was something different. Reading was like a drug, a dope. The novels created moods in which I lived for days. But I could not conquer my sense of guilt, my feeling that the white men around me knew that I was changing, that I had begun to regard them differently.

Whenever I brought a book to the job, I wrapped it in newspaper—a habit that was to persist for years in other cities and under other circumstances. But some of the white men pried into my packages when I was absent and they questioned me.

"Boy, what are you reading those books for?"

"Oh, I don't know, sir."

"That's deep stuff you're reading, boy."

"I'm just killing time, sir."

"You'll addle your brains if you don't watch out."

I read Dreiser's *Jennie Gerhardt* and *Sister Carrie* and they revived in me a vivid sense of my mother's suffering; I was overwhelmed. I grew silent, wondering about the life around me. It would have been impossible for me to have told anyone what I derived from these novels, for it was nothing less than a sense of life itself. All my life had shaped me for the realism, the naturalism of the modern novel, and I could not read enough of them.

Steeped in new moods and ideas, I bought a ream of paper and tried to write; but nothing would come, or what did come was flat beyond telling. I discovered that more than desire and feeling were necessary to write and I dropped the idea. Yet I still wondered how it was possible to know people sufficiently to write about them. Could I ever learn about life and people? To me, with my vast ignorance, my Jim Crow station in life, it seemed a task impossible of achievement. I now knew what being a Negro meant. I could endure the hunger. I had learned to live with hate. But to feel that there were feelings denied me, that the very breath of life itself was beyond my reach, that more than anything else hurt, wounded me. I had a new hunger.

In buoying me up, reading also cast me down, made me see what was possible, what I had missed. My tension returned, new, terrible, bitter, surging, almost too great to be contained. I no longer *felt* that the world about me was hostile, killing; I *knew* it. A million times I asked myself what I could do to save myself, and there were no answers. I seemed forever condemned, ringed by walls.

I did not discuss my reading with Mr. Falk, who had lent me his library card; it would have meant talking about myself and that would have been too painful. I smiled each day, fighting desperately to maintain my old behavior, to keep my disposition seemingly sunny. But some of the white men discerned that I had begun to brood.

"Wake up there, boy!" Mr. Olin said one day.

"Sir!" I answered for the lack of a better word.

"You act like you've stolen something," he said.

I laughed in the way I knew he expected me to laugh, but I resolved to be more conscious of myself, to watch my every act, to guard and hide the new knowledge that was dawning within me.

If I went north, would it be possible for me to build a new life then? But how could a man build a life upon vague, unformed yearnings? I wanted to write and I did not even know the English language. I bought English grammars and found them dull. I felt that I was getting a better sense of the language from novels than from grammars. I read hard, discarding a writer as soon as I felt that I had grasped his point of view. At night the printed page stood before my eyes in sleep.

Mrs. Moss, my landlady, asked me one Sunday morning: "Son, what is this you keep on reading?"

"Oh, nothing. Just novels."

"What you get out of 'em?"

"I'm just killing time," I said.

"I hope you know your own mind," she said in a tone which implied that she doubted if I had a mind.

I knew of no Negroes who read the books I liked and I wondered if any Negroes ever thought of them. I knew that there were Negro doctors, lawyers, newspapermen, but I never saw any of them. When I read a Negro newspaper I never caught the faintest echo of my preoccupation in its pages. I felt trapped and occasionally, for a few days, I would stop reading. But a vague hunger would come over me for books, books that opened up new avenues of feeling and seeing, and again I would forge another note to the white librarian. Again I would read and wonder as only the naive and unlettered can read and wonder, feeling that I carried a secret, criminal burden about with me each day.

That winter my mother and brother came and we set up housekeeping, buying furniture on the installment plan, being cheated and yet knowing no way to avoid it. I began to eat warm food and to my surprise found that regular meals enabled me to read faster. I may have lived through many illnesses and survived them, never suspecting that I was ill. My brother obtained a job and we began to save toward the trip north, plotting our time, setting tentative dates for departure. I told none of the white men on the job that I was planning to go north; I knew that the moment they felt I was thinking of the North they would change toward me. It would have made them feel that I did not like the life I was living, and because my life was completely conditioned by what they said or did, it would have been tantamount to challenging them.

I could calculate my chances for life in the South as a Negro fairly clearly now.

90 I could fight the southern whites by organizing with other Negroes, as my grandfather had done. But I knew that I could never win that way; there were many whites and there were but few blacks. They were strong and we were weak. Outright black rebellion could never win. If I fought openly I would die and I did not want to die. News of lynchings were frequent. 90

I could submit and live the life of a genial slave, but that was impossible. All of my life had shaped me to live by my own feelings and thoughts. I could make up to Bess and marry her and inherit the house. But that, too, would be the life of a slave; if I did that, I would crush to death something within me, and I would hate myself as much as I knew the whites already hated those who had submitted. Neither could I ever willingly present myself to be kicked, as Shorty had done. I would rather have died than do that.

I could drain off my restlessness by fighting with Shorty and Harrison. I had seen many Negroes solve the problem of being black by transferring their hatred of themselves to others with a black skin and fighting them. I would have to be cold to do that, and I was not cold and I could never be.

I could, of course, forget what I had read, thrust the whites out of my mind, forget them; and find release from anxiety and longing in sex and alcohol. But the memory of how my father had conducted himself made that course repugnant. If I did not want others to violate my life, how could I voluntarily violate it myself?

I had no hope whatever of being a professional man. Not only had I been so conditioned that I did not desire it, but the fulfillment of such an ambition was beyond my capabilities. Well-to-do Negroes lived in a world that was almost as alien to me as the world inhabited by whites.

95 What, then, was there? I held my life in my mind, in my consciousness each day, feeling at times that I would stumble and drop it, spill it forever. My reading had created a vast sense of distance between me and the world in which I lived and tried to make a living, and that sense of distance was increasing each day. My days and nights were one long, quiet, continuously contained dream of terror, tension, and anxiety. I wondered how long I could bear it. 95

## Questions on Meaning

1. If you did not know when this essay was published, what words used by Wright would help you identify the time period? What would happen if a black writer used these words today? What about a white writer?
2. What amazed Wright about Mencken? What did the first Mencken book teach Wright about writing?
3. What does Wright mean by his "Jim Crow station in life"?

## Questions on Rhetorical Strategy and Style

1. How does Wright use causation to show how his book knowledge changed his view of the white men he worked for? What kind of power did Wright gain from this knowledge? How did it affect his whites bosses' perception of him?
2. Compare and contrast how reading both inspired and depressed Wright. What frustrations did reading cause him? Why did he become tense and bitter?
3. Find where Wright analyzes his options as a southern black. What would you have done in his shoes? How many of these options apply today to blacks in America?

## Writing Assignments

1. Describe something you learned from personal research (e.g., books, lectures, or the Internet) that had a significant impact on your life—such as something to do with a hobby, travel, religion, or politics. How were you introduced to this new knowledge? How did you satisfy your quest for more knowledge? How has it altered other aspects of your life?
2. Wright mentions that some of the white men he worked with were "Kluxers," a reference to the Ku Klux Klan. Research this organization and its roots. Typically who were members of the Klan? What are the current activities of the organization?
3. Wright had few if any real black role models. Although he knew that "Negro" professionals existed, he never saw them. Write an essay on the importance of successful minority role models for minority youths to achieve success. How would you recommend getting minority teachers, journalists, engineers, doctors, and other professionals involved with youth programs? What could you do as a college student (even if you are not a member of a minority group)?

# COLLEGE PRESSURES

## William Zinsser

*William Zinsser (1922– ) was born in New York City. A graduate of Princeton University (1944), Zinsser has worked as a feature and editorial writer, drama editor, and film critic for* The New York Herald Tribune*; a columnist for* Life, Look, *and* The New York Times*; an editor for the Book-of-the-Month Club; and an English instructor at Yale University. Zinsser's books include* Pop Goes America *(1963),* On Writing Well: An Informal Guide to Writing Nonfiction *(1976),* Writing With a Word Processor *(1983),* Writing to Learn *(1988),* Willie and Dwike *(1984), and* Spring Training *(1989). In the essay that follows, published in* Blair and Ketchum's Country Journal *magazine in 1979, Zinsser describes the pressures experienced by college students in the late 1970s that make them rigidly goal-driven and unable to explore.*

Dear Carlos: I desperately need a dean's excuse for my chem midterm which will begin in about 1 hour. All I can say is that I totally blew it this week. I've fallen incredibly, inconceivably behind.

Carlos: Help! I'm anxious to hear from you. I'll be in my room and won't leave it until I hear from you. Tomorrow is the last day for . . .

Carlos: I left town because I started bugging out again. I stayed up all night to finish a take-home make-up exam & am typing it to hand in on the 10th. It was due on the 5th. P.S. I'm going to the dentist. Pain is pretty bad.

Carlos: Probably by Friday I'll be able to get back to my studies. Right now I'm going to take a long walk. This whole thing has taken a lot out of me.

Carlos: I'm really up the proverbial creek. The problem is I really bombed the history final. Since I need that course for my major I . . .

Carlos: Here follows a tale of woe. I went home this weekend, had to help my Mom, & caught a fever so didn't have much time to study. My professor . . .

Carlos: Aargh! Trouble. Nothing original but everything's piling up at once. To be brief, my job interview . . .

Hey Carlos, good news! I've got mononucleosis.

1 Who are these wretched supplicants, scribbling notes so laden 1
with anxiety, seeking such miracles of postponement and balm? They are men and women who belong to Branford College, one of the twelve residential colleges at Yale University, and the messages are just a few of the hundreds that they left for their dean, Carlos Hortas—often slipped under his door at 4 A.M.—last year.

But students like the ones who wrote those notes can also be found on campuses from coast to coast—especially in New England and at many other private colleges across the country that have high academic standards and highly motivated students. Nobody could doubt that the notes are real. In their urgency and their gallows humor they are authentic voices of a generation that is panicky to succeed.

My own connection with the message writers is that I am master of Branford College. I live in its Gothic quadrangle and know the students well. (We have 485 of them.) I am privy to their hopes and fears—and also to their stereo music and their piercing cries in the dead of night ("Does anybody *ca-a-are?*"). If they went to Carlos to ask how to get through tomorrow, they come to me to ask how to get through the rest of their lives.

Mainly I try to remind them that the road ahead is a long one and that it will have more unexpected turns than they think. There will be plenty of time to change jobs, change careers, change whole attitudes and approaches. They don't want to hear such liberating news. They want a map—right now—that they can follow unswervingly to career security, financial security, Social Security and, presumably, a prepaid grave.

5 What I wish for all students is some release from the clammy grip 5
of the future. I wish them a chance to savor each segment of their

education as an experience in itself and not as a grim preparation for the next step. I wish them the right to experiment, to trip and fall, to learn that defeat is as instructive as victory and is not the end of the world.

My wish, of course, is naïve. One of the few rights that America does not proclaim is the right to fail. Achievement is the national god, venerated in our media—the million-dollar athlete, the wealthy executive—and glorified in our praise of possessions. In the presence of such a potent state religion, the young are growing up old.

I see four kinds of pressure working on college students today: economic pressure, parental pressure, peer pressure, and self-induced pressure. It is easy to look around for villains—to blame the colleges for charging too much money, the professors for assigning too much work, the parents for pushing their children too far, the students for driving themselves too hard. But there are no villains; only victims.

"In the late 1960s," one dean told me, "the typical question that I got from students was 'Why is there so much suffering in the world?' or 'How can I make a contribution?' Today it's 'Do you think it would look better for getting into law school if I did a double major in history and political science, or just majored in one of them?' " Many other deans confirmed this pattern. One said: "They're trying to find an edge—the intangible something that will look better on paper if two students are about equal."

Note the emphasis on looking better. The transcript has become a sacred document, the passport to security. How one appears on paper is more important than how one appears in person. *A* is for Admirable and *B* is for Borderline, even though, in Yale's official system of grading, *A* means "excellent" and *B* means "very good." Today, looking very good is no longer good enough, especially for students who hope to go on to law school or medical school. They know that entrance into the better schools will be an entrance into the better law firms and better medical practices where they will make a lot of money. They also know that the odds are harsh. Yale Law School, for instance, matriculates 170 students from an applicant pool of 3,700; Harvard enrolls 550 from a pool of 7,000.

10 It's all very well for those of us who write letters of recommendation for our students to stress the qualities of humanity that will make them good lawyers or doctors. And it's nice to think that admission officers are really reading our letters and looking for the extra dimension of commitment or concern. Still, it would be hard for a student not to

visualize these officers shuffling so many transcripts studded with *A*s that they regard a *B* as positively shameful.

The pressure is almost as heavy on students who just want to graduate and get a job. Long gone are the days of the "gentleman's C," when students journeyed through college with a certain relaxation, sampling a wide variety of courses—music, art, philosophy, classics, anthropology, poetry, religion—that would send them out as liberally educated men and women. If I were an employer I would rather employ graduates who have this range and curiosity than those who narrowly pursued safe subjects and high grades. I know countless students whose inquiring minds exhilarate me. I like to hear the play of their ideas. I don't know if they are getting *A*s or *C*s, and I don't care. I also like them as people. The country needs them, and they will find satisfying jobs. I tell them to relax. They can't.

Nor can I blame them. They live in a brutal economy. Tuition, room, and board at most private colleges now comes to at least $7,000, not counting books and fees. This might seem to suggest that the colleges are getting rich. But they are equally battered by inflation. Tuition covers only 60 percent of what it costs to educate a student, and ordinarily the remainder comes from what colleges receive in endowments, grants, and gifts. Now the remainder keeps being swallowed by the cruel costs—higher every year—of just opening the doors. Heating oil is up. Insurance is up. Postage is up. Health-premium costs are up. Everything is up. Deficits are up. We are witnessing in America the creation of a brotherhood of paupers—colleges, parents, and students, joined by the common bond of debt.

Today it is not unusual for a student, even if he works part time at college and full time during the summer, to accrue $5,000 in loans after four years—loans that he must start to repay within one year after graduation. Exhorted at commencement to go forth into the world, he is already behind as he goes forth. How could he not feel under pressure throughout college to prepare for this day of reckoning? I have used "he," incidentally, only for brevity. Women at Yale are under no less pressure to justify their expensive education to themselves, their parents, and society. In fact, they are probably under more pressure. For although they leave college superbly equipped to bring fresh leadership to traditionally male jobs, society hasn't yet caught up with this fact.

Along with economic pressure goes parental pressure. Inevitably, the two are deeply intertwined.

15 I see many students taking pre-medical courses with joyless tenacity. They go off to their labs as if they were going to the dentist. It saddens me because I know them in other corners of their life as cheerful people. 15

"Do you want to go to medical school?" I ask them.

"I guess so," they say, without conviction, or "Not really."

"Then why are you going?"

"Well, my parents want me to be a doctor. They're paying all this money and . . . "

20 Poor students, poor parents. They are caught in one of the oldest webs of love and duty and guilt. The parents mean well; they are trying to steer their sons and daughters toward a secure future. But the sons and daughters want to major in history or classics or philosophy—subjects with no "practical" value. Where's the payoff on the humanities? It's not easy to persuade such loving parents that the humanities do indeed pay off. The intellectual faculties developed by studying subjects like history and classics—an ability to synthesize and relate, to weigh cause and effect, to see events in perspective—are just the faculties that make creative leaders in business or almost any general field. Still, many fathers would rather put their money on courses that point toward a specific profession—courses that are pre-law, premedical, pre-business, or, as I sometimes heard it put, "pre-rich." 20

But the pressure on students is severe. They are truly torn. One part of them feels obligated to fulfill their parents' expectations; after all, their parents are older and presumably wiser. Another part tells them that the expectations that are right for their parents are not right for them.

I know a student who wants to be an artist. She is very obviously an artist and will be a good one—she has already had several modest local exhibits. Meanwhile she is growing as a well-rounded person and taking humanistic subjects that will enrich the inner resources out of which her art will grow. But her father is strongly opposed. He thinks that an artist is a "dumb" thing to be. The student vacillates and tries to please everybody. She keeps up with her art somewhat furtively and takes some of the "dumb" courses her father wants her to take—at least they are dumb courses for her. She is a free spirit on a campus of tense students—no small achievement in itself—and she deserves to follow her muse.

Peer pressure and self-induced pressure are also intertwined, and they begin almost at the beginning of freshman year.

"I had a freshman student I'll call Linda," one dean told me, "who came in and said she was under terrible pressure because her roommate, Barbara, was much brighter and studied all the time. I couldn't tell her that Barbara had come in two hours earlier to say the same thing about Linda."

25 The story is almost funny except that it's not. It's symptomatic of 25 all the pressures put together. When every student thinks every other student is working harder and doing better, the only solution is to study harder still. I see students going off to the library every night after dinner and coming back when it closes at midnight. I wish they would sometimes forget about their peers and go to a movie. I hear the clacking of typewriters in the hours before dawn. I see the tension in their eyes when exams are approaching and papers are due: *"Will I get everything done?"*

Probably they won't. They will get sick. They will get "blocked." They will sleep. They will oversleep. They will bug out. *Hey Carlos, help!*

Part of the problem is that they do more than they are expected to do. A professor will assign five-page papers. Several students will start writing ten-page papers to impress him. Then more students will write ten-page papers, and a few will raise the ante to fifteen. Pity the poor student who is still just doing the assignment.

"Once you have 20 or 30 percent of the student population deliberately overexerting," one dean points out, "it's bad for everybody. When a teacher gets more and more effort from his class, the student who is doing normal work can be perceived as not doing well. The tactic works, psychologically."

Why can't the professor just cut back and not accept longer papers? He can, and he probably will. But by then the term will be half over and the damage done. Grade fever is highly contagious and not easily reversed. Besides, the professor's main concern is with his course. He knows his students only in relation to the course and doesn't know that they are also overexerting in their other courses. Nor is it really his business. He didn't sign up for dealing with the student as a whole person and with all the emotional baggage the student brought along from home. That's what deans, masters, chaplains, and psychiatrists are for.

30 To some extent this is nothing new: a certain number of professors have always been self-contained islands of scholarship and shyness, more comfortable with books than with people. But the new pauperism has widened the gap still further, for professors who actually like to spend time with students don't have as much time to spend. They also are overexerting. If they are young, they are busy trying to publish in order not to perish, hanging by their finger nails onto a shrinking profession. If they are old and tenured, they are buried under the duties of administering departments—as departmental chairmen or members of committees—that have been thinned out by the budgetary axe.

Ultimately it will be the students' own business to break the circles in which they are trapped. They are too young to be prisoners of their parents' dreams and their classmates' fears. They must be jolted into believing in themselves as unique men and women who have the power to shape their own future.

"Violence is being done to the undergraduate experience," says Carlos Hortas. "College should be open-ended: at the end it should open many, many roads. Instead, students are choosing their goal in advance, and their choices narrow as they go along. It's almost as if they think that the country has been codified in the type of jobs that exist—that they've got to fit into certain slots. Therefore, fit into the best-paying slot.

"They ought to take chances. Not taking chances will lead to a life of colorless mediocrity. They'll be comfortable. But something in the spirit will be missing."

I have painted too drab a portrait of today's students, making them seem a solemn lot. That is only half of their story; if they were so dreary I wouldn't so thoroughly enjoy their company. The other half is that they are easy to like. They are quick to laugh and to offer friendship. They are not introverts. They are unusually kind and are more considerate of one another than any student generation I have known.

35 Nor are they so obsessed with their studies that they avoid sports and extracurricular activities. On the contrary, they juggle their crowded hours to play on a variety of teams, perform with musical and dramatic groups, and write for campus publications. But this in turn is one more cause of anxiety. There are too many choices. Academically,

they have 1,300 courses to select from; outside class they have to decide how much spare time they can spare and how to spend it.

This means that they engage in fewer extracurricular pursuits than their predecessors did. If they want to row on the crew and play in the symphony they will eliminate one; in the '60s they would have done both. They also tend to choose activities that are self-limiting. Drama, for instance, is flourishing in all twelve of Yale's residential colleges as it never has before. Students hurl themselves into these productions—as actors, directors, carpenters, and technicians—with a dedication to create the best possible play, knowing that the day will come when the run will end and they can get back to their studies.

They also can't afford to be the willing slave of organizations like the *Yale Daily News.* Last spring at the one-hundredth anniversary banquet of that paper—whose past chairmen include such once and future kings as Potter Stewart, Kingman Brewster, and William F. Buckley, Jr.—much was made of the fact that the editorial staff used to be small and totally committed and that "Newsies" routinely worked fifty hours a week. In effect they belonged to a club; Newsies is how they defined themselves at Yale. Today's student will write one or two articles a week, when he can, and he defines himself as a student. I've never heard the word Newsie except at the banquet.

If I have described the modern undergraduate primarily as a driven creature who is largely ignoring the blithe spirit inside who keeps trying to come out and play, it's because that's where the crunch is, not only at Yale but throughout American education. It's why I think we should all be worried about the values that are nurturing a generation so fearful of risk and so goal-obsessed at such an early age.

I tell students that there is no one "right" way to get ahead—that each of them is a different person, starting from a different point and bound for a different destination. I tell them that change is a tonic and that all the slots are not codified nor the frontiers closed. One of my ways of telling them is to invite men and women who have achieved success outside the academic world to come and talk informally with my students during the year. They are heads of companies or ad agencies, editors of magazines, politicians, public officials, television magnates, labor leaders, business executives, Broadway producers, artists, writers, economists, photographers, scientists, historians—a mixed bag of achievers.

40 I ask them to say a few words about how they got started. The students assume that they started in their present profession and knew all along that it was what they wanted to do. Luckily for me, most of them got into their field by a circuitous route, to their surprise, after many detours. The students are startled. They can hardly conceive of a career that was not pre-planned. They can hardly imagine allowing the hand of God or chance to nudge them down some unforseen trail. 40

## Questions on Meaning

1. Why does Zinsser identify "achievement" as the "national god"? What is his wish for students? Who does he say is responsible for getting students out of their achievement trap?
2. In this 1979 essay, Zinsser expresses the opinion that female students are under more pressure than male students. Do you believe that is the case today?

## Questions on Rhetorical Strategy and Style

1. In the second paragraph after the notes to Carlos, Zinsser identifies students who are "panicky to succeed" as often being students at "New England and other private colleges that have high academic standards and highly motivated students." How do you react to this comment? Do you feel that Zinsser becomes more inclusive as he continues the essay, or does he maintain this somewhat elitist perspective?
2. How does Zinsser use the writing strategy of classification and division to describe the various pressures students face? How do these pressures compare to the pressures students feel today? Using his divisions, how would you classify the pressures you feel at school?
3. How does Zinsser compare and contrast the outlook of students in the 1960s to students in the late 1970s? How would you compare and contrast the outlook of students today to those he describes?

## Writing Assignments

1. Find where Zinsser uses an example of an artistic student to illustrate parental pressure. How well do you relate to the trials and tribulations of an artistic student at Yale in the late 1970s? What are the characteristics of a student who would best reflect the pressures *you* feel?
2. Reread paragraph 11 ("The pressure is almost as heavy . . .") and paragraph 20 ("Poor students, poor parents.") and compare and contrast how you are approaching your college years to the approach Zinsser would like to see students take. Explain why you feel you are headed in the right direction or not.

3. It is not difficult for students to get caught up in competing with their peers in terms of time spent studying, pages of reports, and, of course, grades. Describe the peer pressures you have felt at college. How have they affected the way you study and your feelings of accomplishment?
4. In the 1960s, students used to joke that they would like to collect Social Security upon graduation and work a few years extra when they reached retirement age so they could enjoy life while they were young. Write an essay about what you would do if you were given a living allowance and told to take a few years off after college *without penalty on your resume.* Would you take courses you couldn't because of requirements in your major, perform volunteer work, travel, live alone in a cabin and read, help your family at home, wait tables at a resort? How do you think this spontaneous, experimental time would affect your outlook on life? What "unforeseen trails" do you think you might be "nudged down"?